"I've taken my guitar with me on multiple combat deployments to share the power of music. My compliments to those who brought this important work to life."

—*Retired Lieutenant General Bob Ashley, guitar player*

"This should be required reading for music therapists, program directors, and other professionals involved with service provision to military personnel, veterans, their families and caregivers."

—*Concetta M. Tomaino, DA, MT-BC, Executive Director, Institute for Music and Neurologic Function*

"Military music creates a sense of belonging, encouragement, and comfort among those who serve. This well-written and carefully researched book suggests it can do more and charts a compelling way forward for music therapy in the recovery of service members, veterans, and their families."

—*Retired General Martin E. Dempsey, 18th Chairman of the Joint Chiefs of Staff*

"This seminal book has assembled a collection of essays that paint a picture of the evolving phenomenon of music therapy in the military—from pioneering practitioners to national partnerships!"

—*Arthur Bloom, Founder and Director, MusiCorps*

"This much-needed comprehensive resource about music and military-connected communities will surely guide the continued integration of music therapy in military and veteran healthcare."

—*Dr. Nina Kraus, Northwestern University*

of related interest

A Comprehensive Guide to Music Therapy, 2nd Edition
Theory, Clinical Practice, Research and Training
Edited by Stine Lindahl Jacobsen, Inge Nygaard Pedersen and Lars Ole Bonde
Foreword by Helen Odell-Miller
ISBN 978 1 78592 427 9
eISBN 978 1 78450 793 0

Music Therapy Methods in Neurorehabilitation
A Clinician's Manual
Felicity Baker and Jeanette Kennelly
Foreword by Barbara L. Wheeler
ISBN 978 1 84310 412 4
eISBN 978 1 84642 536 3

Music, Music Therapy and Trauma
International Perspectives
Edited by Julie P. Sutton
ISBN 978 184310 027 0
eISBN 978 1 84642 332 1

Post-Traumatic Stress Disorder and Art Therapy
Dr. Amy Backos
ISBN 978 1 78775 204 7
eISBN 978 1 78775 205 4

Art Therapy in the Treatment of Addiction and Trauma
Edited by Patricia Quinn
ISBN 978 1 78592 786 7
eISBN 978 1 78450 730 5

MUSIC THERAPY *with* MILITARY AND VETERAN POPULATIONS

Edited by Rebecca Vaudreuil

Foreword by Barbara A. Else

Jessica Kingsley Publishers
London and Philadelphia

First published in Great Britain in 2022 by Jessica Kingsley Publishers
An Hachette Company

1

A CIP catalogue record for this title is available from the
British Library and the Library of Congress

ISBN 978 1 78775 479 9
eISBN 978 1 78775 480 5

Printed and bound in the United States by Integrated Books International

Jessica Kingsley Publishers' policy is to use papers that are natural, renewable and recyclable products and made from wood grown in sustainable forests. The logging and manufacturing processes are expected to conform to the environmental regulations of the country of origin.

Jessica Kingsley Publishers
Carmelite House
50 Victoria Embankment
London EC4Y 0DZ

www.jkp.com

Dedication/Acknowledgements

This book is dedicated to all of the service members and veterans who serve and have served in the United Stated Armed Forces, as well as their families who serve(d) alongside them. Your courage, honor, and commitment to our country has inspired my professional aspirations to serve as I am able, through my work as a music therapist. Special acknowledgement to the caregivers, clinicians, and staff who provide medical treatment, rehabilitative and mental health services, and coordinate care for military-connected populations. A heartfelt thanks to all of the leaders, colleagues, and patients who have helped me become a better provider and person, all of the professors and professionals who have taught and trained me, my team members who are part of the Force that is Creative, and all of the contributing authors who empowered this book to move from a vision to a reality. To my friends who graciously provided countless pep talks and didn't take broken plans personally during the duration of this book project, thank you for your understanding and support. Huge shout-outs and many thanks to Dr. Barbara Reuer, Ben Tourtelot, Captain Paul Sargent, Hannah Bronson, Demi Bullock, and the Tourtelot/Fagen, Danley, Schneider, and Avila families, who have ventured with me on this journey of establishing music therapy with military-connected populations. Special acknowledgement and gratitude to Mr. Bill O'Brien, the National Endowment for the Arts (NEA), Dr. Sara Kass, the Henry M. Jackson Foundation for the Advancement of Military Medicine, Inc., Americans for the Arts, and the entire Creative Forces®: NEA Military Healing Arts network for unyielding support of integrating creative arts therapies into military and veteran healthcare systems and communities. Lastly, but first in my heart, limitless gratitude to my family—Shirley, Alan, Michelle, and Joseph—who provide endless and unconditional love and dedication to supporting each other in times of triumph and trouble. I wouldn't be who I am without each of you being who you are, and I can't ever thank you enough or express how much I deeply love, respect, and admire you all.

Contents

Section III: Expansion Efforts and Military Music Therapy Research

Foreword

BARBARA A. ELSE

My family, like so many families, has a history of military and civilian civil service for purposes of national defense and peace keeping. My grandfather served in a civilian role with the Merchant Marines in the years leading up to WWII, my father was a weather officer in the Pacific in WWII, and my late brother was a career Air Force officer. My humble part, while limited and conducted remotely, took place with my business partner/brother where I provided logistics and analytic support for his work as a civilian contractor in conflict and post-conflict zones in the Middle East, post-Soviet states, and central and east Africa. It is through this history and lens that I hoped to bridge and advocate for music therapy services, music-based interventions, and the arts more broadly with service members, veterans, family members, civilian non-governmental organization (NGO) workers, and contractors.

In 2006, I was privileged to direct and collaborate on a multi-year program grant sponsored by the American Music Therapy Association (AMTA) and funded through the National Association of Music Merchants (NAMM) Foundation (NAMM Foundation, 2021), *Active Music Making and Music Therapy Services: An Early Intervention and Readjustment Program Among Returning Military Personnel and Their Families*. Its aim was to design and pre-test a music-based intervention as part of a music therapy program for service members and their families involved in frequent deployments in support of Operation Enduring Freedom (OEF) and Operation Iraqi Freedom (OIF). This project was the impetus for many subsequent conversations regarding the need for music therapy programming with military populations on a national scale.

A few years later, I had the pleasure of first meeting Rebecca Vaudreuil, the editor of this book, when she was working as a music therapist in San Diego, California, at Resounding Joy, Inc., founded by Dr. Barbara Reuer in 2004 (Resounding Joy, 2021). During the AMTA 2009 annual conference in San Diego, Dr. Reuer and I discussed the importance of expanding music therapy services to active-duty service members and their families in the region. Although for years prior, Resounding Joy had the desire, drive, and infrastructure to support one-time, stand-alone music therapy experiences for military-connected populations, it wasn't until 2010 that they were able to secure funding for sustainable services. This occurred through a fruitful connection with a local military installation and a non-profit NGO that exclusively supports military populations. Through the power of partnership, Resounding Joy, a military base, and a military-focused NGO joined forces to make it happen. As I continued to become acquainted with Rebecca and her work developing sustainable and sound military music therapy programming for Resounding Joy, it was clear that she was passionate about expanding music therapy programming to serve military populations in Southern California and beyond. She did just that.

More recently, creative arts therapists have enjoyed expanded opportunities to fortify the legacy of service with military populations, thanks to numerous partnerships including federal, state, and local agency support for the arts, creative arts therapies, and integrative wellness programming at military and veteran treatment facilities. Additionally, scores of qualified and credentialed music therapy professionals and creative arts therapists throughout the United States and beyond provide services to active-duty military, veterans, and their families in various communities.

Concurrent to this clinical work, important research initiatives are being investigated and communicated for an array of conditions affecting military-connected and other populations through the Sound Health initiative with the National Institutes of Health and the Sound Health Network. On the research side, one aim of Sound Health is to explore ways to enhance the potential of music as therapy for neurological disorders, including brain injuries and traumatic stress (Sound Health, 2021). The Sound Health Network is a partnership of the National Endowment for the Arts with the University of California, San Francisco, in collaboration with the National Institutes of Health, the John F. Kennedy Center for the Performing Arts, and Renée Fleming. Its aim is to promote research and public awareness about the impact of music on health and wellness (Sound Health Network, 2021).

Given this context, there are three points that merit noting as one explores the contents of this book. First, military service is marked by frequent deployments, temporary duty assignments, and relocations. Despite customary turnovers in command and duty stations, music and purposive uses of music, including therapeutic music-based interventions, are an enduring and consistent thread in military life. Virtually all sections of this book highlight music in military service and history as a foreground to their respective subtopics. Second, military culture serves as a common, shared bond among service members, veterans, family members, and supporting civilian personnel. Military culture transcends the immense diversity of its personnel. Protocol and chain of command provide structure, expectations, rules, and guidelines. It is not coincidental that music is pervasive and integral to military culture. Third, a military job, unlike many civilian jobs, is often one where the service member's job is *the* primary source of identity for the service member with their peers, unit, and branch of service. Similarly, I believe it is fair to say that music therapy is a profession where practitioners represent their profession with pride. Like service members, music therapists identify strongly and passionately with their professional roles. In fact, all contributors to this book, irrespective of their roles, see music and military culture as essential and inextricably bonded.

This book is an important contribution to the literature for two main reasons. The first is that it is diverse in the perspectives of the various contributors who are engaged and involved with music and military populations. Second, is the editor's and contributing authors' aim for the book to be accessible to a wide audience. The book is intended as a resource in academia for purposes of education, training, and skill building, and a source of continued learning among music therapists, and non-music therapists interested in the subject matter.

In closing, I wish to extend my gratitude to the dedicated music therapy professionals, other creative arts therapists, and musicians/artists who currently serve as active members of the military in some capacity and to those who are veterans of military service. I also hold great respect for the music therapists whose spouses/partners are on active duty and who show incredible resilience and strength of character throughout their travels and work. Last but not least, I thank the editor and all the contributing authors for their service and dedication to this subject.

Barbara A. Else, MPA, MT-BC, Consultant, Sr. Advisor Policy & Research, American Music Therapy Association

Preface

REBECCA VAUDREUIL

As I think back to the first music therapy session that I facilitated with a service member, I immediately knew that I wanted to work with military populations and was inspired to create a career path that would accommodate this aspiration. Both of my grandfathers served in the United States (U.S.) military, and my uncle, who served in Vietnam, used music to dampen the impact of his combat-related physical and psychological injuries. Over time, I became increasingly aware of the selfless sacrifice that military service entails, and I learned more about the power of music to help people process life experiences, which ultimately led me to pursue music therapy as a profession. When I began my career in 2009, there were many opportunities and established guidelines for music therapists working in the Veterans Health Administration; however, sustainable music therapy programming offered through the Military Health System for active-duty service members and military families had yet to be formally established. I am grateful that I was able to help pioneer this powerful part of the profession and continue to support its development through clinical practice standardization, multifaceted community collaboration, and innovative research. It has been a long journey to where it stands today, and while there is still ample road ahead, we have found a stride, generated momentum, and will keep on traveling where the road leads to meet the needs of our country's military personnel, veterans, and their families.

Therefore, I have designed this book, *Music Therapy with Military and Veteran Populations*, as a compilation of essential information gleaned from a diverse cadre of subject matter experts to provide a comprehensive review of the historical and theoretical development and application of music therapy positioned within the U.S. Departments of Defense (DoD) and Veterans Affairs (VA). The information presented in each chapter is relevant to any reader who desires to learn about the profession of music therapy with military-connected populations, from inception to current state—information I wish I'd had access to when I started working as a music therapist with these uniquely deserving populations. For example, the DoD and VA are their own cultures with customary traditions, structure, and language; therefore, I have included a list of acronyms used throughout the chapters of this book. This type of resourcing is valuable to learning about and understanding military culture, which is fundamental to working with military-connected populations.

The remainder of this Preface includes the context of need that warrants this book's creation, an overview of content, and chapter descriptions for reader edification. I hope that others enjoy and learn from reading this book as much as the contributing authors and I have from writing and editing it. May it inspire your work, amplify your understanding, and empower your advocacy regarding the impact of creative arts therapies, specifically music therapy, with military-connected populations.

Context of need

Since 2001 when the Global War on Terrorism (GWOT) began, it has transcended past conflicts of the U.S. military, spanning almost two decades and yielding higher survival rates due to advances in medicine and technology. Military personnel are experiencing service-related injuries, including traumatic brain injury (TBI) and post-traumatic stress disorder (PTSD), and recovery processes are often complex, protracted, and require extensive and integrated rehabilitation. Reported incidences of these "invisible wounds of war" have yielded data indicating over quarter of a million cases of TBI within the DoD. Furthermore, it is estimated that up to 20 percent of the almost three million service members deployed in support of GWOT operations—Operation Enduring Freedom (OEF), Operation Iraqi Freedom (OIF), Operation New Dawn (OND), and other conflicts—present with or may develop symptoms of PTSD.

Book overview

This book chronicles how music therapy is used to treat service members and veterans and provide family and caregiver support by sharing best practices in the areas of clinical application, multi-site program replication, and innovations in music therapy practice, community engagement, and research specific to military populations supported by local, state, and national arts initiatives. In addition to military cultural competencies and methods of integrating music therapy into the DoD and the VA, this book presents the importance of music in military culture and the role that it has played since the inception of the U.S. Armed Forces for ceremonial traditions, training purposes, communication during combat operations, and motivation on the battlefield.

Currently, music therapy is applied to treat service members and veterans as they rehabilitate, recover, and reintegrate into their families, communities, and society. Considerations for individual and group music therapy contexts and distinctions of short-term and longitudinal care models for treating TBI and PTSD are discussed in this book, along with examples that exist on a spectrum of services ranging from clinical treatment to community-based arts engagement, referred to as the clinic to community continuum. Recommendations for resourcing and capacity-building within government systems, national programs, and local communities are also presented. Music therapy research with military populations is introduced, and knowledge gaps and need areas for future research are identified to assist in projecting where the field of music therapy within military and veteran healthcare systems can focus efforts for continued success.

Contributing authors include military personnel and veterans from multiple branches of the U.S. Armed Forces, U.S. Public Health Service, family members, medical providers, and music therapy professionals including clinicians and researchers. This book is intended for a diverse audience that spans a spectrum of students, interns, new professionals, and board-certified music therapists interested in and currently working with military-connected populations. This book can also serve as a reference for non-music therapy professionals and rehabilitation specialists who want to gain more understanding of music therapy with military populations. It can provide a training resource and basis for curriculum development in academia and a tool for program development and advancement in clinical practice.

Book outline and chapter descriptions

Section I: The History of Music Therapy in the Military

Chapter 1: The Role of Music in Military Culture. This chapter provides a historical account of how music has been used in the military dating back to the inception of armed forces across the world. Music has been used on battlefields for over 2500 years. The role of music in supporting training and combat, camaraderie building, ceremonies, and public outreach is presented. Every country with a standing military has at least one military band to serve the needs of the military and bridge the gap to the civilian sector. Current positioning and use of U.S. military bands is described, including outreach efforts across the U.S. and international areas of interest. This chapter concludes by presenting the benefits of music on health, wellness, resilience, and readiness.

Chapter 2: The Evolution of Music Therapy in Military Medicine. This chapter details the roots and evolution of music therapy as a profession in military medicine. Anthropologic and folkloric depictions of the healing properties of music date back to the Paleolithic era. Prominent Classical Greek philosophers cited music in their texts, and later, in the 1800s, the restorative influence of music was indicated by Florence Nightingale's seminal guide to nursing, regarding the wounded and ill soldiers in her care. Music therapy, as a profession, originated from military medicine dating back to the U.S. Civil War and both World Wars when community musicians performed live music, rendering comfort and connection to convalescing soldiers. Its evolution into a holistic healing profession crosses Veterans Health Administration medical centers and military treatment facilities in the U.S. Music therapy is a viable therapeutic option in the current medical model, and its inherent properties that impact the mind, body, and spirit make music therapy increasingly relevant to emerging, whole person approaches to health, healing, and wellbeing.

Chapter 3: Music Therapy in the Department of Veterans Affairs. This chapter provides the historical foundation and evolutionary development of music therapy in the Department of Veterans Affairs . Acknowledgement of music therapy as a clinical intervention is an ongoing process in the Veterans Health Administration, and occupational positioning of board-certified music therapists is becoming increasingly aligned with the education, training, and skills that music therapists employ to treat veterans from all service eras and across diagnoses.

Chapter 4: Creative Forces®: NEA Military Healing Arts Network—Expanding Creative Arts Therapies in the Departments of Defense and Veterans Affairs. An initiative of the National Endowment for the Arts (NEA), Creative Forces®: NEA Military Healing Arts Network is a partnership with the Departments of Defense (DoD) and Veterans Affairs (VA), and state and local arts agencies that seeks to improve the health, wellness, and quality of life for military and veteran populations exposed to trauma, as well as their families and caregivers. Creative Forces supports creative arts therapies programming via a network of embedded creative arts therapists at DoD and VA clinical sites across the U.S., including telehealth services that provide access to remote and rural military and veteran populations.

Section II: Music Therapy Clinical Application and Community Integration

Chapter 5: Military Music Therapy in Individual Settings. This chapter explores individual music therapy sessions with service members and veterans. The clinical process of music therapy treatment—from assessment to termination—tailored to individual patients' needs is described. The facilitation of music therapy to address disruptions in neurologic and psychological functioning is explored, including clinical examples of goal-based interventions used to address TBI, PTSD, and other areas impacting the physical and psychological health of military-connected populations.

Chapter 6: Military Music Therapy in Group Contexts. This chapter introduces group music therapy protocols implemented in both intensive outpatient programming and longitudinal treatment within the Departments of Defense (DoD) and Veterans Affairs (VA). Through engagement in active/expressive and passive/receptive music therapy interventions, service members and veterans experience music in a new context and make deliberate choices to develop their sense of agency through collaborative creative expression. Cohesion and camaraderie are critical values for military populations, essential for survival during military service and continued wellbeing throughout post-military life. Highlighting these values is of vital importance in the treatment processes of stand-alone and co-treatment music therapy groups, where there are often multiple diagnoses and presenting symptomatology. The impact of group music therapy and co-treatment on overall functioning and performance optimization in military (unit, team), familial (nuclear, extended), occupational (military, civilian), and social (community, society) environments is explored.

Chapter 7: Caring for the Caregiver: Supporting Military Families Through Music. This chapter describes the impact on military families who care for their loved ones through experiences of injury, rehabilitation, and reintegration. It portrays how family involvement in rehabilitation can predict better outcomes, and examines the crucial role that music plays in supporting military families as a whole throughout service members' and veterans' recovery processes. This chapter is authored exclusively by military family members and provides parental and spousal perspectives of how music can be used as a transformative tool to reshape family structure and re-establish familial bonds.

Chapter 8: Music Therapy and Telehealth: Serving Remote Military Populations. This chapter explores the use of music therapy telehealth to facilitate remote clinical music therapy services and community music models with military populations in the U.S. and Uganda. Music therapists' efforts to employ traditional interventions facilitated via virtual platforms in clinical and community environments are discussed. This chapter reports on the historical context and integration of music therapy and telehealth and acknowledges the promptness with which music therapists across the world have pivoted their practices to virtual platforms in response to the COVID-19 global pandemic, which emerged during the writing of this chapter. This chapter presents facilitation techniques of didactic and applied clinical experiences, competencies, and past and present models of music therapy telehealth, and reviews current literature. Brief vignettes of remote music facilitation with one service member deployed in Afghanistan and a group of liberated child soldiers in Uganda are shared.

Section III: Expansion Efforts and Military Music Therapy Research

Chapter 9: From Clinic to Community: The Social Impact of Music. This chapter illustrates the transformational trajectory from clinical treatment to community reintegration through programmes that extend opportunities for music engagement outside the clinical setting. Examples include: 1) the formation of bands comprising service members, veterans, community musicians, and industry professionals that perform together at local and national venues in support of reintegration and awareness building, and 2) veteran music retreats that provide socialization, shared experiences, and psychoeducation regarding the ongoing utilization of music to positively impact overall functioning. The impact of music performance to support long-term health benefits is highlighted through applied community programming.

Chapter 10: Music Integration with the National Guard, Military Reserve Force, and First Responders. This chapter explores the need for music programs intentionally designed for use within the National Guard and Military Reserves, with implications for first responders. These populations experience intensive training that is completed in an abbreviated amount of time compared with other military service branches. Due to irregular training schedules and regular deployments, these populations receive limited access to healthcare, hence traditional music therapy programming is not practical for implementation. The need for customized music therapy-informed programming is discussed and examples of interventions, resources, and programming to accommodate Guardsmen, Reservists, and first responders are shared.

Chapter 11: Historical Overview and Research Trends and Gaps in Military Music Therapy. This chapter provides an overview of historical research, synthesizes the current state of research in military music therapy, and presents gap areas in the research pertaining to music therapy with military-connected populations. An overview of a model clinical and research program to inform future studies regarding music therapy with military populations is presented.

Chapter 12: Looking Ahead: Continued Advancement of the Military Music Therapy Continuum. This chapter takes the book full circle—from commencement to completion—by highlighting historical developments, reviewing current applications of music therapy in military and veteran health systems, and making recommendations for continued music therapy applications and research with military-connected populations. Recommendations are provided from current scholarly literature, with insights gleaned from surveying creative arts therapists, service members, veterans, military families, and uniformed healthcare providers regarding their perspectives of the future of music therapy and priority need and gap areas in the realms of education, training, practice, and research. Integration of an innovative arts-based wellness model into the military healthcare system is introduced, and the implications for extended impact on community and society at large are discussed.

List of Acronyms

A

AAF	Army Air Force
AAMT	American Association for Music Therapy
ACT	Acceptance and Commitment Therapy
AFTA	Americans for the Arts
AFTB	Army Family Team Building
AIH	Arts in Health
AMMT	Associative Mood and Memory Training
AMTA	American Music Therapy Association
APT	Auditory Perception Training
ASF	Army Service Force

B

BLUF	Bottom Line Up Front
BM-GIM	Bonny Method of Guided Imagery and Music

C

CARA	Comprehensive Addiction and Recovery Act
CAT	Creative Arts Therapist
CIH	Complementary and Integrated Health
CONOPS	Concept of Operations
CPT	Army Captain
CPT	Common Procedural Technology
CW4	Chief Warrant Officer Four

D

DMH	Doctor of Medical Humanities
DoD	Department of Defense
DPH	Directors of Psychological Health

E

EAS	End of Active Service
EO	Executive Order

F

fMRI	Functional Magnetic Resonance Imaging
FY	Fiscal Year

G

GS	General Schedule
GWOT	Global War on Terror(ism)
GySgt	Marine Gunnery Sergeant

I

ICU	Intensive Care Unit
IED	Improvised Explosive Device
IOP	Intensive Outpatient Program
ISC	Intrepid Spirit Center

L

LCSW	Licensed Clinical Social Worker

M

MA	Master of Arts
MACT	Musical Attention Control Training
MAP	Mission, Aspiration, and Purpose
MEd	Master of Education (or EdM)
MEFT	Musical Executive Function Training
MEG	Magnetoencephalography
MHS	Military Healthcare System
MIDI	Musical Instrument Digital Interface
MIT	Melodic Intonation Therapy
MM	Master of Music
MME	Master in Medical Education
MMT	Master of Music Therapy
MMT	Musical Mnemonics Training
MOS	Military Occupational Specialty
MP	Military Police
MPC	Music in Psychosocial training and Counseling
MSOT	Music Sensory Orientation Training
MST	Military Sexual Trauma
MT	Music Therapist
MT-BC	Board Certified Music Therapist
MTF	Military Treatment Facility
MTR	Music Therapy of the Rockies

N

NAMM	National Association of Music Merchants
NAMT	National Association of Music Therapy
NEA	National Endowment for the Arts
NGO	Non-Governmental Organization
NHDVS	National Homes for Disabled Volunteer Soldiers
NIAHM	National Initiative for Arts & Health Across the Military
NICoE	National Intrepid Center of Excellence
NMC	National Music Council
NMT	Neurologic Music Therapy
NOAH	National Organization for Arts in Health

NRC	National Resource Center (Creative Forces)
NVCAF	National Veterans Creative Arts Festival

O

OEF	Operation Enduring Freedom
OIF	Operation Iraqi Freedom
OMREX	Oral Motor and Respiratory Exercises
OND	Operation New Dawn
OPM	Office of Personnel Management
OWI	Office of War Information

P

PCLM	PTSD Checklist for Military and Veteran Populations
PCM	Primary Care Manager
PCS	Permanent Change of Station
PEB	Physical Evaluation Board
PM&RS	Physical Medicine and Rehabilitation Service
PREP	Post-Deployment Rehabilitation and Evaluation Program
PSE	Patterned Sensory Enhancement
PTRP	Polytrauma Transitional Rehabilitation Program
PTSD	Post-Traumatic Stress Disorder
PVT	Army Private

Q

q-EEG	Quantitative Electroencephalography

R

RJoy	Resounding Joy, Inc.
RMT	Registered Music Therapist
RPS	Rehabilitation and Prosthetic Services
RT	Recreational Therapist
RT/CAT	Recreation/Creative Arts Therapist
RTS	Recreation Therapy Service
RVTRI	Rural Veterans Telehealth Rehabilitation Initiative

S

SSG	Army Staff Sergeant
SUD	Substance Use Disorder

T

TBI	Traumatic Brain Injury
TIMP	Therapeutic Instrumental Music Performance

U

U.S.	United States
USA	United States Army
USAF	United States Air Force
USCG	United States Coast Guard
USERA	Uniformed Services Employment and Reemployment Rights Act

USMC	United States Marine Corps
USN	United States Navy

V

VA	Department of Veterans Affairs
VAHCS	Veteran Administration Health Care System
VAMC	Department of Veterans Affairs Medical Center
VHA	Veterans Health Administration
VISN	Veterans Integrated Service Network
VIT	Vocal Intonation Therapy
VSO	Veterans Service Organization
VVC	VA Video Connect

W

WAC	Women's Army Corps
WARCAT	Warrior Administered Retrospective Casualty Assessment Tool
WDPH	Wing Director of Psychological Health
WRNMMC	Walter Reed National Military Medical Center
WWI	World War I
WWII	World War II

Y

YMWI	Yamaha Music and Wellness Institute
YRRP	Yellow Ribbon Reintegration Program

SECTION I

The History of Music Therapy in the Military

Chapter 1

The Role of Music in Military Culture

JONATHAN L. CRANE

Disclaimer: The information contained in this chapter was compiled from publicly available sources and does not necessarily reflect official policy or position of the United States Department of Defense or the United States Military Academy.

Introduction to the author: my experience as a military musician

I enlisted in the United States (U.S.) Army as a 42R Army Musician, with a specialty of electric bass, on July 22, 2009, which happens to be my birthday. My wife and I were two musicians living on an unpredictable income with no health insurance and had just been blessed with our first child. In the U.S., it is almost impossible to afford the costs of medical care without health insurance, and as parents, we felt it was our duty to provide this for our family. With no prospects of full-time work that included benefits, we decided that we needed a change. In the back of my mind, I always knew that the military hired musicians. In high school, I remember a few older students who joined active or reserve military bands. In fact, my elementary school music teacher was a former member of The President's Own Marine Corps Band; he served during the Kennedy, Johnson, and Nixon administrations. I met more former military band members who were professors at Lebanon Valley College in Pennsylvania, where I completed undergraduate studies in music education. My teachers and peers demonstrated that it was possible to attain a stable career as a professional musician in the military. I am grateful for these connections, as they directed me towards the recruiter's office, a journey that shaped the rest of my life.

I wish I could say that I initially joined the Army out of a sense of duty to my country or to support ideals that the nation was founded on. However, at the time I enlisted, the decision was based more on practical purposes. I needed to support my growing family, which I was better positioned to do with job security, a predictable paycheck, and benefits. The Army provided these fundamental needs and also paid off a significant portion of my student loan debt. I had spent nine years in college during which time I obtained three degrees, and, despite having some scholarships, I was still very much in debt and saw little chance of being able to pay it all off. At the time I enlisted in the Army, the Global War on Terrorism (GWOT) warranted significant portions of the U.S. military to be deployed across the world. Thinking back on that time, the thought that I was joining the front lines didn't occur to me and based on what I heard from my teachers and peers, I had preconceived notions of the duties and responsibilities of military bands.

My first year in the Army focused on being indoctrinated into the lifestyle and learning. I was stationed at Schofield Barrack, Hawaii, with the 25th Infantry Division Band. The band mostly performed for ceremonies and didn't connect directly with audiences. I played the bass drum in the marching band and spent very little time performing on my primary instrument, electric bass. In July 2010, we received orders that the band was deploying with the Division Headquarters which, little did I know, had been a common occurrence over the previous six years. I asked one of the Sergeants how long we would be gone (I had assumed about a month, to play at various bases). He laughed and said, "At least 12 months, maybe 15..." The prospect of being separated from my family for that long was initially traumatic, and this is when the reality of military service started to sink in. Even though I wouldn't be directly fighting the enemy, I knew that my deployment would be focused on using my musical talents and skills to bring comfort, familiarity, and a sense of "home" to my fellow soldiers in the fight.

On December 3, 2010, I boarded a plane en route to Iraq with 300 other Division Soldiers. We were stationed at the sprawling Camp Liberty/Victory complex in Baghdad, a former residence of Saddam Hussein. Most of my fellow band members had been deployed at least once before and were accustomed to the unconventional travel, and they shared tips that made the journey as comfortable as possible. After landing on the military side of Baghdad airport, we traveled by bus to temporary tents at Camp Liberty. Getting our equipment into theater was no easy task. One container (about one quarter the size of a tractor trailer), shipped by air, that was there when we arrived. Our other two containers, which were full size and had been shipped by boat, would not arrive for another two months. It took me many weeks to acclimate to the magnitude of the base. It was a functioning city with residential neighborhoods, shopping and recreation centers, and military offices. We had the choice of four dining facilities, with the option to purchase fast food or eat local cuisine on base. There were traffic intersections with stop signs and speed limits, and the Military Police (MP) would issue citations for rolling through a stop sign! On learning that, I thought to myself, "This is a friggin' war, isn't it?" It was not the austere environment that my fellow soldiers endured circa 2003–2005. In fact, it felt very similar to being on a military installation within the U.S., with the exception that I carried an M4 rifle with 30 rounds everywhere I went.

I was assigned to a rock band. We decided to exclusively play cover songs by artists such as Metallica, Avenged Sevenfold, Tool, and Bon Jovi. Our repertoire was based on our strengths, preferences, and assumptions that the battle-hardened troops stationed at Camp Liberty wanted aggressive music. We came to find that our audiences were much more diverse than we had anticipated, which expanded our performing opportunities. We never talked much about our goals for performing in a war zone, and I had expected that we would perform solely for fellow soldiers at organized concerts and events. However, our audience consisted of not only U.S. Soldiers, but also contractors, third-country nationals, Iraqi citizens, civilian government officials, and foreign military members, and with each performance we learned more about how music resonated with different groups of people.

Figure 1.1: Performing heavy metal for a group of soldiers in central Iraq, April 2011 (photo credit: SFC(R) Erin Betz)

Some of our shows felt defeating, and, in hindsight, this was because they were not appropriate for the environment. For example, in one situation we traveled to a nearby base for a scheduled performance not knowing that a day earlier that base had been attacked, which resulted in a casualty. Each challenging performance was often followed by one of transcendental proportions. Experiencing soldiers and foreign nationals joining together in friendly "moshing" and spirited "headbanging" to the music we played was amazing! The increase in understanding between widely separated cultures through shared musical experiences was played out in real time, as shown in Figure 1.1. This is a main purpose of integrating music in conflict areas, and I am honored to contribute to this mission as a U.S. Soldier, leader, musician, and researcher. The cross-pollination of music throughout the globe has created areas of commonality in which diverse groups of people can unify. This chapter focuses on the role of music in the history of military culture and how it continues to shape this culture today.

The historical uses of music in the military

Music is a ubiquitous part of human existence; however, defining exactly what music consists of remains a challenge. According to Morley (2013), archeologists have unearthed flutes made from animal bones that date back at least 40,000 years, which was around 150,000 years after the first anatomically modern humans appeared. It is likely that humans used their vocal cords in speech-like ways and for singing before creating instruments. As we have evolved as a species, so has our relationship with sound. Morley (2013) states:

> ...musical activities rely on the ability to voluntarily produce sequences of sounds moderated for intensity and/or pitch and/or contour, generated by metrically organized muscular movements (often coordinated/entrained with an internally or externally perceived pulse), plus the ability to process and extract information from such sounds. (p.8)

For the purposes of this chapter, music is defined as sound that is organized either through human design or perception. There are ongoing arguments about whether animals and humans perceive sound in similar ways, and studies of the advanced human brain indicate development towards affinity for organized sound. The ways in which humans manipulate sound have influenced our biological, psychological, and social processing systems. In his book, *This Is Your Brain on Music*, Daniel Levitin states, "The power of music to evoke emotions is harnessed by advertising executives, filmmakers, military commanders, and mothers" (2006, p.22). He further proposes that "...despite this manipulation of our emotions, we accept and enjoy [music's] ability to create emotional experiences" (2006, p.22). All cultures have some degree of musical associations embedded in their identities, either by adopting pre-existing songs or creating their own.

Throughout history, humans have sought power and defended their interests through force. Additionally, we tend to integrate music into all aspects of life, so inevitably it has become a cultural aspect of those who engage in militant conflict. Lethality and survival are central to serving in a military capacity. Individuals and groups develop cultural identity to enhance their ability for social cooperation, of which music is a crucial component. A military force has two states of being: training for and conducting war. Music exists in both states and has grown in different capacities over time. Prior to the 20th century, music was used during war as a communication tool and for psychological manipulation. Imagery from Greek and Roman times depicts soldiers playing drums and horns, as shown in Figure 1.2, which were used to maintain orderly ranks on the march and instill devotion to duty as encouragement for the battle to come (Camus, 1975).

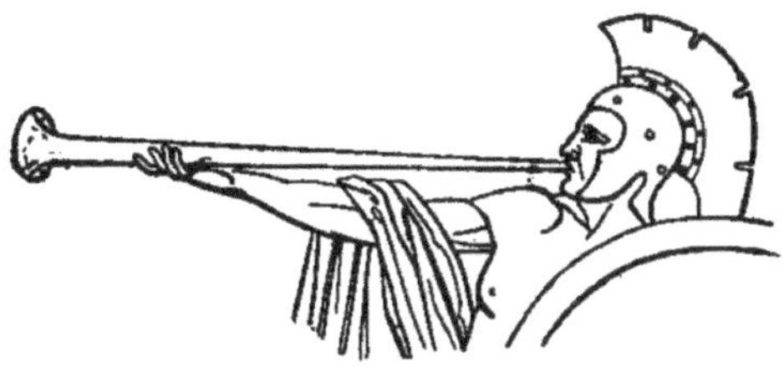

Figure 1.2: Greek/Roman warrior with salpinx trumpet from the fourth edition of Meyers Konversations-Lexikon (1885–1890)[1]

After the widespread distribution of gunpowder by the end of the 13th century, powerful drum and trumpet sounds were used to transmit information over loud blasts and long distances to large forces. Sending unique commands through musical signals was an efficient way to ensure men in battle knew what to do and where to go. Playing unit-specific drumbeats and bugle calls was a distinct battlefield advantage. Communication through sound came to be known as field music, a style used until the beginning of the 20th century. Today, field music has been relegated to ceremonies, with only a few groups within the U.S. military specializing in its performance, such as the U.S. Army Fife and Drum Corps. World War I brought the end of music signaling in battle, as issuing commands through sound became impractical and dangerous. Secrecy of movement became the paramount tactic, and that continues in today's battle strategies.

As the new American colonies were settled, each community had a militia for protection. These militias adopted the military music traditions from their countries of origin, dominated by British, Prussian, and French influence. Skilled musicians were in high demand both for community and militia purposes. Many people played music in the local taverns at night, then picked up a drum for their day job of required militia training. In 1687, the Virginia Colony voted to purchase drums, trumpets, and colors for their militia through taxes imposed on the residents; however, colonists still had to purchase their own arms and

1 https://commons.wikimedia.org/wiki/File:Meyers_b14_Salpinx_trumpet_230.jpg

equipment. This law demonstrated the importance of music to the community in addition to military use (Camus, 1975). Since a standing military did not exist at the time, defense of the colony was the responsibility of all its inhabitants. The colonists' musical activities reflected experiences in battle and everyday life.

Decades later in 1775, the various militias across the colonies began to organize. The provincial congress appointed General George Washington with this mighty task, and the General Orders of July 14, 1775 ensured that drummers and fifers were provided to all units. Each regiment was allowed drum and fife majors to instruct and maintain discipline among the musicians (White, 1944). General Washington was a known amateur flautist and recognized the effect music had for military purposes, as evidenced by his quote below.

> "Nothing is more agreeable, and ornamental, than good music...every officer, for the credit to his corps, should take care to provide it." George Washington, June 4, 1777

During the U.S. Civil War, military bands were the main source of musical activity. Field music, brass bands, and group singing were the main ways that soldiers experienced music during the Civil War. Soldiers became the arbiters of popular musical taste in the north and south. The documentation of their musical experiences had a profound effect on the entire population's perception of war, which is still evident today (McWhirter, in Kraaz, Ch.4, 2019). At the time, each militia regiment had a band, and when combined to form a division, there could be as many as 45 bands for each division (White, 1944). One of the most recognizable sounds of military music was composed during the Civil War—the bugle call known as "Taps." The call that we know today was adapted by General Daniel Butterfield, from a longer call titled "Tattoo," which was used at the end of the day to signal to cease drinking and return to barracks. Butterfield's call was immediately well received and spread throughout the Union and Confederate Armies. It became the official call for the extinguishing of lights soon after its first use in 1862. By 1891, it became the official musical composition used at military funerals (Villanueva, n.d.). The melodic contour of "Taps" has made it the default sound of triumphant melancholy, as shown in Figure 1.3. In news reports, television shows, movies, and advertisements, the melody represents death and sadness, and simultaneously, honor and dignity. Little music from within the military culture permeates the public consciousness, with "Taps" being the exception, as it is instantly recognizable across the U.S. to this day.

Figure 1.3: "Taps" notation

The reason "Taps" has such a strong effect on listeners is beginning to be understood. As neuroscientists have begun to identify the effects of sound on the brain, music's persuasive power is still used today to influence friendly and enemy forces. Military forces often use music for motivation to rally service members for a common purpose. This music also functions to intimidate the enemy. As electronic reproduction of sound became possible in the 20th century, music was sometimes used to demoralize the enemy in order to drive them out of hiding or obtain information from captives. Appropriate music selections applied in specific situations can be an incredibly powerful force to motivate as well as cause intense frustration and inflict psychological pain.

The use of music as military propaganda peaked during World War II (WWII) within the music department of the Office of War Information (OWI). The OWI had a mission to influence both foreign and domestic audiences generally through print, film, and radio. It was important to counteract the negative influence campaigns of the Germans, which claimed that the U.S. was "uncultured." The OWI's 50,000-item music library provided the raw materials for the promotion of U.S. musical culture to the world (Fauser, in Kraaz, Ch.9, 2019). The folklorist Bess Lomax Hawes was a constant throughout the office's existence. Many of the prominent U.S. composers rotated through OWI, including Henry Cowell, Roy Harris, Samuel Barber, and Elliott Carter. The Allied forces co-opted the opening motive from Beethoven's 5th Symphony, which consisted of three short notes and one long, a major third lower. This motive, shown in Figure 1.4, corresponded nicely with the three short, one long Morse code "V" for victory (Trotter, 2005). This signal could be used both over closed communications and public announcements so that all in earshot would immediately understand the Allies were winning.

When a military unit is not directly fighting, it is training. During training, music is used to motivate and build common identity among the members. Part of the training phase is synchronization of movement (e.g., marching). Prior to the modern era, marching was the sole method of movement on the battlefield. This has since been relegated to ceremonies and parades; however, this synchronization of movement is critical to building a cultural identity for military units. Music experiences such as marching to a drum and cadence (call-and-response singing) unifies troops and causes a release of endorphins (Launay *et al.*, 2016). This type of military indoctrination ensures troops function as a team to achieve the mission. Shared music-making before and after battle also serves the purpose of entertainment. This is the most common application of music across many western cultures and the foundation of the modern music industry. Music entertainment exists in the forms of listening to live or recorded music, composing, and performing music, which often includes elements of choreographed dance and sequenced movement. These musical forms also have potential wellness benefits, which will be further discussed later in this chapter.

Figure 1.4: Morse code and Beethoven excerpt

Each service branch of the U.S. military conducts ceremonies with slightly different procedures, and music is a consistent and integral attribute to their success. Cultures around the world recognize the pairing of music and ceremonies to mark important occasions in the lives of individuals and groups. In fact, some cultures do not distinguish between music and ceremony; they have no understanding of holding ceremonies without music or making music outside ritualistic (ceremonial) experience. Music used in military ceremonies is preferably performed by live musicians, but recordings are often used since there are not enough military musicians to cover all of the ceremonies conducted across the military. Including music performed by an ensemble signifies a higher importance to the ceremony, usually due to the higher level of command or hosting organization. Live performances of ceremonial music are radically different than experiences of typical music listening. For example, music is used for marching troops during ceremonies.

Marching music is selected from the early 20th century, often composed by John Philip Sousa or Karl King. An oddity in this style of music is that the bass drum is played louder, despite the dynamic contours of the other instruments, for a purely functional reason, namely that troops strike their left foot on the ground each time the bass drum sounds. Another unique variation in U.S. military ceremonial music is stopping the march on any starting beat of a measure, regardless of musical phrase; the music stops when the troops stop moving. This often results in awkward sounding cuts to the music. The sole purpose of the music is for synchronization of movement, not enjoyment by the listener. It is common practice today to invite the civilian public to observe military ceremonies but, historically, the music performed was meant only for operational purposes. Some ceremonies have evolved over time and serve entertainment purposes, such as the military tattoo, depicted in Figure 1.5. The military tattoo was originally just a drum signal but is now an elaborate show involving many organizations, such as the Twilight Tattoo held at Fort Myer, Virginia, and the Royal Edinburgh Tattoo in Scotland.

Figure 1.5: Fireworks explode in the sky over Edinburgh Castle for the Annual Royal Military Tattoo in 2011 (photo credit: Sally Stimson/MOD)

The image that comes to mind for most people when they think of military music is the marching band. These groups feature musicians in elaborate uniforms playing and moving in tight synchronization with an emphasis on percussion instruments. The origin of the military marching band can be attributed to Turkey during the time of the Ottoman empire. Several accounts from the reign of Suleyman the Magnificent (1520–1566) describe the construction of these military bands known as *mehterhane* or *janisarry* (new troops) music. They typically had double-reed oboe-like instruments, trumpets, large and small kettle drums, a large bass drum, cymbals, and a stick rattle with small metal bells (Lichtenwanger, 1948). These bands played during battle for internal motivation and to intimidate the enemy. The large kettle drum was especially important as it signified the Sultan. When troops mobilized, this drum was often carried by a camel or elephant due to its large size, as opposed to being carried by a soldier or on horseback. The *mehter* played in locations proximate to the headquarters, reflecting the power of the Sultan and generating martial enthusiasm among the troops (Bowles, 2006). Additionally, the bands played formal music to accompany morning, afternoon, and evening prayers.

These groups most likely existed for hundreds of years before the Ottoman empire and European Christian armies appropriated the instruments and sounds for their own military bands. These musical groups remained largely unchanged throughout the 17th century. The modern military band began to take shape by the end of the 18th century when the *hautbois* (predecessor of the modern oboe) joined with clarinets, horns, and bassoons in the courts of Europe. This group became known as *Harmoniemusik*, which referred to an ensemble of winds and percussion and was also used for military purposes. "Turkish" sounds of cymbals, tambourine, triangle, trumpets, and drums were added to the ensemble to make a somewhat standard military band (Gleason, 2015). The groups were often referred to as "outdoor" or "military" even if they were not specifically tied to an armed force.

U.S. military service songs

Each service within the U.S. military has official songs designed to promote the spirit, service, and history of each branch. The U.S. Army song, "The Army Goes Rolling Along," was adapted from "The Caisson Song." John Philip Sousa modified the music from an old Civil War tune in 1917, and new lyrics were added by Harold Arberg on its adoption as the official song of the Army in 1956. It is performed at the end of all reviews, parades, and honor guard ceremonies (Army Regulation 600–25). The U.S. Navy adopted the fight song, "Anchors Aweigh," from its Naval Academy in Annapolis, MD, written in 1906 by Charles Zimmerman, with lyrics by Alfred Miles. The hymn, "Eternal Father, Strong to Save," has also been adopted by both the U.S. and UK Navies. The U.S. Marine Corps designated the "Marine Hymn" as its official song in 1929. The music comes from an aria in the opera, "Genevieve de Brabant," composed by Jacques Offenbach. The lyrics changed over the years, with the current version authorized in 1942. "The U.S. Air Force Song" was originally adopted in 1939 as the "The Army Air Corps Song," when the Army and Air Force were a unified branch. After the Air Force became an independent branch in 1947, the song title was changed to "The U.S. Air Force Song." The music and lyrics were written by Robert Crawford. Since 1990, it has become popular to play all the songs as a medley during events that honor all service members and veterans across branches and service eras. The Coast Guard song, "Semper Paratus," is also part of the medley, since the organization used to fall within the Department of Defense (DoD). It is now under control of the Department of Homeland Security.

The Army is the largest of the U.S. military branches and hence is divided into multiple smaller organizations, many of which have their own official songs. Some of these date further back than the Army Song itself, including: "The All-American Soldier" (82nd Airborne Division), "Rendezvous with Destiny" (101st Air Assault Division), "The Signal Corps Song" (U.S. Army Signal Corps), "Essayons" (U.S. Army Engineer Corps), "The Caissons Go Rolling Along" (U.S. Army Field Artillery Corps), and "Dogface Soldier" (3rd Infantry Division). The large number of songs and unique iconography within each sub-organization of the Army demonstrate the variety of organizations required to maintain such a force. Soldiers tend to identify more with the music of their unit rather than that of the larger organization. The Army is founded on the principle of small teams joining together to serve the larger mission. In contrast, for example, many Marines collectively identify with being a Marine rather than the sub-organization to which they belong.

U.S. military bands in focus

Over 6000 service members' primary military occupational specialty (MOS) is "musician." There are 130 different military music organizations spread across the Army, Navy, Marine Corps, and Air Force, including both active (i.e., full-time) and reserve (i.e., part-time) service members. The stationing of these bands is a complex web of historical precedent and strategy. The roots of U.S. military bands can be traced to the militias of the original 13 colonies. As early as 1633, drummers in the Virginia colony received tobacco and corn in exchange for their musical services (Camus, 1975). Since every able-bodied man was required to fulfill military service, those with musical abilities carried their talents into drills.

The first recorded appearance of the military band in the U.S. was the "hautboys and fifes" of the Regiment of Artillery Company in Philadelphia commanded by Colonel Benjamin Franklin. Drumbeats were an effective way to facilitate synchronous movement and train specific musical calls that allowed for commands to be readily understood. This functional use of music was an essential part of forming an army and gaining battlefield advantage. Music also served a recreational purpose, and therefore, *Harmoniemusik* groups were formed. The men in these groups were classically trained musicians, whereas field musicians could be any soldier tasked with the duty of playing music. Today, two units carry on the tradition of field music including the U.S. Army's 3rd Infantry Regiment "Old Guard" Fife and Drum Corps at Joint Base Myer-Henderson Hall in Virginia and The Hellcats of the West Point Band at the U.S. Military Academy in New York. The Old Guard ensemble consists of fifes, one-valve bugles, and rope-tension drums. Similarly, the Hellcats perform on one-valve bugles and rope drums but use piccolos instead of fifes. The U.S. Military Academy is the only military installation in the U.S. that still uses a live bugler to sound various calls throughout the day; all others use digital recordings played over loudspeakers.

The modern-day bands of the Army and Air National Guard come from original militia groups who use their musical skills in service to the U.S. military on a part-time basis and at the behest of the state government. Every state besides Alaska, Montana, and Nevada has a National Guard band, including the territories (i.e., Puerto Rico, Guam, the Virgin Islands). The U.S. Army is the only service branch to maintain Reserve Bands. They are located throughout the continental U.S. and serve their respective geographic commands. All four military branches include bands that serve specific commands and/or geographic regions. For example, the Marine Corps Bands serve their local command, while Navy and Air Force bands tend to be geographically assigned. The Army uses a mix of both methods. The U.S. military also carries "special" bands in its inventory. The Navy has one of these bands, the Marines and Air Force each have two, and the Army has four. The U.S. Coast Guard Band currently falls under the Department of Homeland Security, but previously it was a part of the DoD; therefore, its band follows a similar structure and purpose to other military "special" bands. At the time of this publication, the U.S. Space Force does not have its own band.

The concept of "special" bands arose after WWI, largely attributed to General John J. Pershing. He heard the bands of Europe and marveled at their excellence. He knew that for the U.S. to be respected on the global stage, their bands needed to be of equal or superior caliber. This led to the founding of the U.S. Army Band "Pershing's Own." However, many of America's finest musicians were already serving in a military capacity including James Reese Europe's 369th "Harlem Hellfighters" Infantry Division Band, U.S. Military Academy Band (now the West Point Band), and the "President's Own" Marine Corps Band. Even though American military bands were patterned after the Turkish and, later, European bands, they became the global gold standard of prestige and versatility.

What began as music exclusively played for war and ceremonial duties has seen exemplary evolution largely due to the tremendous flexibility of modern military bands. No other musical organization is expected to play music from all genres to accommodate any and all occasions. In a single week, the typical military trumpeter might perform in a brass quintet for a military training graduation ceremony, march as part of large ensemble for a local town parade, play in a jazz combo for a formal military ball, and perform "Taps" at a military funeral. Most professional musicians are highly specialized in the type of music they perform.

The military musician must be a chameleon and a consummate professional in all missions. The U.S. DoD recruits the highest quality musicians because the utmost skill is required to promote its national interests and project the prestige of the country's military. Leon Botstein, an eminent conductor and President of Bard College, remarked on the important work of military bands, "They project a common image of the nation, inspiring faith in the national ideals put in place by the founders of the country" (Botstein, verbal communication, 2020).

On November 21, 2019, the U.S. President awarded the National Medal of the Arts to all past and present musicians of the U.S. military. This is a unique honor, as the medal is traditionally awarded to civilian artists who are highly recognized for achievements that span their careers in the arts. Past recipients include Dizzy Gillespie, B.B. King, Ray Charles, Tito Puente, Harry Belafonte, Barbra Streisand, Johnny Cash, and Bob Dylan, to name a few. This award validates the long-standing contributions and dedication of military musicians to their respective services. Military bands are the keepers of musical heritage for the U.S. DoD and ambassadors of American culture to the world.

The musical soldier

All members of the U.S. military are musical in some way or another, as is the entire human population. Human brains are finely adept at identifying patterns in sound and deriving pleasure from auditory organization. Call-and-response singing or calling cadence has a link to native cultures in sub-Saharan Africa and is possibly the oldest form of music-making (Wikipedia contributors, 2020). These shared songs make arduous tasks seem more enjoyable and contribute to the building of camaraderie. Songs sung by enslaved people in the Americas directly influenced the evolution of the Blues genre, still relevant in popular music culture today. The success of these songs often depends on the leader or facilitator, who must possess skill and dedication to inspire others who are likely unenthused about the work to be accomplished. All service members participate in cadence calling at some point throughout their careers. A historical review of military cadences (History of Military Cadences, n.d.) indicated that almost all current cadences can be attributed to variations of a chant created by Private (PVT) William Duckworth in 1944. PVT Duckworth was an African American who served in the U.S. Army during segregation who likely recalled work songs of prior generations. These chants resonate with military members, as they are designed to distract and uplift spirits through emotional expression during difficult or oppressive times. There is preliminary evidence to suggest that shared vocalizations bring people together, whether they are enduring slavery or war

(Launay *et al.*, 2016). Research into the relationship between synchronization, exertion, endorphins, and social bonding is ongoing.

While much of U.S. military music is created by professional musicians, many service members with a non-musical MOS create and record original compositions, often inspired by their service. Service members have always found ways of creating music in training and combat environments, particularly during the GWOT. An imagery analyst stationed in Kandahar, Afghanistan, 2011, used his guitar and singing skills to boost the morale of his fellow soldiers. A soldier can be seen in the Sebastian Junger film, *Restrepo*, playing his guitar in the narrow confines of his sleeping quarters. The desire to make music, even in the most dangerous of places, demonstrates its deep-rooted integration into military culture.

Radio and recorded music listening were not feasible until WWII, and even then, live performance continued to dominate the musical landscape. Songs written to support U.S. troops fighting in Korea during the early 1950s came mostly from the country genre (Tribe, in Kraaz, Ch.11, 2019). Songs by Ernest Tubb and Jimmy Osborne's "God, Please Protect America," for example, depicted the inherent polarization of war, in that we wish for victory, but also mourn for those who make the ultimate sacrifice: their lives.

The Korean War did not come to a definitive conclusion as evidenced by the continued division of the peninsula. U.S. citizens were enjoying newfound prosperity, which made it easy to ignore the conflicts overseas. Rock 'n' roll music became the dominant genre, much of which would find its way into the military. However, rock 'n' roll's rebellious spirit did not align with military leaderships' desire for order and discipline. This contradiction would play out during the Vietnam War. Radio and recorded music became the primary source through which deployed troops experienced music. Service members listened to both approved military stations as well as "pirate" radio, which played the protest music that most people associate with this time in history.

The wars in Iraq and Afghanistan following the terrorist attacks on September 11, 2001 spawned a new way that service members could interact with music, through the use of portable music devices. These eventually evolved from portable CD players, to laptop computers, to mp3 players (e.g., iPods), and now smartphones. This was the beginning of an era in which the internet was readily accessible for both business and leisure purposes. Service members now have individual access to massive libraries of their own curated music playlists customized for any and every situation. As in previous conflicts, military bands and celebrity musicians perform concerts; however, personal digital music devices dominate the musical experience. Being in the restricted environment of a military base in a war zone strips away the control of the individual service member, but digital music devices and software allow the service member to have complete control of one very critical element—their preferred music. Access to personal music is familiar, soothing, and an essential part of maintaining cultural and self-identity with social groups outside the military. Technological advancements in the last two decades have increased the ubiquity of music listening and expanded ways for individuals to create personal music narratives while preparing for, participating in, and recovering from war (Gilman, 2016).

Music is so readily accessible that sharing common musical tastes is becoming less prevalent. Algorithms that recommend music based on prior listening are constantly refined by digital music platforms (e.g., Spotify, Pandora, Apple, Google, and Amazon) to create a completely individualized music experience for each unique listener. Continued growth of concert ticket sales and community music-making conflicts with the custom music trend. Today, service members can barely remember the official songs of their branch/sub-organization, much less include them on their playlist, and they continue to find music aligned with their personal narratives. Official songs have become subconscious organizational and motivational influencers, much like music used in commercials and sonic branding, to constantly associate a core set of values with the larger organization. The musical culture of the U.S. military is a blend of the official songs chosen by the highest authority, and the personal choice of civilian music by service members of all ranks, ages, and jobs. Certain songs may be tagged with a very specific memory of service for military members, while they may identify their overall service with the official songs of their respective branch or organization.

Music and health in the U.S. military: a primer

The American Music Therapy Association (AMTA) attributes the development of music therapy as a profession to musical exercises conducted by the U.S. Army during WWII (American Music Therapy Association, 2014). The U.S. War Department Bulletin 187 outlined the reasons and methods for the use of music in veterans' hospitals and reconditioning clinics. The document cites: "… bringing a group together, releasing emotions, creating a spirit of fellowship, and esprit de corps. Music is suggested to be used throughout hospital settings for: physical reconditioning, occupational therapy, education, and recreation" (U.S. War Department, 1945, p.1). Key to this effort were the bands of the Women's Army Corps (WAC), Marine Corps Women's Reserve, and Women Accepted for Volunteer Emergency Service. These bands were originally formed to support the segregated gender roles of men and women during WWII; however, as the war drew to a close in 1945, these bands were increasingly used in hospitals and ports to perform music for returning male service members (Sullivan, 2011). In particular, the 400th, 401st, 402nd, and 403rd WAC Bands were mobilized and stationed at military hospitals at the end of the war. Following their service, some of the women in these bands were the first students educated in the inaugural academic music therapy programs. The effect these bands had on injured and recovering troops was observable through changes in morale and demeanor. First-hand accounts from the soldiers in the 403rd WAC Band, captured in Figure 1.6, said they made certain to include the audience in their performances through playing instruments, singing, or dancing. These women were innovators who crafted new ways of using music to interact with convalescing soldiers and helped to create the foundation for the current field of music therapy.

Figure 1.6: 403rd Women's Army Corps Band (photo credit: Dr. Jill M. Sullivan)[2]

Innovations in music therapy and military populations are being furthered through an initiative of the National Endowment for the Arts (NEA), called Creative Forces®: NEA Military Healing Arts Network. Creative Forces is a partnership with the U.S. Departments of Defense and Veterans Affairs, and state and local arts agencies and managed in partnership with Americans for the Arts, and the Henry M. Jackson Foundation for the Advancement of Military Medicine. Creative Forces, the National Institutes for Health, Kennedy Center's Sound Health Network initiative, and many other organizations continue to build bridges between music, neuroscience, and military health that the founding women soldiers of the WAC and other military bands started constructing over a century ago. What began as a military-based initiative has come full circle to include local and national non-profits and other government organizations working towards a shared mission: to provide programming, build community connections, and support research that demonstrates the use of music to improve wellness across all branches of the U.S. military, to include service members, veterans, National Guard and Reserve populations, as well

2 http://jillsullivan.faculty.asu.edu/?page_id=139

as families and caregivers. These areas of advancement are discussed in depth throughout subsequent chapters of this book.

Summary

Creating and engaging with music dates back to the earliest humans and has made its way into military culture. The idea of military service, both voluntary and conscripted, includes musical constructs unique to the military lifestyle. Signal or field music was needed to communicate information over long distances at a louder volume than that of battle. Highly rhythmic music is used to aid synchronization of movement through internal and external entrainment, such as marching. Prior to WWI, military formations always moved in specific ways to successfully outmaneuver the enemy. Military ceremonies require specific music and signals, which remind service members of their heritage while demonstrating prestige and honor to the civilian public. The adoption of popular songs for supporting individual emotion regulation and building group cohesion is a critical part of military culture. This includes the use of music to specifically deliver messages that influence the decisions and beliefs of an audience. The composition of music for and by military members allows for expression of experiences and helps to maintain the values of military culture.

All the various uses of music throughout the military, particularly in the U.S., contribute to the individual and social health of the fighting force. The U.S. Armed Forces are ultimately reliant on the people who make up the system. Their health and wellbeing directly determine the military's ability to accomplish the tasks requested by the civilian government and successfully achieve the mission. The systematic and intentional use of music to maintain the health of the military has been and will continue to be critical to its success in all endeavors. Botstein (1991) recognized the continued creation of music during war for its ability to remind us of the best in humanity, sustain our sense of hope, and preserve our sense of dignity against the fiercest odds.

Chapter 2

The Evolution of Music Therapy in Military Medicine

JUSTIN FRANCIS AND DONNA FARAONE

Disclaimer: The viewpoints articulated in this chapter are those of the authors and do not reflect on official policy of the Department of Veterans Affairs, Department of the Army, Department of Defense, or the United States Government.

Music in medicine: Antiquity through to the 21st century

Prominent figures in science and humanities regard music as a language that traverses cultural boundaries. Since the age of Antiquity, musical behaviors have been entrenched in tradition across cultures bestowing wisdom, virtue, and morality. Simply recall a melody or song that never ceases to uplift your spirits and fathom how evoking or inspiring music can be. Throughout human civilization, many cultures integrate musical properties and qualities in practices of medicine (Levitin, 2006). In fact, Babikian *et al.* (2013) claimed that music is one of the earliest known restorative art forms practiced by ancient healers. The influence of music in medicine can be traced back to the Paleolithic era, approximately 10,000 to 50,000 years ago. It was believed that music harbored mystical and supernatural properties over the spirit world. The early hunter-gathering societies were haunted by superstition, and alleged disease was a paradigm of spiritual imbalance. Paleolithic societies believed that music held magical properties capable of expelling evil spirits that inflicted human suffering (Levitin, 2006). Moreover, many viewed music as a conduit to commune with spiritual realms and nature.

Spanning human civilization, early medicine men, also known as *shamans* or *witch doctors*, infused music into their everyday medicinal and ceremonial rituals dating back for tens of thousands of years (Davis & Gfeller, 2008). West (2000) posits that ancient societies relied on the wisdom of shamanic healing for natural cures since a biomedical model of medicine was not yet envisioned.

Thus, illnesses were perceived as manifestations of spiritual or demonic possession rather than caused by infectious disease (Davis & Gfeller, 2008; West, 2000). Shamans shared in-depth knowledge of spiritual possession and of medicinal, herbal, and musical remedies. They would often play musical instruments during rituals for the purposes of communing with nature to cleanse and heal spiritual imbalances that were responsible for impeding their patient's health. Ancient instruments such as early model flutes, drums, and horns served an intentional purpose in conjuring and influencing the spiritual realm (West, 2000). Furthermore, archeological evidence supports claims of ancient "music healers" incorporating various drumming and chanting incantations in healing practices (Boxberger, 1962; Davis & Gfeller, 2008; Winkelman, 2017).

Modern-day music therapists subscribe to the notion that the foundations of music therapy are informed by early musical practices. Dr. Michael Thaut, an internationally recognized authority in music and neuroscience and the founder of neurologic music therapy (NMT), asserted that "the notion of music as therapy is based on ancient cross-cultural beliefs that music has a therapeutic effect on the mind and body" (2005, p.114). Likewise, early civilizations spoke of the therapeutic benefits of music on the physical and psychological wellbeing of the wounded, ill, and injured (American Music Therapy Association, 2011). In ancient Egypt, priests considered music as medicine for the soul, and the period of Antiquity sought the demarcation between magical healing and that of "rational medicine" (Davis & Gfeller, 2008). West (2000) surmised that musical healers were held in the highest regards during Antiquities, often performing in trance-like states which ritualized the inclusion of drumming in healing ceremonies, community events (Hawkins, 1994), and significant rites of passages (Douglas, 1966). Thus, music held an important role in healing practices throughout early preliterate and literate human societies.

The interplay of music, medicine, and philosophy

Ancient Greece

The Ancient Greeks revered music as a gift from the Muses: deities of wisdom, intuition, and the arts and sciences. They believed music held medicinal properties, therefore priest-healers performed soothing music and dance rituals to appease the god Apollo to provide relief to the sufferers of the deadly plague of 500 BC (Schoen-Nazzaro, 1978). Greek physicians, Pythagoras and Hippocrates, prescribed musical remedies to treat both physiological and psychological ailments (Babikian *et al.*, 2013) Greek philosophers, Aristotle and Plato, understood that music deeply held a humanistic and medicinal significance to human existence (Babikian *et al.*, 2013; Schoen-Nazzaro, 1978). Aristotle's treatise "De Anima" revealed philosophy of the musical soul as life's essence. Likewise, Aristotle's third rationale proclaimed music as a "...remedy of pain caused by toil" (Schoen-Nazzaro, 1978, p.266). In contrast, Plato viewed music as an expression of human emotions (Babikian *et al.*, 2013). Particularly, Plato thought that "rhythm and music generally are a reproduction expressing the moods" (Schoen-Nazzaro, 1978, p.267). Sacks (2008) argued that that human spirit is uplifted by music because people are biologically innate and culturally conditioned to emotionally respond to music. Plato's conception of music in medicine persisted and evolved through the Middle Ages, as did music.

Music from the Middle Ages to psychoanalytic theory

The Middle Ages (AD 476–1450) were an intriguing time for the arts in medicine, as music was thought to aid in the regulation of homeostatic function (West, 2000). Medieval physicians realized the therapeutic benefits of music in the treatment of mental illnesses (ibid.). Through the Renaissance period (14th–17th centuries), music in medicine adopted a more psychosomatic role in treating mental illness (Cochrane *et al.*, 2013). Cochrane and colleagues posited that therapeutic music was used to manage physical and psychosomatic pain during the time of the Great Plague in Europe in the mid-14th century. According to West (2000), the tarantella was a music and dance ritual prescribed by medieval physicians perceived to heal hysteria inflicted by spider bites. The effect of music on the human psyche was studied by many prominent figures in the psychological community during the late 19th century. From a psychoanalytical perspective, Sigmund Freud theorized that unconscious thoughts could potentially materialize and resolve through musical experiences (Reik, 1954). Moreover, it has been well established that listening to music helps restore emotional regulation and self-awareness (Schäfer *et al.*, 2013).

Early emergence of music, military, and medicine

The psychological underpinnings of music and wellbeing differed from that of the medical philosophy in the early 20th century. Arrington (1954) presented theoretical principles of music psychology that are focused on music's abilities to affect human behavior and emotional intelligence. This has influenced current practices, as many physicians, psychologists, and music therapists seek to rationalize the connection between the body's *fight-or-flight* response mechanisms in relation to musical consciousness, neurocognitive function, and behaviors (Sacks, 1998; Schneck & Berger, 2006). Throughout both World Wars, music therapists considered soothing music as calming and appropriate for use in psychiatric clinical work and discouraged the use of dissonance and minor keys as these musical elements were perceived to be emotionally damaging to convalescing soldiers. Even physicians of the Renaissance warned against the misuse of music, indicating that unsuitable music could provoke undesirable effects during treatment. The contemporary music therapist utilizes music to contextualize environments and shape moods of their patients and implements standards of clinical practice that mitigate risk of harm. The field of music therapy acknowledges the ability of music to evoke emotion used for healing, and also its power to elicit undesirable responses.

The music therapy profession has branched out into the areas of cognitive neuroscience to explore the neural circuitry of musical behaviors and physiological and neurological responses to music (Sacks, 2008). The 21st century has observed major technological advances in neuroimaging research that greatly impact the modern music therapy profession (Thaut, 2005). Furthermore, Thaut suggests that music is processed in the brain through a complete neural network that includes the sensory, auditory, motor, visual, and prefrontal cortex, along with the amygdala, hippocampus, and cerebellum (Schneck & Berger, 2006). Thaut's (2005) research of connectivity between music and neurological, physical, and emotional function further demonstrates beneficial outcomes on memory, behavior, and cognition through the application of standardized and evidence-based NMT treatment techniques. The emergence of psychological and cognitive neuroscience research has further promoted the role of music in human behavior, elevating disciplines such as music therapy in integrative healthcare models. Much about the ancient world's use of the arts in medicine remains unknown, yet practices such as ceremonial chanting and drumming, active and receptive listening, creative improvisation, ritualized dance, and art-making have inspired the establishment of creative arts therapies professions. These disciplines employ practices that preserve humanistic and holistic traditions of the long past.

Music therapy in American military medicine: a historical perspective

Music is intertwined in American military culture and military medicine (Forrest, 2008). Although music therapy as a profession lacked regulation and legitimacy until the mid-20th century, it has been influential in the military system since the 19th century. The capacity of music to shape interpersonal relationships and inspire troop morale was a relevant factor for its inclusion in military medicine. The earliest recorded recognition of music therapy appeared in the 1789 *Columbian Magazine* article entitled "Music Physically Considered," which alleged the potential benefits of music for grief-afflicted service members (Davis & Else, 2019).

Throughout the 19th and 20th centuries, music therapy continued to evolve as a creative arts discipline for service members impacted by physiological and psychological injuries (American Music Therapy Association, 2011).

Multiple capacities of music

During the American Revolution and Civil War, music served in dual capacities for both ceremonial and strategic purposes (Dobney, 2008). Military musicians sounded vital signals on the battlefield and regulated daily routines in garrison through use of specific songs. Musicians serving in the military proved to be an invaluable psychological asset for instilling courage, patriotism, pride, and loyalty among injured troops (Bradford, 2006). During the Crimean War (1853–1856), Florence Nightingale favored hospital music—a type of music composed to contain calming and restorative properties, which was played while rendering medical treatment to the wounded (McWhirter, 2012). In 1886, the National Homes for Disabled Volunteer Soldiers (NHDVS) were established to care for disabled Civil War veterans, and volunteer musicians visited Union hospitals (later Confederate hospitals) to entertain convalescing soldiers (Davis, 2003; Olson, 1981). The NHDVS provided injured veterans "home[s] specially adapted to the needs" of convalescence (van de Wetering, 1984, p.14). According to Kelly (1997), music programs offered in the NHDVS homes served multiple purposes of alleviating institutional boredom, acclimating to a new environment, and providing sociable means of entertainment, leisure, or educational pursuits (e.g., music lessons). Different NHDVS homes established bands that offered veterans opportunities for connection through socialization and community outreach (ibid.). Celina (1977) suggests that these bands provided entertainment and accompaniment for site-wide military ceremonies and social functions. The bands and other recreational programs provided meaningful engagement for veterans and enhanced morale at the NHDVS homes. The NHDVS remained operational until 1931, when it merged with the newly formed Veterans Administration, which is part of the Department of Veterans Affairs (VA).

For centuries, most European countries had well-established hospital music programs and America started to catch up by the outset of the 20th century (Browne, 1954). Music therapy gained notable momentum during World War I (WWI), particularly through integration into psychiatry practices (Light, 1946). As WWI ushered in the age of mechanized warfare, traumatic combat exposure left military physicians scrambling to investigate root causes of mental illness as prevalence increased (Tyson, 1981). Music therapy served primarily as an adjunctive treatment that worked alongside physical and occupational therapies to support respiratory recovery (Light, 1946); promote relaxation prior to surgical procedures (Light *et al.*, 1954; Tyson, 1981); and foster mental health recovery in psychiatric institutions (van de Wall, 1936). Dr. Willem van de Wall (1946) claimed that music therapy was well suited for psychiatric rehabilitation as it could awaken memories and stimulate emotional responses. Furthermore, music programs on hospital wards were generally well received by service members convalescing in psychiatric institutions and were believed to render patients "more agreeable" to receiving clinical services (van de Wall, 1936, p.26). Modern-day music therapy is recognized to increase treatment compliance in service members' overall treatment plans, especially when delivered through an interdisciplinary care model (Vaudreuil *et al.*, 2019a).

Emerging concepts in early music therapy

By the 1930s, the scientific upsurge in allopathic medicine obscured the once traditional close relationship observed between music and medicine. Although some still believed that biomedicine had dehumanized the practice of modern medicine, physicians began to recognize the importance of neuropsychiatry and the need for specialized treatment of mental health disorders (Taylor, 1981). A decade earlier, Dr. Esther Gatewood advocated for the neuropsychological benefits of music therapy in institutional settings. Remarkably, Gatewood's research into the neuro-receptive response to musical stimuli helped formalize the iso-principle, an actionable concept distinctive to the music therapy profession. The iso-principle method attends to clients at their individual emotional levels and gradually shifts their mood states via music intervention (Taylor, 1981). Contemporary music therapists apply music-based clinical interventions to match the emotional states of their clients to foster and achieve desired therapeutic goals. In the years preceding World War II (WWII), government hospitals rapidly expanded recreational music programs (Davis & Gfeller, 2008). Gilliland (1945) justified that early recreational music programs, though beneficial, were not to be confused with prescribed music therapy treatment. It seemed to be the innate fusion of creative arts and medicine that formalized music therapy as a clinical discipline during WWII. The War Department recognized the therapeutic potential of music therapy and sought its inclusion into the Army's Reconditioning Program (Boxberger, 1962).

Music in reconditioning during World War II

Efforts made by music technicians (i.e., inaugural music therapists) in the aftermath of WWII foreshadowed the development of the contemporary music therapy profession. Music programs in civilian medical facilities received broader acceptance at military hospitals in the 1940s as supportively safe milieu therapy for recovering service members (American Music Therapy Association, 2014; Taylor, 1981). Conversely, the War Department remained skeptical towards exaggerated claims surrounding music therapy (Davis & Else, 2019). Army leadership considered military music used on the battlefields obsolete in the age of mechanized warfare (Ainlay, 1948). Furthermore, between 1942 and 1943, the military deemed private music instruments as contraband and prohibited them on overseas deployments (Rorke, 1996). In 1942, the Army and Navy established the Music Advisory Council to organize hospital music and recreational programing (Sullivan, 2007). By early 1943, perceptions shifted, and Army doctors revisited the morale-boosting and clinical benefits of music therapy. Medical administrators acknowledged the complexities surrounding psychiatric care; henceforth, Surgeon General Norman T. Kirk explored alternative adjunctive interventions to meet the growing demands on healthcare systems based on the needs of returning service members. The Army's Special Services Branch, in collaboration with the Surgeon General's Office, formally integrated music therapy as part of the Army's Reconditioning Program (Rorke, 1996).

Volunteer musicians

An increasing number of amateur and professional musicians volunteered in hospitals on medical and psychiatric wards to aid in the recovery of the wounded (American Music Therapy Association, 2014). Michel and Pinson (2005) conveyed that music "provided a kind of solace for the war-weary soldier" (p.5). By 1942, the Reconditioning Program offered planned programs aimed at physical fitness, educational resourcing, and recreation therapy intended to restore wounded service members' fitness for active duty and optimize psychological and physiological health for safe discharge (Barton, 1945). The inclusion of music in the Reconditioning Program aspired to aid in morale, reduce symptoms of homesickness, and develop creative outlets to address medical, physical, and neuropsychiatric clinical needs (U.S. War Department, 1945).

Hospital music programs have demonstrated efficacy in alleviating somatic tension during wartime (van de Wall, 1946), promoting self-expression, developing healthy social habits, and stimulating emotional recall in psychiatric treatment (Simon, 1945). Contemporary music therapists are qualified to provide meaningful evidence-based interventions informed by clinical goals to evoke similar physiological and psychological responses that contribute to successful treatment outcomes. Ainlay (1948) asserted that "if the healthy Soldier wanted and needed music to keep up his spirits, how much more did the wounded man need it to keep up his morale?" (p.323). Military figures like Captain Guy

V.R. Marriner, with support from Colonels George W. Ainlay and Howard Bronson, vigorously advocated for the inclusion of music therapy as formal treatment in military medicine. Together, they drafted the U.S. War Department Technical Bulletin 187 in 1945, signifying the Army's official doctrine for music in reconditioning.

In 1942, Lieutenant Marriner, a commissioned Army officer, was appointed to the position of Music Liaison under Colonel Howard Bronson, Chief of the Music Branch in the Office of Special Services, where they spearheaded the Music in Reconditioning Program (Ainlay, 1948; Davis & Else, 2019; Fauser, 2013). In 1943, Marriner arranged a nationwide tour of military hospitals to ascertain the musical tastes and preferences of returning wounded service members ("Music for Rehabilitation of War Casualties," 1944). Marriner served in the New Zealand Army during WWI before settling in America where he worked as a professional concert pianist and presided as Director of Music at the Franklin Institute (Fauser, 2013). He rationalized that an integrative hospital music program, led by qualified music technicians, could offer therapeutic relief from the "imprints of battle" in neuropsychiatric patients ("Music for Rehabilitation of War Casualties," 1944, p.10). Between 1944 and 1946, Marriner carried out longitudinal studies to investigate the scientific merit of music as therapy. Collaborators included Dr. van de Wall at the La Garde General Hospital in New Orleans (Fauser, 2013) and Frances Paperte at Walter Reed General Hospital (Paperte, 1946). Furthermore, the Army formalized the Women's Army Corps (WAC) and Army Service Force (ASF) bands in 1944 to entertain the wounded and perform concerts at military hospitals (Sullivan, 2007). Sullivan reported that WAC bands were well received by the wounded, and hence military band performances increased as part of the Reconditioning Program by 1945.

Music technicians

By 1945, the newly promoted Captain Marriner was appointed Chief of the Hospital Section of the Music Branch (Ainlay, 1948). The U.S. War Department issued the Technical Bulletin, TB MED 187, which specified that "music should be provided along with other activities offered to patients because it is one of the most effective vehicles for bringing a group together, for releasing emotions, and for creating a spirit of fellowship and esprit de corps" (1945, p.1). The bulletin endorsed a well-rounded music program for use in rehabilitative and neuropsychiatric wards. Structurally, music officers served as knowledgeable consultants and overseers of all hospital music programming, which was facilitated by volunteer music technicians. These technicians provided direct therapeutic music engagement prescribed by physicians to patients in hospitals, and maintained instrument inventories (Ainlay, 1948). Therapeutic engagements consisted of active, passive, and audio-receptive music programs. For example, Figure 2.1 depicts a service member playing a marimba as a component of his physical reconditioning program (National Museum of Health and Medicine, c. WWI). Individualized leisure educational programs were supported by volunteer organizational partnerships, such as the American Red Cross, that offered supplementary programming or entertainment in the event that technicians were unavailable (Rorke, 1996).

Figure 2.1: Patient playing marimba to assist with physical rehabilitation, circa WWI (photo credit: Otis Historical Archives, National Museum of Health and Medicine)

As a physician and amateur musician, Colonel Ainlay noted that military doctors held misconceptions of music as therapy beyond its aesthetic value until the 1950s (Bunt & Stige, 2014). In an effort to train musicians on basic medical training and scientific inquiry, university-level music therapy curriculums were developed by 1944 (Ainlay, 1948). In 1945, the National Music Council (NMC) created a music therapy committee, and by 1950 the National Association of Music Therapy (NAMT) was founded to advocate for credentialing, professional standards, research, and clinical training (Bunt & Stige, 2014). Despite lack of formal training and empirical evidence, music technicians continued to implement prosperous therapeutic programming nationwide at military and veteran hospitals (Green, 1949b; Paperte, 1946). At Walter Reed General Hospital, Paperte conducted a six-month longitudinal study with neuropsychiatric patients (*n*=50) to ascertain whether controlled applications of music could enhance clinical outcomes (Paperte, 1946). Following an interview, subjects were classified by symptoms and placed into small treatment groups, with no more than six subjects in each group. Treatment groups met once a day, five days a week, for approximately three months. Music therapy interventions included both active and receptive methods indicated by the iso-principle. Although findings were inconclusive, a psychiatrist reported that music hastened recovery rates of his patients. In sum, the study reinforced the need for the development of professional clinical standards in music therapy (Paperte, 1946).

Early music therapy programming assisted occupational therapy treatment through the use of percussion instruments to train varying levels of attention, wind instruments to support chest injury recovery, and the provision of music to bolster group participation and relaxation methods on neuropsychiatric wards (Marriner, 1945). Music technicians increased educational opportunities through developing resources such as *The Minute Self-Instructor for Tonette, Ocarina, Harmonica, and Ukulele* and the Army's *Hit Kits*, used to promote receptive listening skills (Ainlay, 1948). Additional audio-receptive programs included recordings and V-Disks supplementing educational and music appreciation courses. Unfortunately, wartime statistics of hospital music programs remain unknown; however, between 1946 and 1950, TB MED 187 guidelines remained viable throughout all 122 VA hospitals (American Music Therapy Association, 2014; Rorke, 1996). A survey of VA sites across the U.S. conducted by Ray Green in 1946 found that 80,000 veterans participated in music programs. Of those, approximately 7538 veterans were prescribed or referred to music programming by physicians, 1447 veterans were offered instrumental instruction, 331 veterans engaged in songwriting programs, 1431 veterans were offered vocal instruction, and nearly 275,000 veterans attended educational, diversional, or music appreciation programs (Rorke, 1996). Green reported that by December of 1947, 83,121 veterans attended music programming across 126 VAs and neuropsychiatric wards reported an approximate active patient participation ratio of 1:4 (Green, 1948a). The same report found that by December of 1946, 875,000 veterans participated in passive music programs throughout 122 VAs. Music performed a vital role in the Army's Reconditioning Program and music technicians made considerable strides working with patients who presented with neuropsychiatric dysfunction and proved music's flexibility to support rehabilitative medicine.

The role of music therapy in the post-war era

During WWII, the military offered hospital music programs in tandem with other clinical disciplines such as physical therapy, occupational therapy, and psychiatric care (Light, 1946). Michel and Pinson (2005) claim that music administered in adult psychiatric settings gained wider acceptance among the healthcare community and population during the post-war years and grew into a vital creative outlet for veterans receiving care through the VA (Boxberger,

1962). In the post-war era, there were music technicians operating in 122 military and VA hospitals nationwide (American Music Therapy Association, 2014). According to Fauser:

> In Marriner's and the Army's post-war world, alternative forms of therapy had to measure up to recently developed standards of scientific and medical research that sought to isolate causes and quantify effects... The increased suspicion of a direct connection between music and emotion was rooted not only in the new paradigms of medical research; once it had become clear to what extent such regimes as the Nazis had instrumentalized music for political gain, music's emotional side became deeply suspect and demanded careful investigation. (2013, p.134)

By late 1945, the Army Air Force (AAF) Convalescent Hospital at Fort Logan, Colorado established music therapy programming to address the mental, physical, and spiritual needs of returning airmen (McKay, 1945). The program was led by eight enthusiastic enlisted personnel and provided group and individual therapeutic music programs, instrumental lessons, radio broadcasts, and jam sessions. Additionally, they established a Tinker Shop to assist in rehabilitation by making improvised instruments such as the Xylette, as depicted in Figure 2.2, which is a two and one-third octave, 15-pound, miniature piano invented by AAF Private Harold Rhodes (Newsweek, 1944). Following the war, psychiatric facilities explored music for procedural support with patients undergoing insulin and electroshock treatment as well as a component of administering anesthesia during oral surgery. Results revealed that receptive music helped patients recover quicker from procedures (Lewis *et al.*, 1947; Taylor, 1981).

Figure 2.2: A convalescing soldier receiving short-cut method music instruction on the Xylette. Newsweek, December 1944

An article in the New York Times (June 1, 1946) titled "Music Helps Veterans with Impaired Hearing," indicated that music therapy had beneficial outcomes when integrated into treatment that addressed helping veterans adapt to hearing loss, improve vestibular function via music and movement programs, and achieve speech language goals including vocal control and modulation training. Bernstein (1946) suggested that music therapy interventions aided in social readjustment and instilled confidence in veterans with visual impairments. The article discussed the case of Lieutenant "X," a soldier who expressed a desire to study voice after being rendered completely blind and suffering severe injuries to his upper extremities including complete loss of his right hand and most of his left. In addition to vocal lessons, the music technician offered trombone lessons to assist Lieutenant X's occupational therapy by creatively adapting his new prosthetic device to play the musical instrument. He also learned to read braille music. At Percy Jones General Hospital in Battle Creek, Michigan, music programs were recognized to be a beneficial component of service members' speech and language therapy to treat aphasia, as group singing was effective in stimulating associational pathways through old and familiar songs (Sheehan, 1946).

Music and music therapy: post-WWII to the Global War on Terrorism

Advances in the quality and portability of technology increased access to music for military personnel serving during conflicts following WWII, from Korea (1950–1953) to Operation Enduring Freedom (2001–2014). This emphasizes the importance of music as a vehicle for social and emotional expression and a means to stay connected to home. The music of the Korean War era was generally patriotic and uplifting; however, there was a growing "shift from the overly patriotic lyrics of WWII to the anti-war protest melodies of the Vietnam Era" (Wolfe, 2016, para.1). Soldiers in Vietnam had increased access to music compared with those who served in previous eras. Bradley and Werner note that access to music via technology and live performances provided U.S. service men and women in Vietnam with a means to remain somewhat connected to home and, for many, a safe outlet to express feelings of uncertainty and ambivalence (as cited in Wolfe, 2016).

Music serves to reflect the ebb and flow of support for the military as well as the changing face of the service member, transcending the Vietnam draft to the voluntary force of modern times. Each era of unique conflict yields its own specific considerations that impact the concentration and application of military medicine. For example, due to the persistent duration of the Global

War on Terrorism (2001–present), it is common for contemporary service men and women to experience multiple deployments; therefore, treatment is focused on maintaining mission readiness of the fighting force. The severity of invisible wounds, such as post-traumatic stress disorder (PTSD), traumatic brain injury (TBI), and military sexual trauma (MST), and the heightened incidence of amputations due to improvised explosive devices, as well as the increasing suicide rate are only a few of the casualties of combat. More than 500,000 men and women of the U.S. Armed Services are living with TBI or PTSD, including 10–20 percent of all service members deployed to Iraq and Afghanistan. TBI, PTSD, and MST contribute to anxiety and depression, which are major contributing factors to veteran suicide (U.S. Department of Veterans Affairs, 2019a). Creative arts therapists are being integrated into interdisciplinary treatment models to provide comprehensive care for service members and veterans rehabilitating from physiological and psychological injuries (Vaudreuil *et al.*, 2019a). NMT techniques are well suited to meet the unique needs of service members and veterans and, additionally, there is a growing trend in expanding the academic curriculum to meet the increasing need for qualified music therapists to deliver effective music therapy services for military and veteran populations.

Advancement of music therapy in the 20th century

By the 1950s, the NAMT advocated for the progressive advancement of music therapy clinical standards and the development of ethical guidelines for music therapy practice and research. In 1951, the VA internally surveyed hospitals system-wide to ascertain outcomes of music therapy services since 1949 (Quinto, 1951). The survey indicated the following results:

- Five hospitals reported providing receptive music in operating rooms to comfort patients.
- Seventy hospitals incorporated music therapy into insulin and electroshock therapy treatments.
- Forty-seven hospitals provided active music-making with "regressed patients" on neuropsychiatric wards.
- Sixty-eight hospitals offered receptive music in chow halls and frequently provided musical entertainment during evening programming.

According to Larson (1953), the NMC endorsed the intelligent use of music as a therapeutic modality in healthcare and advocated for the full-time employment of music technicians at VA hospitals (Quinto, 1951). By 1951, the profession of music therapy was officially recognized by the VA (Davis & Else, 2019), and from the 20th century on, veteran demand for the creative arts has continued to grow.

Today, music is used across military and civilian medical sectors. It is used receptively, as it is infused into waiting areas and procedure rooms of modern-day medical clinics (e.g., doctors, dentists, osteopaths), and it is used expressively through interactive music-making, such as lively drum circles. Regulation of the music therapy profession has evolved throughout the 20th century through establishment of the national associations to provide governance, as shown in Figure 2.3. Regulation and governance ushered music therapy as a viable treatment and profession into military medicine, veteran healthcare, and civilian medical centers nationwide. Oversight, advocacy, and research have enabled the field of music therapy to demonstrate the efficacy of music as an accommodating and powerful tool for rehabilitation across physical, psychological, neurological, and spiritual domains.

Figure 2.3: Timeline of music therapy governance

Pioneers in music therapy

The 20th century brought about major methodological and integrative treatment approaches to rehabilitative and psychiatric health. During this time, Browne (1954) noted steady growth and interest among musicians pursuing music programs in military hospitals. These early hospital musicians laid the foundation for the modern music therapy profession and positioned the field to be recognized for its therapeutic value in healthcare. Several pioneers in music therapy from the early 20th century stand out as exemplary early music therapists who worked with military populations. These include Isa Maud Ilsen, Margaret Anderton, Dr. Willem van de Wall, Harriet Ayer Seymour, and Frances Paperte, whose contributions to the field of music therapy in military medicine have had lasting impacts.

Isa Maud Ilsen

Early in her career, Isa Ilsen provided music therapy to wounded Canadian Soldiers during WWI. She developed clinical music therapy protocols for use in adult rehabilitative and psychiatric settings and was an advocate for the use of music therapy in surgical and post-operative care (Davis & Gfeller, 2008). In 1918, Ms. Ilsen vigorously promoted music therapy services with wounded American service members while carrying out her role as Director of Hospital Music for the Reconstruction Hospitals (Davis, 1993). Following the war, Ms. Ilsen taught "musical therapy" at Columbia University and in 1926 she founded the National Association of Music in Hospitals (Davis, 1993).

Margaret Anderton

Much like her colleague, Isa Ilsen, Margaret Anderton provided care to wounded Canadian Soldiers recovering from their tours of duty in WWI. Ms. Anderton lectured on music in medicine at Columbia University in 1919 (Davis & Gfeller, 2008). She advocated for the use of active musical engagements in support of physical reconditioning, and passive receptive methods for psychological reconditioning (Davis & Gfeller, 2008; Taylor, 1981).

Dr. Willem van de Wall

Dr. Willem van de Wall started his career in music therapy in 1919. During WWI, he enlisted with the Marine Corps Band where he witnessed first-hand the therapeutic and morale-lifting benefits of music (van de Wall, 1936). His work was influential in developing music therapy programs in mental health institutions (Browne, 1954). By 1927, Dr. van de Wall established a clinic at the Allentown State Hospital and taught a music and health course at Columbia University. In 1944, he served as the Chairman on the Committee for the Use of Music in Hospitals and postulated that musical behaviors were directly correlated to psychological and physiological health (van de Wall, 1946). Dr. van de Wall's efforts directly influenced music therapy in mental health recovery at military hospitals during the first half of the 20th century.

Harriet Ayer Seymour

Harriet Ayer Seymour provided music therapy to service members with shellshock—what we now know to be PTSD. According to Davis (1993), Ms. Seymour noted positive psychological benefits of music therapy while providing care to wounded service members. She founded the National Foundation for

Music Therapy in 1941 and later published the first academic texts illustrating clinical and professional standards (Boxberger, 1962). This publication provided valuable insight into the clinical applications of music therapy with various treatment populations, and prioritized the need for musical competencies, ethics, and clinical standards.

Frances Paperte

While maintaining a prominent singing career, Frances Paperte volunteered to comfort the wounded during WWI through musical performance. While volunteering, Ms. Paperte directly observed the therapeutic benefits of music and pursued a career in music therapy (Rorke, 1996). By WWII, she was a pioneer of the concept that music therapy had a valuable and restorative role to play in military medicine.

The future of music therapy in the evolving clinical approach

It is easy to find daily commentary on medicine across multimedia forums and it is even more prevalent during times of a healthcare crisis, such as the COVID-19 global pandemic. Medical breakthroughs, healthcare reform, and access to care are polarizing topics for political platforms, media blitzes, and dinner table conversation. In a broad stroke, healthcare focuses on activities that maintain and restore health; however, the U.S. spends nine times more on medical care than it does on optimizing or promoting health. This approach is contraindicated by the growing body of research demonstrating the benefits of adopting healthy lifestyles and affirming the power of an individual focus on behavioral change (Kovner & Knickman, 2008). This unbalanced focus should not impede continuous efforts for greater access to care that patients and healthcare systems alike can promote, including collaborations of scientists, providers, patients, and communities that can substantially impact quality of life through informed intervention and research innovation (MISSION Act, 2018).

The clamor for U.S. healthcare reform has been overtly apparent for decades as evidenced by cost escalation and increasing difficulty for Americans to attain and maintain quality healthcare. The waste and redundancy-riddled system is calling for modernization with focus dedicated to patient-centered care (Institute of Medicine, 2001). As part of the national movement towards value-based and accountable care, healthcare systems are working to incorporate patient-centered approaches to improve patient wellness and increase engagement in self-care (Bokhour *et al.*, 2020a, p.1). The opioid crisis and escalation of suicide among military personnel and veterans are motivating change, and have challenged the current healthcare paradigm to meets the needs of America's military, including elevating the function of 21st-century medicine.

Models of modern medicine: VA Whole Health initiative

The VA's Whole Health initiative is an example that empowers and enables a person to take charge of their health and wellbeing in order to live life to the fullest (U.S. Department of Veterans Affairs, n.d.-h). Identifying what is important to the individual, their mission, aspiration, and purpose (MAP), is crucial to implementing a Whole Health approach (Bokhour *et al.*, 2020a). An individual's MAP may change as needs and life circumstances evolve, which aligns with a relational versus transactional model of care. Whole Health incorporates health coaching and complementary and integrative treatment options for patients and empowers the individual to engage in and integrate self-care into daily living by providing skill building and support through clinical and psychoeducational resources. This healthcare design is fertile ground for the growth and acknowledgement of music therapy as a therapeutic tool in clinical care and a dynamic treatment that supports development of self-care skills to enhance wellbeing and optimize quality of life.

On July 22, 2016, the Comprehensive Addiction and Recovery Act (CARA) was signed into law, establishing funding to support strategies to address the opioid epidemic (CARA, 2016). In response, the VA's Office of Patient-Centered Care and Cultural Transformation formalized an approach to care called the Whole Health System of Care, which incorporates patient-centered care and complementary and integrative health, as depicted in Figure 2.4 (Bokhour *et al.*, 2020b, p.1). A two-year progress report on 18 VA flagship sites, funded through CARA, indicated: progress in implementation of the Whole Health system; increased utilization of Whole Health services, especially among veterans with chronic pain; a positive impact on reducing opioid use among veterans; and early trends towards improvement in patient reported outcomes (Bokhour *et al.*, 2020b).

There are many opportunities for music therapists to contribute to the Whole Health system. Music therapists are trained to value the patient–therapist therapeutic relationship and to make impactful connections that benefit the patient's overall treatment plan. The art and science of music is composed of verbal and non-verbal and non-threatening and inviting structures that lend themselves to building trust. Music therapy is often facilitated at the bedside, in clinics and communities, and across environments to stimulate creative processes and enhance healthy communication.

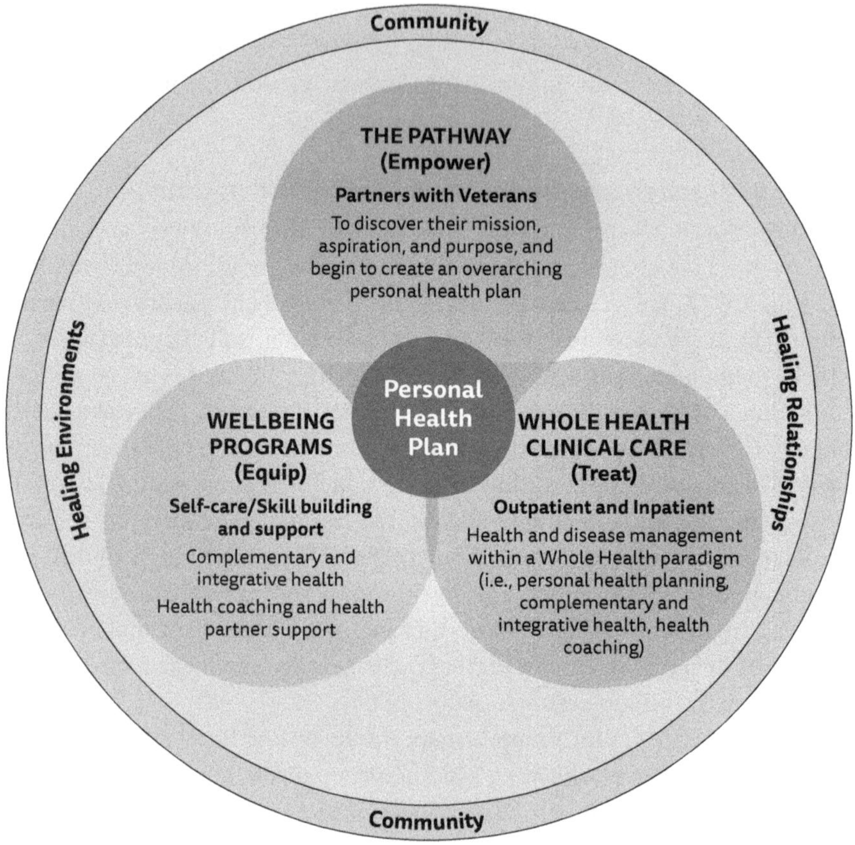

Figure 2.4: VA Whole Health system of care (image credit: Bokhour and Hyde, 2020b)

Music therapists can play a major role in facilitating the development of patients' MAP through the use of music and the application of therapeutic interventions to facilitate relaxation, incite reflection, inspire goal identification, and define health in the context of goal accomplishment. Music listening, improvisation, songwriting, and music imagery are just a few of the interventions that support the development of the MAP as a foundation for Whole Health. In addition, specific NMT techniques are grounded in theory that supports music interventions to treat areas of cognition, sensorimotor, and speech and language dysfunction as well as behavioral, emotional, and psychological dysregulation through music in psychosocial training and counseling techniques (Vaudreuil *et al.*, 2020a). The approach of integrating music and traditional rehabilitation domains lends itself to treating military populations, as they experience high occurrences and comorbidities of physical, psychological, and neurological injuries, such as TBI and PTSD. Interdisciplinary care models are implemented widely across military and veteran healthcare systems, and music therapy is positioned as a standard of care to assist in multiple areas of rehabilitation through stand-alone and co-treatment sessions (Bronson *et al.*, 2018). Building skill in self-care practices requires experiential and educational opportunities to train and support patients in actions relevantly aligned to the MAP and goals included in the patient's treatment plan. Music therapists can lead patients through the proactive components of health and wellbeing, as indicated in the Circle of Health displayed in Figure 2.5, using music in a variety of forms and functions to facilitate goal accomplishment.

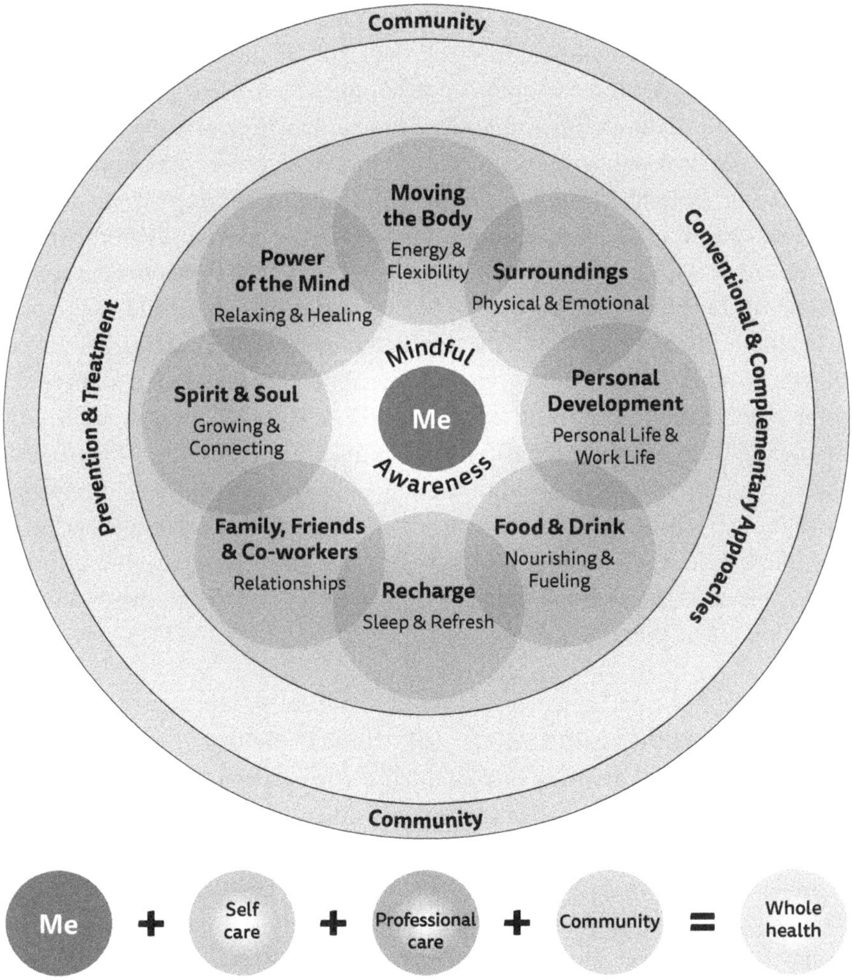

Figure 2.5: Circle of Health (image credit: www.va.gov/WHOLEHEALTH/circle-of-health/index.asp)

The integration of components of whole health and music

Many scholars have been curious about the function of music from varying perspectives (e.g., social, physiological, psychological), resulting in an array of theories and proposals on how to classify the functionality of music (Schäfer *et al.*, 2013). In 1964, Alan Merriam discussed scholarly theories for the categorization of music's uses and functions, and proposed ten functions of music, including 1) emotional expression, 2) aesthetic enjoyment, 3) entertainment, 4) communication, 5) symbolic representation, 6) physical response, 7) enforcing conformity to social norms, 8) validation of social institutions and religious rituals, 9) contribution and stability of culture, and 10) constitution to the integration of society (Merriam, 1964, pp.232–239). Distinct parallels can be made between these ten categories and the eight components of the Circle of Health that suggest the use of music to support the patient in clinical treatment and in the development of self-care practices. For example, music can motivate physical activity through entertainment, empower the mind through stimulating thought, influence the spirit and soul by enhancing rituals (e.g., religious, traditional), evoke emotion, and create a conducive environment for conversation with family, friends, or co-workers. Music therapists can coach patients in developing self-care practices relevant to their MAP and health plan to habituate lifelong patterned behaviors that nurture wellbeing. The delivery of evidence-based, quality clinical care informed by a patient's MAP remains a key component in the Whole Health system. In Whole Health clinical care, an entire healthcare team supports the patient's plan of care and develops shared goals aimed at supplementing wellbeing and addressing the needs of the whole person. In a Whole Health system, the clinical provider considers holistic approaches in addition to evidence-based medical protocols and pharmaceutical interventions, and emphasizes research-associated complementary and integrative treatment, including music therapy.

Increasing visibility and validity of music therapy

For decades, music therapy has retained a strong presence in the VA and continues to grow its presence in the DoD. Music therapy is practiced with military populations to treat a myriad of diagnoses, including physical and mental health needs. In a Whole Health approach, music therapists may find themselves increasingly considered as a credible clinical partner to facilitate music therapy interventions that address patient goals, thus positioning music therapy as a viable option in the treatment of medical conditions and disease as well as a clinical practice that promotes health maintenance. Military and veteran institutions are embracing collaborations across systems levels—micro (e.g., individual, families), mezzo (e.g., communities), and macro (e.g., government)—to coordinate efforts in support of the same mission of meeting the needs of patients' overall health and wellbeing and improve quality of life. These partnerships aim to increase access to the arts and music therapy in communities nationwide.

Community advocates and partners

Arts advocacy organizations, such as Americans for the Arts, National Organization for Arts in Health, and Resounding Joy, Inc., acknowledge and support the holistic and healing properties of the arts in medicine and the use of music and music therapy. Governmental efforts and community partnerships will be further described in later chapters of the book (Chapters 4 and 9) indicating viable connections between music therapists collaborating with community artists to assist processes of transition from military and veteran healthcare settings into the community using a strategic clinic and community continuum that supports reintegration (Vaudreuil *et al.*, 2019b).

Summary

As demand for music therapy services continues to evolve at DoD and VA facilities, it is essential to reflect on the unique contributions that early music therapists and music technicians have made to the development of the modern-day music therapy profession. The history of music in military medicine and its subsequent metamorphosis into a therapeutic profession is a fascinating area of inquiry for future investigators wishing to explore this subject in more depth. Music's heritage in ancient medicine, military service and culture, and its contribution to military medicine can attest to the rich historical and humanistic connections that music has on health and wellbeing. Following WWII, the Army anticipated the critical need for music therapy services in response to the health needs of returning service members and veterans. Despite initial skepticism, the modern music therapy profession has evolved into a standardized evidence-based treatment at DoD and VA facilities.

The future of developing health systems to employ patient-centered approaches requires moving beyond the traditional medical model to incorporate and integrate health promotion and wellness. The DoD and VA are committed to modernizing systems and envisioning a new paradigm of care delivery that embraces health and wellbeing for America's military service members, veterans, and military families. A key VA transformation strategy is a systemic shift from a focus on disease management to one that embraces whole health models of care (U.S. Department of Veterans Affairs, 2019a, p.21). VA's Whole Health initiative regards that which is important to the patient as the foundation for healthcare delivery and integrates complementary and integrative treatment approaches where patient goals are incorporated into planning and decision-making and supported with skill building and coaching (Bokhour *et al.*, 2020a). There is a wealth of evidence to support the impact of music on health and the efficacy of music therapy in both promoting and restoring health. The music therapy profession is a viable and effective component in a Whole Health system, as it can facilitate the accomplishment of personal and clinical goals using music and therapeutic interventions to optimize health and wellbeing.

Chapter 3

Music Therapy in the Department of Veterans Affairs

LISBETH WOODWARD AND DAVID OTTO

Disclaimer: The viewpoints articulated in this chapter are those of the authors and do not reflect on official policy of the Department of Veterans Affairs, Department of the Army, Department of Defense, or United States Government.

The foundation of music as therapy in the Veterans Administration

In the 1920s, following World War I, the United States Veterans Bureau, Bureau of Pensions of the Interior Department, and National Home for Disabled Volunteer Soldiers were established for the delivery of veterans' benefits, including disability compensation, insurance, and vocational rehabilitation (U.S. Department of Veterans Affairs, 2005). These three agencies, along with the Public Health Service Veterans' hospitals, were later consolidated by Congress in 1921 to establish the Veterans Bureau. Significant efforts followed to accommodate WWI veterans, many of whom required specialized care due to chemical exposure, tuberculosis, and mental health issues. On July 21, 1930, President Herbert Hoover signed Executive Order (EO) 5398, authorizing consolidation and coordination of governmental activities affecting war veterans (U.S. Department of Veterans Affairs, 2005). Under this EO, the Bureau of Pensions, the National Home for Disabled Volunteer Soldiers, and the U.S. Veterans Bureau were merged to create the Veterans Administration (VA), known today as the U.S. Department of Veterans Affairs (VA). As the VA is referenced throughout this and other chapters in this book, it is important to note that any mention before March 15, 1989 refers to the Veterans Administration and any mention after that date refers to the Department of Veterans Affairs. At the time that this EO was passed there were 45 hospitals in the VA system, which expanded to 97 by 1945 (U.S. Department of Veterans Affairs, n.d.-a). The increase in VA hospitals continued into World War II (WWII).

The WWII era brought further changes to veterans' benefits and in 1943, vocational rehabilitation programs were legislatively approved for service-related injuries. This created employment opportunities for allied health professions, including the developing profession of music therapy (Davis & Else, 2019). On July 26, 1945, the War Department released a Technical Bulletin entitled *Music in Reconditioning in ASF Convalescent and General Hospitals* (U.S. War Department, 1945). The purpose of this bulletin was to outline a music program for reconditioning in active service forces convalescent and general hospitals within the VA. The bulletin highlighted several methods and techniques for program delivery, including: music activities and objectives; duties and responsibilities; program participation; audio-reception; music with calisthenics; special activities; music preferences; programs for different cadres of patients; and musical equipment. The bulletin included the notation, "The Office of The Surgeon General cannot consider music a therapeutic agent until further scientifically controlled tests have proved its values as therapy" (U.S. War Department, 1945, p.1). This motivated research in music as a therapeutic medium.

In September of 1945, two months after the publication of Technical Bulletin 187, the Committee on the Use of Music in Hospitals was created by the National Music Council (NMC) under the direction of Howard Hanson, then NMC President and Director of the Eastman School of Music (Boxberger, 1962). By November 1945, the VA established the Office of Special Services (Green, 1947). This program included bringing to the VA "recreation leaders, chaplains, canteen workers, librarians, sports instructors, music specialists, motion picture projectionists, entertainment and radio specialists and other trained personnel, who provide a program for the wellbeing and enjoyment of patients" (Green, 1947, p.36). Ray Green was appointed as Chief of Music, Recreation Service, Special Services, and was tasked with the job of introducing and developing a VA music program within the Recreation Service department, under the Office of the Assistant Administrator for Special Services (Green, 1947). General F.R. Kerr, the Assistant Administrator for Special Services, was overall supportive of music activities for veterans and delineated that participation should be focused on recreation and entertainment, as well as aligned with a general medical program.

The music therapy profession continued to evolve within the military, VA, and civilian sectors. In 1946, Chicago Musical College developed a training course including an internship at Downey, Illinois, VA Hospital "where two thousand veterans [were] treated by the latest psychiatric methods, under a training program directed by Dr. Jules H. Masserman of Northwestern University Medical School" (Gilliland, 1952, p.vii). The Downey VA music program was considered an exemplary model and received national recognition. In 1947, just two years after formation of the VA Office of Special Services, Ray Green was invited to serve as acting chairman of the Committee on the Use of Music in Hospitals (Boxberger, 1962). The Committee published the first *Hospital Music Newsletter* in May of 1948 (Boxberger, 1962; Green, 1948a). One of the first volumes included the results of a nationwide survey by Dr. Roy Underwood, Head of the Department of Music at Michigan State College and Chairman of the Music Teachers National Association Committee on Music in Hospitals (Green, 1948b). Dr. Underwood reported on a survey outcome from 117 hospitals nationwide that employed full-time music specialists. Of the 117 hospitals, 51 music specialists were employed in 41 of the 126 VA hospitals and centers by the end of 1947. Table 3.1 reflects findings from Dr. Underwood's survey and identifies 38 of the 41 hospitals cited in his report.

Table 3.1: VA hospitals with full-time music specialists circa 1947

VA Hospital, North Little Rock, AR	VA Hospital, Bath, NY
VA Hospital, Wilshire and Sawtelle, Los Angeles 25, CA	VA Hospital, Bronx, NY
VA Hospital, Palo Alto, CA	VA Hospital, Canandaigua, NY
VA Hospital, Fort Lyon, CO	VA Hospital, Castle Point, NY
VA Hospital, Danville, IL	VA Hospital, Halloran, Staten Island, NY
VA Hospital, Downey, IL	VA Hospital, Northport, Long Island, NY
VA Hospital, Marion, IN	VA Hospital, Fayetteville, NC
VA Hospital, Knoxville, IA	VA Hospital, Cleveland, OH
VA Hospital (Winter), Topeka, KS	VA Hospital, Portland, OR
VA Hospital, Wichita, KS	VA Hospital, Vancouver, OR
VA Hospital, Fort Thomas, KY	VA Hospital, Coatesville, PA
VA Hospital, Togus, ME	VA Hospital, San Juan, PR
VA Hospital, Perry Point, MD	VA Hospital, Columbia, SC
VA Hospital, Bedford, MA	VA Hospital, Fort Meade, SD
VA Hospital, Minneapolis, MN	VA Hospital, Murfreesboro, TN
VA Hospital, St. Cloud, MN	VA Hospital, Nashville, TN
VA Hospital, Biloxi, MS	VA Hospital, Salt Lake City, UT
VA Hospital, Jefferson Barracks, MO	VA Hospital, Lincoln, NE
VA Hospital, Lyons, NJ	VA Hospital, Sheridan, WY

The report stated, "The music program in the Recreation Service, Special Services, in the Veterans Administration is probably the most comprehensive single hospital music program in operation today" (Green, 1948c, para.1). A variety of music activities were described, including active participation in various instrumental and vocal groups, ward sing-alongs, concerts, recitals, community sings, songwriting, and orchestration (Green, 1948c). The report provided statistics of active and passive participation and indicated that by the end of 1947, there were 609 patient-performing groups in VA hospital nationwide (Green, 1948c).

The May 1948 *Hospital Music Newsletter* also included an "Activity Chart of Music Program in Veterans Administration Hospitals and Centers" shown in Figure 3.1 (Green, 1948d, para.18). This chart presented a "two-way approach to the use of hospital music, (1) music as recreation, and (2) music activities requested by medical authorities" (Green, 1948d, para.18). Music programming, including music entertainment, was activity and educationally based, except for specialized services. According to a 1948 VA report, music personnel collaborated with medical staff to conduct projects "in which music was used in insulin shock treatment, hydrotherapy and…during operations" (U.S. Veterans Administration, 1949, p.34).

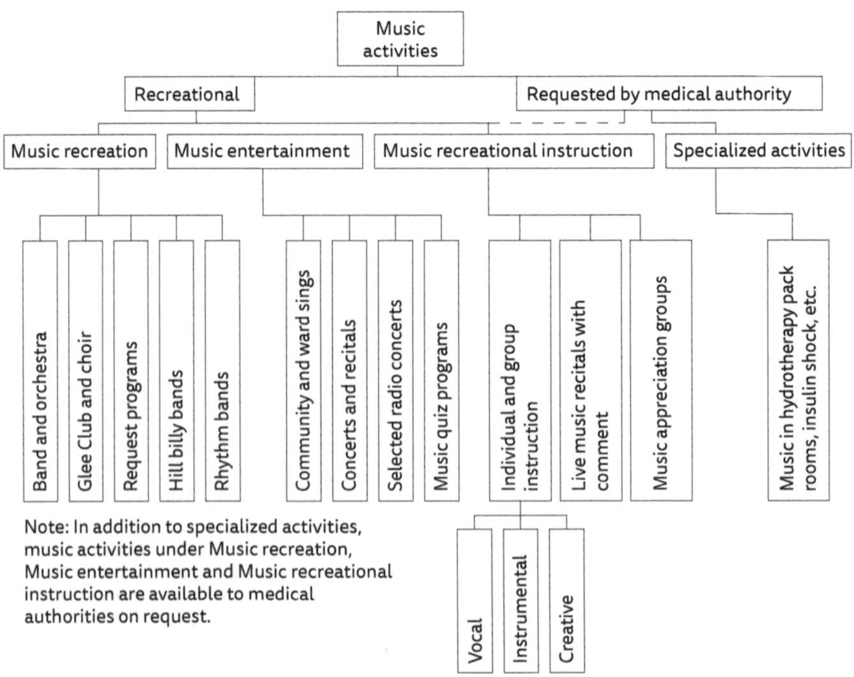

Figure 3.1: Music program in VA hospitals and centers (Green, 1948d)

Subsequent hospital music newsletters promoted the need for increased investigation into how music programs within the VA implemented various therapeutic uses of music. The Recreation Director at the VA Hospital in Northampton, Massachusetts, B.F. Fiore, submitted an article describing a project that integrated music and sports (Green, 1948e). Fiore's description included the project outline, multidisciplinary collaboration, and program outcomes. The program conjoined the use of specifically selected uptempo recorded music to accompany on-ward (e.g., calisthenics) and off-ward (e.g., adaptive sports) physical activities. Programmatic outcomes were measured in terms of increased participation and desire to participate in mild outdoor sports. Although improvements in physiological outcomes were not cited, the importance of music selection and driving rhythm were indicated as primary factors in positive outcomes, thus illustrating early considerations of tempo and rhythm to cue motor control. Modern neurological music therapy (NMT) techniques such as patterned sensory enhancement (PSE) use "the rhythmic, melodic, harmonic and dynamic-acoustical elements of music to provide temporal, spatial, and force cues for movements that reflect functional exercises and activities of daily living" (Thaut *et al.*, 2008, p.270). Fiore's report identified coordination between the hospital Special Services and Medical Service as another primary factor in the project's success, demonstrating increasing multidisciplinary support within the Northampton VA (Green, 1948e).

The emergence of music therapy as a profession continued to progress. In 1948, the University of Kansas established a master's degree in music education that specialized in functional music, which incorporated a six-month affiliated internship program at the Winter VA Hospital in Topeka, Kansas (de l'Etoile, 2000; Gilliland, 1952; Sears, 1960). Donald E. Michel, the Director of Music Therapy at the Topeka VA, directed the internship in consultation with E. Thayer Gaston. According to de l'Etoile (2000), "the combination of clinical training and early course offerings was instrumental in the establishment of the first degree offered in music therapy at the University of Kansas in 1948" (p.59). Music specialists, supported by other professionals in the VA, actively sought to identify methods to validate perceived therapeutic outcomes. In January 1949, the *Hospital Music Newsletter* Vol. 1, No. 3 included the submission, "Patient Behavior Scales," by Maurice Lorr, M.S. from the Clinical Psychology Department at the VA in Washington, DC (Lorr, 1949). Dr. Lorr developed the set of scales based on aspects from several psychiatric and psychology rating scales, as well as the Raymond Cattell personality variables. The article highlighted 17 questions using a six-point behavior rating scale, as reproduced in Appendix A. The first nine components were credited to Anne Roe, although her credentials and position were not indicated in the publication. Music technicians or volunteers facilitated interventions and conducted evaluations using the scale to indicate patient progress. The article included the purpose, a description of the rating process, guide points for rating, factors related to training the raters, and the rating scales (Lorr, 1949). The new role of music technicians and qualified music volunteers as facilitators of behavior scales denoted a trend towards qualifying and quantifying therapeutic aspects of music interventions in VA hospitals.

In September 1949, the Hospital Music Committee of the NMC submitted the article "Hospital Music Research" (Green, 1949a). This article detailed an expanded activity chart that delineated recreational versus therapeutic activities for implementation in conjunction with music program objectives. The program chart and objectives were intended to aid in establishing a foundation for research. Green cited several music-based research articles and projects including "The Use of Music in the Insulin Shock Ward" conducted at the VA Hospital in Richmond, Virginia. The research was led by Darrell Joachim, former Chief of the Music Section, Recreation Division, VA Branch Office No. 4, in collaboration with neuropsychiatric staff at the hospital. The article detailed examples of music used during three stages of treatment: sedation, excitation, and coma recovery. The research team concluded that patient wellbeing was enhanced by adhering to recommended procedures and "the use of music during insulin shock treatment is desirable and...recommended" (Green, 1949a, para.17).

Programmatic and professional development

During the 1950s, significant groundwork to establish music as a therapeutic and efficacious practice was initiated within VA hospitals and civilian medicine. According to Boxberger (1962), during the 1950 Music Teachers National Association conference in Cleveland, OH, music therapy leaders met with the intention of creating a national organization to represent the field. The outcome of this convention propelled the inception of the National Association of Music Therapy (NAMT) in June 1950 in New York City (Gilliland, 1952; Boxberger, 1962). Ray Green was selected as the first president and the NAMT constitution was formulated to "promote the progressive use of music in medicine, to establish educational standards, and to encourage research" (Gilliland, 1952, p.xv).

Music therapy programming and research efforts continued to progress in several VA hospitals. According to Hanson-Abromeit and Davis (2007), in 1951 Leonard Quinto, the Chief of Music, Recreation Service, Special Services in the VA, published an article in the hospital newsletter detailing a music therapy program for VA hospitals nationwide. It stated that standardized VA music therapy programs were designed to meet long- and short-term patient needs through goal-oriented sessions. The importance of coordinating with other disciplines was also accentuated. Five functional goal areas were delineated including to: 1) aid in adjusting to hospital life; 2) grant physician observation of patient behavior during sessions; 3) assist in adjustments to physical/mental conditions; 4) improve mental health and physical functioning; and 5) support social readjustment. The article further described active and prescriptive music interventions being delivered in the Knoxville, Iowa VA. The prescriptive applications of music were provided pre- and post-medical procedures, including electric and insulin shock treatments, lobotomies, hydrotherapy, and anesthesia.

Between 1951 and 1953, VA music programs progressively expanded and participation in active music-making through various types of engagement experienced new growth (U.S. Veterans Administration, 1952, 1953, 1954). Increased requests were generated from medical staff for specialized applications of music during procedural support, dental work, and treatment of tuberculous patients. The VA also used music programs in dining facilities, libraries, religious services, radio programs, social events, sports activities, and on hospital wards. During this period of professional growth, the VA's Special Services (e.g., recreation, chaplaincy, voluntary, library, canteen) went through an organizational transition. In the fall of 1955, the Special Service Program was realigned under the Department of Medicine and Surgery (U.S. Veterans Administration, 1964).

The following tables contain information compiled from VA annual reports from 1947 to 1957. Tables 3.2 and 3.3 demonstrate the overall growth of the music program by number of participating patients in different activity periods; however, the specific types of music activities were not disclosed (U.S. Veterans Administration, 1948, 1949, 1950, 1951, 1952, 1953, 1954). It is likely that the consistent increase in participant numbers reflected variables such as the addition of music specialists or technicians, overall higher numbers of admitted veterans, and the establishment of new music programs across VA hospitals. Table 3.4 is divided by three patient types (tuberculous, neuropsychiatric, general medical and surgical), and the fourth column is a total number of all patient types per number of activity periods and patient participations. This indicates an overall growth in early VA music programs; however, it does not discern between types of music activities or other variables (U.S. Veterans Administration, 1956, 1957a, 1957b).

Table 3.2: Music activities for VA hospitals and domiciliaries

Month and year	Number of activity periods	Estimated attendance	Patient participations
1947: April–June	48,286	1,683,920	296,551
1947: July–December	92,330	3,725,050	568,636
1948: January–June	97,408	3,875,674	609,018

Adapted from Annual reports: 1947–1948, by the Veterans Administration, United States Government Printing Office (www.va.gov/vetdata/Report.asp). In public domain.

Table 3.3: Music activities for VA hospitals and domiciliaries

Month and year	Number of activity periods	Different patients actively participating	Patient participations
1948: July–December	54,568	169,126	*320,346
1949: January–June	53,922	135,479	1,018,555
1949: July–December	54,637	151,975	976,769
1950: January–June	51,890	134,721	823,499
1950: **October–Dec.	30,153	145,897	554,077
1951: January–June	65,068	314,820	1,212,514
1951: July–December	67,738	324,964	1,431,096
1952: January–June	80,634	346,212	1,342,425
1952: July–December	67,300	328,858	1,582,403
1953: January–June	73,654	355,919	1,362,660

*Note: *Data only available from November–December 1948. **Data not available for July–September 1950. Adapted from Annual reports: 1948–1953, by the Veterans Administration, United States Government Printing Office (www.va.gov/vetdata/Report.asp). In public domain.*

Table 3.4: Music activities for VA hospitals and domiciliaries by patient type

Music activities	Tuberculous		Neuropsychiatric		General medical and surgical		Number of patient types combined	
	Activity periods	Patient partici-pations	Activity periods	Patient partici-pations	Activity periods	Patient partici-pations	Activity periods	Patient partici-pations
FY 1955	27,260	488,659	98,143	2,102,258	42,197	947,274	167,600	3,538,191
FY 1956	36,237	514,973	123,157	2,357,785	46,362	962,825	205,756	3,835,583
FY 1957	28,887	356,001	141,789	2,660,346	44,223	842,718	214,899	3,859,065

Note: Data not available for FY 1954. Adapted from Annual reports: 1955–1957, by the Veterans Administration, United States Government Printing Office (www.va.gov/vetdata/Report.asp). In public domain.

Efforts to validate music therapy continued to gain momentum. In September 1958, Alice Nelson, Recreation Leader (Music) at the VA Hospital in Knoxville, Iowa, published a six-month informal study, "Mental Patients Can Like New Music!" (Nelson, 1958). The study included male veterans (n=24) aged 35 to 45 years residing on a mental health unit for an average of 15 years who presented as withdrawn and uncommunicative. The group met once a week for 45 minutes and was facilitated by recreation and music therapists who presented patients with music choices ranging from familiar/well-known, to recent/popular, to new/unfamiliar songs. Results revealed that when presented with new material, the patients selected unfamiliar songs as often as familiar songs. The article suggested that efficacious practice includes providing the patients with the opportunity to learn new music and make choices, while maintaining the authority of music directors and therapists to make clinically informed judgments related to their practices. Nelson stated, "A mental patient who has long since given up striving for self-realization might, while on a creative quest, rediscover himself" (Nelson, 1958, p.8).

Music therapy and VA alignment

Professional growth continued to be an initiative of NAMT and VA recreation and music therapy staff. According to a report by Robert F. Unkefer in the 1961 NAMT Bulletin, all VA activity therapists were aligned under the Chief of Physical Medicine and Rehabilitation Service (PM&RS) (Unkefer, 1961; U.S. Veterans Administration, 1964). The title of Special Services was discontinued, and the various activities specialists were now identified as rehabilitation specialists and administratively recognized as equal to other rehabilitation therapists (U.S. Veterans Administration, 1964). The PM&RS was supervised by the service chief and operated under the hospital chief of staff, which benefitted recreation therapy personnel as valued clinicians and improved recruitment of activity professionals who possessed advanced qualifications. New applicants were required to meet civil service requirements, which specified minimum standards of a bachelor's degree in recreation or 24 supervised hours in creative arts, recreation, or allied disciplines.

From 1960 to 1966 there was marginal documentation regarding progress and disposition of the VA recreation therapy program. The Recreation Therapy Service (RTS) had been previously criticized for its diversional methodology; however, 1967 revealed a new initiative for the service to become therapeutically oriented (U.S. Veterans Administration, 1967). Recreational therapy gained recognition for patient education related to leisure time management and community reintegration, and in 1968, the PM&RS devised patient-flow concepts that orchestrated progression between treatment specialties during rehabilitation, depicted in Figure 3.2. Veterans were initially seen by physical and occupational therapy and, if indicated, advanced to (creative) arts therapy and corrective therapy, followed by educational and recreational therapies (U.S. Veterans Administration, 1969). Rehabilitation outcomes were believed to be more effective through purposeful flow between treatments, and the patients developed abilities to function independently in their communities.

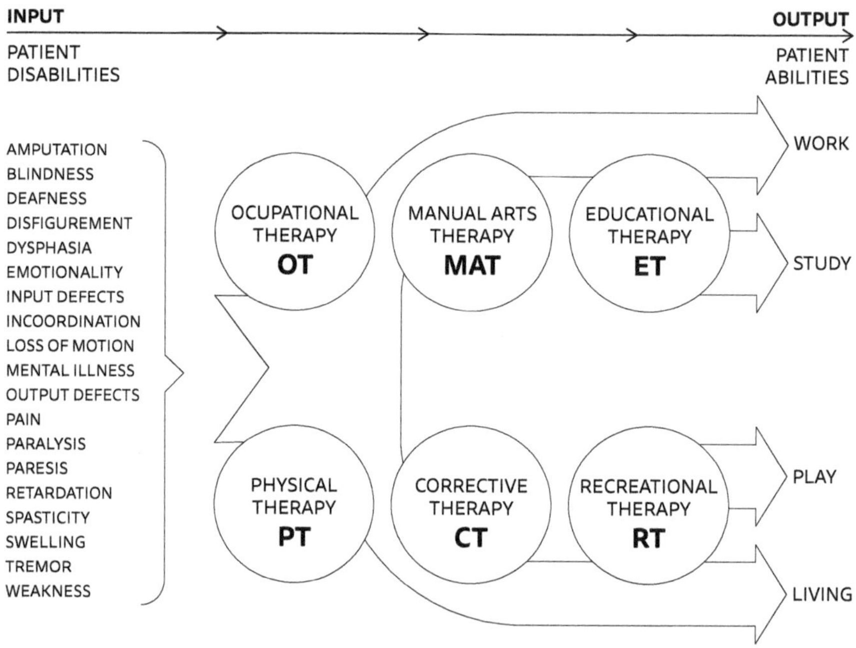

Figure 3.2: PM&RS patient flow chart (VA, 1969)

September 1979 indicated the first significant change since 1960, impacting professionally trained and educated music therapists within the VA. The U.S. Office of Personnel Management (OPM) Multiseries Classification Standard for Therapies Series General Schedule (GS) 0633-0639 was established for therapist positions. Recreation/Creative Arts Therapist (RT/CAT) Series, GS-0638 designated the required professional training and knowledge of concepts, principles, and practices of the specialized creative arts therapies field as a Title 5 occupation (U.S. Department of Personnel Management, 1979). The creative arts therapist position established standards regarding the appropriate use of specialized activities to maintain or achieve physical and mental health in patients' rehabilitation. These standards provided the framework of professional clinical skills, whereby the therapist possessed knowledge and expertise in assessment, developing care plans, clinical treatment provision, and therapeutic outcome evaluation. The grade level of the therapist in the RT/CAT Series was between levels of GS-5 and GS-9.

Between 1980 and 1995, roles of recreational therapists (RT) and creative art therapists (CAT) evolved significantly in the treatment and rehabilitation of veterans (U.S. Department of Veterans Affairs, 1996). The role of therapist experienced increased responsibilities and assignments within the hospitals, now called VA medical centers (VAMCs), that were more complex than OPM's occupation series established in 1979. Role expansion was attributed to related factors such as requirements of the Joint Commission on Accreditation of Hospital Organizations, revised standards for professional practice, and staff qualifications/competencies specified by the National Council for Therapeutic Recreation Certification, Certification Board for Music Therapists, and other credentialing bodies. VAMCs experienced significant changes in healthcare environments, and veterans presented with more complex physical and psychological health conditions such as post-traumatic stress disorder (PTSD). As a result, numerous requests for assisting in re-evaluation of RT/CAT positions were made and subsequently, RTS in VA Headquarters and Position Management and Classification Service departments initiated an in-depth study of arts and recreation-based occupations. Due to increased requirements of therapist education, skill level, and clinical abilities, Human Resources Management Letter No 05-96-01, January 22, 1996, provided an updated position classification. The role of RT/CAT Series, GS-068 significantly changed and revealed the need to improve consistency in occupational classification, which resulted in a standard position description and classification recommendation of a GS-10.

The mission statement for the VA human resources strategic plan continues to affirm that the VA's goal is to "recruit, develop, and retain a competent, committed, and diverse workforce that provides high quality healthcare services to veterans and their families" (U.S. Department of Veterans Affairs, n.d.-b, p.5). The Title 38 Hybrid employment system allows the VA to recruit and appoint high-quality therapists with appropriate professional credentials in an efficient and timely manner. Hence, the RT/CAT, GS-0638 qualification standard was published on June 7, 2019 in the *VA Handbook 5005* Part II, Appendix G60. With the publication of the new qualification standards, the occupations converted from Title 5 to Hybrid Title 38 effective as of June 9, 2019 (U.S. Department of Veterans Affairs, 2019c). Under Title 38, CATs are recruited and hired utilizing the qualification standard, processes, and guidance, and all new VA music therapists must be board certified (MT-BC). Specific knowledge, skills, and clinical experience have been defined for pay grades ranging from GS-7 to GS-14. New position levels above GS-11 have been defined to promote recognition of specialization in various areas of assignments. For example, specialty treatment areas include advanced improvisational music therapy training, NMT, Bonny method of guided imagery and music (BM-GIM), and certifications in palliative care, dementia care, and substance abuse. Additionally, other occupational assignments such as clinical education coordinator, program coordinator, lead CAT, supervisory CAT, assistant and service chief, and clinical research specialist are recognized through higher pay grades. These qualification standards contributed to the most significant change in positioning of music therapy within the VA, effectively benefitting thousands of veterans and their families by advancing the clinical services and professional competencies of the providers who treat them. The Hybrid Title 38 position conversions ensure that our nation's veterans receive the highest level of specialized care.

Continuity of care through national program development

The profession of music therapy continued to grow and develop throughout the Veterans Health Administration (VHA). In addition to expansion, consistency of services is imperative in regulating music therapy practice. Rehabilitation and Prosthetic Services (RPS) oversees program and policy development for VHA rehabilitation services, coordinating the provision of a full continuum of medical, rehabilitative, and prosthetic services to promote health, independence, and quality of life for veterans. RPS administers program and policy development for eight national VA programs with 11 different rehabilitation disciplines, and aligns clinical expertise, clinical practice guidance, and specialized procurement resources to provide comprehensive rehabilitation and prosthetic services across the VHA in an economical and timely manner (U.S. Department of Veterans Affairs, n.d.-c). The National Veterans Sports Programs and Special Events Office hosts six annual national events, one of which is the National Veterans Creative Arts Festival (NVCAF) (U.S. Department of Veterans Affairs, n.d.-d). The NVCAF is part of the VA's continuum of care, which provides opportunities for veterans to improve their independence, wellbeing, and quality of life through therapeutic arts. Veterans' clinical goals are integrated into community programming to maximize rehabilitation potential, increase independence, and support community transition and reintegration processes.

The NVCAF was founded in 1981 at two VA facilities (U.S. Department of Veterans Affairs, n.d.-e). Muriel Barbour, Chief of RT at McGuire VAMC in Richmond, Virginia, created a visual arts competition named VET ARTS in 1981 in conjunction with the International Year of Disabled Person observance. That same year, Shirley Jefferies, an RT at the Waco, Texas, VAMC, created the National Music Competition with a focus on the performing arts, which resulted in the first live stage show held in the VAMC in Tuskegee, Alabama. In 1982, a second live show was held at the Coatesville, Pennsylvania, VAMC. The competition was renamed The Music Festival in 1985 and was hosted live at Constitution Hall in Washington DC (U.S. Department of Veterans Affairs, n.d.-e). In 1989, VETS ARTS and the Music Festival merged, and new divisions of performing arts in drama and dance were added, constituting the formation of what is currently known as the NVCAF (U.S. Department of Veterans Affairs, n.d.-e). Today, thousands of veterans representing VAs across the U.S. submit works of art, music, dance, drama, and writing for the opportunity of their work being showcased at annual premier national events, which culminate with live performances, writing exhibitions, and a gallery-style showcase of artwork recognizing the veteran artists and the role of creative art therapists. Workshops for veterans and therapists are offered throughout the week-long event.

Evidence-based music therapy research

The Colmery O'Neil VAMC in Topeka, Kansas, was a leader in the development of clinical protocols and evidence-based research in creative arts therapies, as Chief of RTS, William Givens, had the foresight of building a program grounded in evidenced-based practice. In 1990, Alicia Clair, PhD, MT-BC, Director of Music Therapy at the University of Kansas, was contracted as a research consultant to work with clinical RTs and CATs. An extensive bibliography of research published from 1990 to 2015 includes work by Dr. Clair, Gary Johnson, MME, MT-BC, Barry Bernstein, MT-BC, and David Otto, MME, MT-BC. Two full-time music therapists supported the facility research program as a member of the Human Subjects Committee of the Research and Development Program (i.e., Gary Johnson) and voting committee member of Research and Development Committee (i.e., David Otto). Their committee membership was essential in represented leadership at the Colmery O'Neil VAMC and supporting the foundational research efforts of RT/CAT services. Early research conducted by music therapists studied the effects of music interventions on veterans with dementia and Alzheimer's, as well as geriatric populations (Clair *et al.*, 1995; Otto *et al.*, 1999). In the late 1900s to 2000s, interest in research, rehabilitation, and protocol development using NMT techniques began to emerge. The establishment of research consultant positions assisted with development of a music therapy evidence base that promoted the field by demonstrating the value of these therapeutic services (Hayden *et al.*, 2009; Johnson *et al.*, 2001).

Occupational taxonomy of VA music therapists

Music therapists and all CATs in the overarching Veteran Administration Health Care System (VAHCS) are part of VHA RTS and hired under the RT/CAT Series. Efforts are underway to ensure that VA facilities properly identify therapists using designated taxonomy codes representative of their clinical education and training. This allows for the collection of meaningful statistics such as number of music therapists employed throughout the VHA, position locality, and Common Procedural Technology (CPT) codes. In order to determine the current status of music therapist positions within the VHA, the authors of this chapter collected data from music therapists working in the VHA including their designated Veterans Integrated Service Network (VISN); VA facility; and specific creative arts therapies disciplines (e.g., art, dance/movement, drama, expressive, music) at their sites (Otto & Woodward, 2020a; Gooding & Langston, 2019).

Data results

Results indicated that as of February 2020, there were 72 music therapists functioning in the capacity of their profession within the VHA, including one RT/CAT Service Chief and two RT/CAT supervisors (Otto & Woodward, 2020a). These results are similar to a report that there were 73 music therapists working in 49 VAMCs across the U.S. (Gooding & Langston, 2019). VA music therapists currently working in 17 of the 18 VISNs. According to the VHA, there were currently 170 VAMCs and 1074 outpatient sites providing care within the VAHCS (U.S. Department of Veterans Affairs, n.d.-f). The 72 employed music therapists were aligned with 52 of the 170 VAMCs. There was one music therapist in 38 of the 52 VAMCs, two music therapists in 10 of the 52 VAMCs (including one service chief and two supervisors), and three music therapists in 4 of the 52 VAMCs (including the NVCAF Director). Survey results indicated that 62.5 percent of VA music therapists were accurately identified under the proper occupational taxonomy and 37.5 percent were classified under a title other than CAT music therapy, of which 34.7 percent were classified as RTs.

Therapist reported trends in the delivery of VA music therapy services: a survey

Method

In addition to data collection to inform occupational positioning, a 38-question survey was distributed via email to current music therapists embedded at VAMCs along with several retired VA music therapists to glean information regarding their past and current professional experiences and identify common trends, procedures, clinical indicators, and personal perceptions of their practices (Otto & Woodward, 2020b). A total of 28 music therapists responded, six of whom retired between 1997 and 2019, and 22 of whom were actively working in the VAHCS. Music therapists represented 12 of 18 VISNs and their years of service averaged 16 years. VA music therapists increasingly exemplify educational standards necessary to facilitate treatment of veterans with complex, and often co-morbid physical and psychological conditions, as the responses identified that 100 percent of actively practicing VA music therapists had a current MT-BC credential and 83 percent of retired music therapists were currently credentialed or were prior to retirement. Other retired music therapists held the credential of Registered Music Therapist (RMT). The survey revealed that from the sample of music therapists (*n*=28), 12 had bachelor's degrees in music therapy, 14 had master's degrees related to the field (e.g., MEd. MA, MME, MM, MMT, MS), one had a master's in social work, one achieved a Doctor of Medical Humanities (DMH), and one earned a PhD in human development and family studies. Three music therapists were licensed within their state. Several respondents confirmed earning additional certifications in specialized areas of music therapy and related professions. Three music therapists served as internship directors, maintaining American Music Therapy Association national roster internships, and many served as clinical training supervisors of university-affiliated internship programs.

Clinical setting

Many of the surveyed music therapists reported that they were the only CATs working within their respective VA facilities, providing individual and/or group therapy to a diverse group of veterans in inpatient and outpatient settings. Survey data indicated that 22 of the music therapists worked in inpatient and outpatient settings, three primarily on inpatient and one primarily on outpatient basis. All of the music therapists reported working with veterans who had a wide range of acute and chronic mental health diagnoses, including PTSD, anxiety disorders, depressive and mood disorders, adjustment disorders, substance use disorders, serious mental illness, personality disorders, schizophrenia, and schizoaffective disorder. Music therapists cited PTSD (82%) as the primary diagnosis of their patients. In conjunction with treating mental health diagnoses, 79 percent reported stand-alone and co-treatment of acute and chronic medical conditions, neurological disorders, and other diagnoses, including mild cognitive impairment, Alzheimer's disease, Parkinson's disease, other dementias with and without behavioral disturbances, movement disorders, multiple sclerosis, amyotrophic lateral sclerosis, traumatic brain injury, acute and transitional spinal cord injury, cerebral vascular accidents, chronic obstructive pulmonary disease, cardiovascular diseases, visual impairments, and various cancers.

Survey responses about the use of specific music therapy interventions identified several consistent trends, as indicated in Table 3.5. Active music-making in individual, group, performance-based, and community-based frameworks was reported in 100 percent of the responses, of which the majority designated treatment goals as both clinical and educational. A variety of musical instruments were used during active music-making, primarily drums and percussion instruments, guitar, keyboard/piano, and voice.

Table 3.5: Common VA music therapy interventions

Cited interventions/techniques	Percentage used by surveyed music therapists
Active music-making	100%
Songwriting	71.43%
Lyric analysis	64.29%
Music assisted relaxation	64.29%
Active/Intentional/Guided listening	35.71%
Music assisted imagery or guided imagery	28.57%
Music and movement exercises	28.57%
NMT techniques	21.43%
Music-based cognitive training	17.86%
Mood vectoring/regulation	<17.86%
Musical life review/Personal music inventory	<17.86%
Breath entrainment	<17.86%
Music for psychosocial expression	<17.86%
Music for pain management	<17.86%
Music for reminiscence	<17.86%

Community partnership programs have been integral to the VA RTS since its inauguration as the Office of Special Services in 1945. VA music therapists continue to collaborate with community members, local agencies, Veterans Service Organizations (VSOs), and the Department of Defense (DoD). These partnerships establish music collaborations that increase resources and opportunities at facility and community levels to promote successful transition through gradational participation and continued support through community engagement (Otto & Woodward, 2020b). According to the VA's Office of Community Engagement, the development of public and private partnerships for creation of shared resources supports the VA's mission and enhances services to veterans and their families (U.S. Department of Veterans Affairs, 2020a).

Survey results specified numerous partnerships between VA music therapists and various community entities, public agencies, and VSOs, including organizations that serve military and veteran populations through music such as the Center for American Military Music Opportunities, Concerts in Motion, Guitars for Vets, MusiCorps, Musicians on Call, Operation Song, Songwriting with Soldiers, and Voices of Valor, to name a few. Localized community programs included partnerships with symphony orchestras, music institutes and societies, choirs, nursing facilities, recording studios, colleges and universities, and community jam opportunities including drum circles with local musicians. One example of a collaboration included a unique partnership between the U.S. Air Force Heritage of America Band and the music therapy program at Salem VAMC in Virginia, where veterans in music therapy engaged with Air Force Band members. Figure 3.3 captures a heartfelt exchange between Army Veteran Bobby Ray Wheeler, Technical Sergeant Jason Cale, and Airman 1st Class Guy James.

Figure 3.3: Music therapy engagement with the U.S. Air Force Heritage of America Band (photo credit: Shannon Wheeler, 2016)

Collaboration and partnerships: increased interest and growth of creative arts therapies

The focus of creative arts therapies in the treatment of veterans, active-duty service members, and their families has been heightened by congressional interest. In 2018, the VHA selected a music therapist, David W. Otto, MME, MT-BC, as the National Program Director, RTS. This position serves as the principle advisor to the Office of the Under Secretary for Health, Deputy Under Secretary for Health for Policy and Services, Assistant Deputy Under Secretary for Health for Patient Care Services, and Deputy Chief Patient Care Services Officer for RPS. This position is responsible for all matters related to RT/CAT services and care in the VA. On September 19, 2019, David Otto provided a presentation concerning the role of creative arts therapies within the VA to legislators, key stakeholders, and distinguished leaders from the DoD, VA, and National Endowment for the Arts (NEA) as shown in Figure 3.4 (The White House, 2019). This meeting highlighted the effectiveness of creative arts therapies for military populations who struggle with trauma and mental health issues.

Figure 3.4: David Otto briefing congressional stakeholders, White House (photo credit: Amy Rossetti)

During his first two years as the National Program Director of RTS, David Otto worked in collaboration with the VHA Office of Rural Health, Rural Veterans Telehealth Rehabilitation Initiative (RVTRI), and Creative Forces®: NEA Military Healing Arts Network to expand CAT positions to provide care for rural veterans through the distance delivery of creative arts therapies via telehealth. In 2020, CAT positions were created to extend services to rural veterans receiving treatment at the following VA facilities: Richard L. Roudebush VAMC in Indianapolis, Indianna; G.V. (Sonny) Montgomery VAMC in Jackson, Mississippi; and Northeast Ohio VAHCS in Cleveland (National Endowment for the Arts, 2019). Many of these VAMCs are the primary treatment facilities for veterans living within 75 to 100 miles of the facility, hence it is not always feasible to travel for necessary treatment. This indicates the immense need for remote services, such as those offered through the RVTRI and Creative Forces partnership (Vaudreuil *et al.*, 2020b). Further program development is currently in progress for expansion at new locations across the enterprise, with additional locations slated for the fiscal year (FY) 2021.

Congressional interest in supporting creative arts therapies for military-connected populations continued with The Committee on Appropriations on Military Construction, VA, and Related Agencies Appropriation Bill, 2020 to accompany H.R. 2745 (Schultz, 2019). The 116th Congress 1st Session of the House of Representatives Report 116-63 acknowledged the "effective use of creative arts therapies in treating Veterans with traumatic brain injuries and psychological health conditions" (Schultz, 2019, p.52). On May 15, 2019, the Committee stated they recognized and supported VA efforts in expanding creative arts therapy programs and services across the VA enterprise. On December 17, 2019, the U.S. House of Representatives and leaders of the House and Senate Appropriations approved $5 million in direct appropriations for creative arts therapies, expansion of Whole Health initiatives, and treating veterans for FY 2020 (Lynch, 2019).

The future of music therapy in the VA

VA music therapists continually strive to facilitate safe, effective, and evidenced-based interventions in the care of our nation's meritorious veterans. The year 2020 introduced new challenges for CATs, as well as healthcare professionals worldwide, as a result of the COVID-19 global pandemic. Fortunately, the VA has a long history of remote videoconferencing and since the1960s has been a leader in the delivery of telehealth (Godleski *et al.*, 2012). The expansion of teleconferencing has continued throughout the VHA to date, providing innovative platforms such as the VA Video Connect (VVC) mobile application used to facilitate remote treatment for veterans (Elliot, 2019). Current VHA telehealth initiatives and RVTRI support VA music therapists in actively learning to navigate VVC for safe and effective treatment of veterans in local and rural locations. An article by Vaudreuil *et al.* (2020b) details a partnership between Creative Forces, the DoD, VA, and various state and local arts agencies that supports virtual delivery of creative arts therapies. Findings endorsed positive outcomes of creative arts therapies telehealth treatment and increased community engagement of active-duty and veteran participants. Furthermore, this article highlighted treatment applications, clinical and ethical considerations, and recommendations for navigating technological limitations. The increasingly complex future of music therapy in the VA is continuously expanding and anticipates incorporation of new technologies and practices, such as the Whole Health initiative detailed in Chapter 2 of this book.

Summary

November 2020 marked 75 years since the inauguration of the Office of Special Services in the VA, and throughout this time, VA music therapists have significantly contributed to the evolution of the music therapy profession. Music therapists working in the VAHCS will continue to progress, as well as be challenged as a result of ever-changing veteran demographics and the complexity of their healthcare needs. The innate capacity of the music therapy profession supports creativity, innovation, adaptability, and resiliency in the development and delivery of best practice models and frameworks. VA music therapists will continue their dynamic path of evolution while answering the call of duty to support the men and women who have selflessly served the United States of America.

Acknowledgements

A special note of appreciation for survey contributors who provided content of Therapist Reported Trends in the Delivery of VA Music Therapy Services: A Survey, including active and retired VA music therapists: Roberta Blake, Joia Byrnes-Tellez, Jerry Coyne, Sherill Cross, Joseph Crumrine, Virginia Dougherty, Kelsey Eisenhauer, John Foley, Justin Francis, Gary Johnson, Hope Kumme, Elizabeth Mackey, Barbara Maclean, Tom Mogyordy, Stephen Montgomery, Sarah Pitts, Sarah Pugliese, Chad Reichert, Judith Good Sherwood, Sheri Smith, Jillian Thompson, Erin Todd, and Rachelle Vishneowski.

Appendix A: Rating Scales of Patient Behavior (Lorr, 1949)

1. Activity: amount

   a. Motionless for considerable periods or stuporous. Does not spontaneously undertake any activity.

   b. Underactive; seldom moving and then slowly.

   c–d. Active according to the situation. Able to rest quietly, or to sit, read, talk, and play games.

   e. Usually restless and busy but may be quiet for periods up to half an hour. Has short outbursts of marked activity. Easily stirred up by newcomers, mild commotions.

   f. Acutely restless, and excited. Rarely remains more than a few minutes in one place. May have prolonged periods of running about. Requires sedation or restraint.

2. Appearance

   a. Extremely untidy and slovenly. Never changes clothes or cleans self unless forced. Clothes soiled with feces, food, or dirt. May be forcibly bathed and changed.

   b. Slovenly and unconcerned about appearance but will clean up when told to do so. Clothes soiled with food or dirt and disarranged.

   c–d. Gives reasonable attention to appearance. Washes when necessary without being told and keeps clothes tidy.

   e. Over-scrupulous about tidiness and cleanliness.

   f. Excessively concerned about cleanliness and neatness. Spends much time on clothes and personal appearance.

3. Activity interest (rate on special ward work or occupational therapy)

   a. Tends to become completely absorbed in and enthusiastic about the activities in which he engages (occupational therapy, games, drawing, music, etc.).

   b. Shows marked interest and desire to participate in special ward and occupational activities.

   c–d. Participates in, and shows normal curiosity and interest in the activities provided in the ward and elsewhere.

   e. Passive and acquiescent but without active interest. Requires urging and supervision to maintain any activity started by ward personnel. May read a little or watch games.

   f. Shows no interest in activities around him. Stops activity immediately if supervision is relaxed. Will not participate unless actively urged.

4. Cooperation

   a. Actively cooperative. Finds ways of cooperating despite difficulties. Generally tends to say "yes" when invited to cooperate. Willingly follows ward routine.

b. Passively resistant or obstructive. Tends to be "difficult." Will not help in ward routine beyond minimum. Requires much urging and persuasion in dressing and undressing, food taking, and before complying with requests.

c. Actively resistant to all routine procedures. Must be dressed and undressed, fed and bathed. Will comply with no request.

5. Speech: production

a. Noisily overtalkative. Shouts and yells. Incessantly productive.

b. Talks excessively. Periodic outbursts of talking.

c–d. Will start a conversation or enter into it readily in a normal manner and in a moderate tone of voice.

e. Does not start a conversation, but will respond to a direct question or remark. May limit himself to a very brief response.

f. Mute, for one or more days at a time.

6. Speech: coherence

a. Speaks in a coherent, relevant and logical fashion. Conversation is logically consistent and connected by some common idea or relationship.

b. Tends to speak in an incoherent fashion. Successive elements of thought are frequently inconsistent or do not hang together. Conversation rambles or is irrelevant.

c. Speech is incoherent to a high degree. It appears to have little or no associative continuity. Speech appears to be scattered, disconnected, or confused. Sentences seem to make "word salads."

7. Social behavior

a. Constantly with others; actively avoids being left alone. Attracted by and moves towards people.

b. Frequently with others. Not fond of being alone. Seeks out people for the sake of company.

c–d. Moves towards people in social situations. Enters into group activities but does not mind being left alone.

e. Moves away from people in social groups and isolates himself.

Will occasionally talk to others but does not join in games or ward activities. Usually seclusive.

f. Nearly always seclusive and isolated. Stays alone and never talks or plays with others.

8. Mood level

a. Exhilarated, cheerful, exuberant, laughing and singing. Ignores unpleasant aspects and difficulties of any situation.

b. Euphoric, happy, persistently cheerful even under inappropriate circumstances.

c–d. Mood appropriate to the situation. Neither very cheerful nor very blue.

e. Generally sad, depressed. Cries easily.

f. Very depressed and melancholic. Cannot be cheered.

9. Mood stability

a. Maintains much the same mood throughout the day whether cheerful or depressed.

b. Shows some rapid changes in mood apparently caused by conditions within the patient. Becomes happy, blue or excited within a short time interval.

c. Frequent and rapid changes in mood and feeling within a short period of time, apparently uncaused by outside events. May become cheerful, tearful, or angry during a conversation.

10. Assertiveness

a. Orders the other patients around and/or tells the nurses and the attendants what to do. Tends to be officious.

b. Tends to dominate or influence other patients. Makes decisions in relations with other patients.

c–d. Makes own decisions. May be assertive or submissive depending on the realistic situation.

e. Tends to let other patients have their way and backs down in a conflict. Lets others make decisions for him.

f. Submissive and docile. Pushed around or easily dominated by other patients.

11. Friendliness

a. Friendly and approachable. Trustful and free of suspicion. Easy to speak to and to and get along with.

b. Often unfriendly and difficult to approach or to talk with. Tends to be suspicious, hostile, and antagonistic. Quick to believe that he is being unfairly treated.

c. Usually unfriendly and difficult to approach or to get along with. Suspicious and unreasonably hostile without apparent justification. May feel persecuted.

12. Self-sufficiency

a. Self-sufficient; does not lean on others in situations calling for independent decisions and action. Accepts responsibility and does what he says he will do.

b. Dependable and consistent in day-to-day behavior.

c. Partially dependent on others in situations calling for independent decisions and action. Requires frequent reassurance, support and supervision in whatever he does. Can accept responsibility for carrying out simple tasks.

d. Completely dependent for support and direction of all activities. Unable to make own decisions. Cannot be depended on to carry out even simple tasks. Requires constant supervision.

13. Self-esteem

a. Continually expresses feelings of unworthiness, inferiority and inadequacy. Makes numerous self-depreciatory remarks.

b. Frequently expresses feelings of unworthiness, guilt and inadequacy.

c. Expresses neither self-depreciatory nor expansive remarks.

d. Often expresses feelings of self-importance, power and confidence in capabilities not warranted by circumstances.

e. Usually boastful, expansive and over-confident. Expresses feelings of self-importance despite circumstances.

14. Destructiveness

    a. Frequently destructive of clothing and furniture. Has destroyed more than one object or garment.

    b. Occasionally destructive or careless and unconcerned.

    c–d. Reasonably careful of property and others.

    e. Very careful of property and clothes. Will not lend own property.

    f. Disturbed by destructiveness of others, or by own torn or damaged clothes; will not permit others to touch or look at his property.

15. Emotional behavior: appropriateness

    a. Frequent and unpredictable silly giggling or laughter without appropriate stimulation. Emotional reactions typically out of harmony with the situation.

    b. Occasional giggling or inappropriate smiling. Emotional reactions and expressions not in keeping with the situation.

    c. Spontaneous and natural responses to the demands of the situation.

16. Emotional behavior: amount

    a. Apathetic and indifferent. Exhibits no feeling to any situation.

    b. Dull and phlegmatic. Reacts with very little effect; rarely shows any feelings and then inadequately, despite the situation.

    c–d. Reacts adequately. Shows feeling sufficient for the situation.

    e. Overreacts emotionally to situation, sometimes explosively. Expresses feelings readily, easily upset.

    f. Overreacts markedly with little or no stimulation. Expresses feelings quickly; becomes cheerful, angry or tearful. May have spontaneous outbursts.

17. Attention

    a. Markedly distractible by internal or external conditions. Difficult or impossible to hold attention to any objective.

    b. Easily distracted by environmental stimuli such as sounds, and movements of other patients. Spasmodic and scattered attention.

c–d. Normally alert to changes in the environment. Shows usual attention span. Able to give attention.

e. Detached or preoccupied. Answers questions briefly and relapses into reverie. Difficult to hold attention.

f. Completely withdrawn and apparently occupied with own thoughts. Cannot be drawn to pay attention.

Chapter 4

Creative Forces®: NEA Military Healing Arts Network—Expanding Creative Arts Therapies in the Departments of Defense and Veterans Affairs

SARA KASS, ELIZABETH K. FREEMAN, REBECCA VAUDREUIL, AND MELISSA WALKER

Disclaimer: The views expressed in this chapter are those of the authors and do not reflect the official policy of the Department of Defense, the National Endowment for the Arts or the U.S. Government. The identification of specific products or scientific instrumentation is considered an integral part of scientific endeavor and does not constitute endorsement or implied endorsement on the part of the authors, DoD, NEA, or any component agency.

Introduction

Creative Forces®: NEA Military Healing Arts Network is an initiative of the National Endowment of the Arts (NEA) in partnership with the Departments of Defense (DoD) and Veterans Affairs (VA), and state and local arts agencies that seek to improve the health, wellness, and quality of life for military and veterans exposed to trauma as well as their families and caregivers. Creative Forces is managed in partnership with Americans for the Arts and the Henry M. Jackson Foundation for the Advancement of Military Medicine.

Creative Forces places creative arts therapies at the core of patient-centered care at clinical sites throughout the U.S., including telehealth services, and increases access to community arts opportunities. As of 2021, Creative Forces supports programming at over a dozen DoD and VA clinical sites, including multiple telehealth programs that provide creative arts therapies to remote and rural military and veteran populations (Vaudreuil *et al.*, 2020a).

Innovations and advancements in military healthcare

In 2010, a new medical facility, proffered by the Intrepid Fallen Heroes Fund to the DoD, opened its doors, as a center for the treatment and research of military service members with traumatic brain injury (TBI) and associated psychological health conditions. The facility—aptly named the National Intrepid Center of Excellence (NICoE)—challenged its staff to boldly explore and identify the most promising treatments for the invisible wounds of the Global War on Terrorism (GWOT), known as TBI and post-traumatic stress disorder (PTSD). Leading clinicians and researchers were brought together under one roof to provide innovative diagnostic and rehabilitative services in the form of an immersive, holistic, and interdisciplinary treatment model. Methods of care included conventional, evidence-based military medicine and neuroimaging as well as complementary and integrative mind–body treatments such as yoga, acupuncture, and meditation. Various forms of psychotherapy were also introduced at the time of program inception, to include creative arts therapies.

The NICoE provides high-tech and high-touch, comprehensive care through a four-week intensive outpatient program model, which is overall touted as beneficial by patients in self-assessment surveys. Art therapy was the first of the creative arts therapies to begin to establish the Healing Arts Program at the NICoE. Art therapy treatment was then, and is now, standardized and scheduled throughout the four weeks, and based on patient experience survey data, it emerged as one of the top five (out of 30+) interventions that patients found impactful in their recovery (Jones *et al.*, 2018). The art therapy studio also housed various musical instruments for patient use, and a volunteer musician from Warrior Cry Music Project offered music lessons per patient request. The positive response to extended arts offerings was a clear indicator that there was room for growth to integrate other creative arts therapies, such as music therapy and dance/movement therapy, within the NICoE Healing Arts Program. In addition, there was emerging inquiry regarding research into how the arts, and specifically creative arts therapies, were affecting the NICoE's patient population.

Engagement of the arts endowment

The NEA's partnership with the DoD started in 2004 when the NEA created a writing program called Operation Homecoming: Writing the Wartime Experience. Operation Homecoming helped military service members and their families write about their wartime experiences through workshops provided at military installations, VA medical centers (VAMCs), military hospitals, and affiliated centers across the U.S. In 2012, the NEA Military Healings Arts Partnership, known today as Creative Forces, started with the integration of the Operation Homecoming writing workshops into the clinical program at NICoE. The writing interventions were well received by patients, and they reported perceiving the process as enjoyable and experiencing mostly positive emotions during and after the workshops and sessions (Landless *et al.*, 2018).

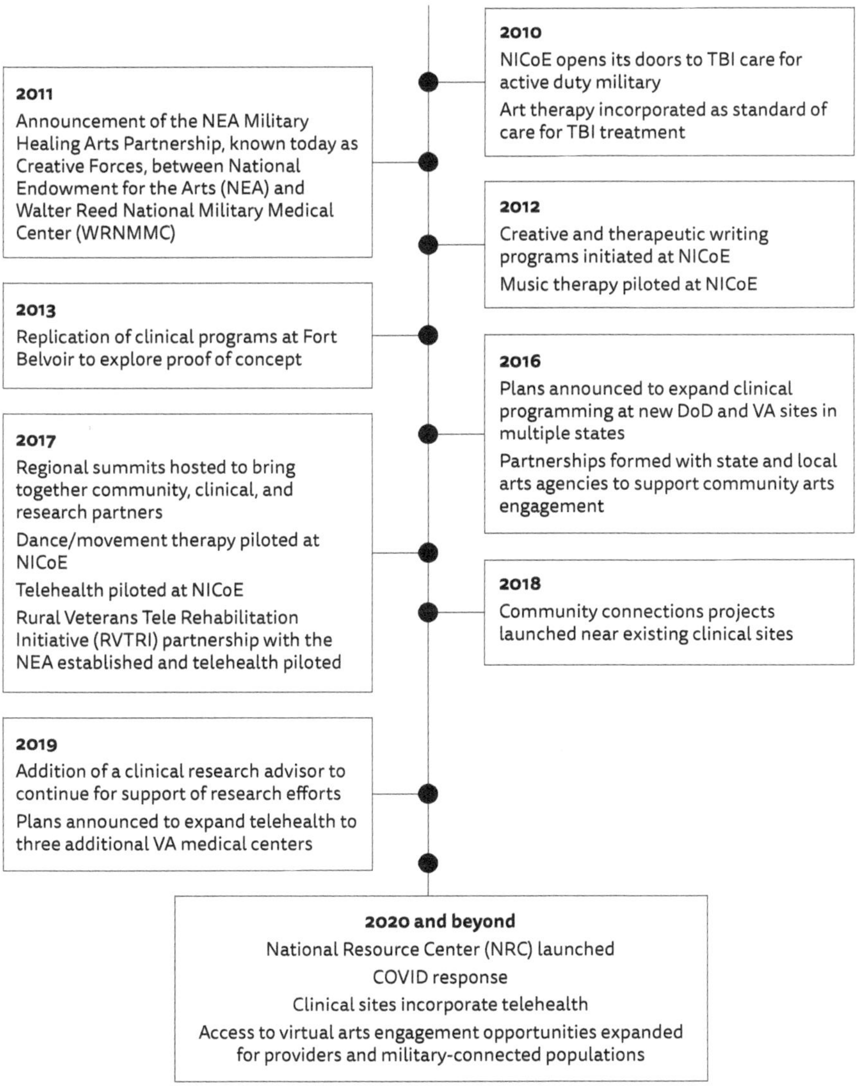

Figure 4.1: Timeline of growth of Creative Forces (image credit: National Endowment for the Arts, 2020a)

Due to the results of the Operation Homecoming writing program, coupled with awareness of the impact of the art therapy program and requests for additional creative arts therapies by patients and high-level officials, the NEA determined that further support was warranted. To meet this identified need, it created a position for a music therapist to work alongside the art therapist at the NICoE. This initial programming set the foundation for the intentional replication of creative arts therapies programming across other DoD and VA sites—allowing Creative Forces to extend from the National Capital Region to create a national footprint. This exploratory endeavor proved successful, and using this proof of concept, dance/movement therapy was piloted at the NICoE shortly thereafter. The timeline of programmatic expansion between 2010 and 2020 started with one creative arts therapist (CAT) at one clinical site and extended to 25+ CATs across 13 different military sites within the DoD and VA, with plans for continued growth. This timeline of growth is demonstrated in Figure 4.1.

Integration of creative arts therapies and military medicine

Historical context

Throughout history, advances in medical care have emerged from times of war. Ambulances, anesthesia, and amputations are medical developments credited to past military conflicts. Modernization of battlefield interventions and prosthetic limbs are among the significant advances of contemporary conflicts. Additionally, integrated care, specifically with the inclusion of the creative arts therapies, should be considered a recent medical innovation. The creative arts therapies have existed for decades; in fact, the histories of art therapy, dance/movement therapy, and music therapy date back to World Wars (WW) I and II (American Art Therapy Association, 2020; American Music Therapy Association, 2014; Chaiklin, 2020). The advent of improvised explosive devices and roadside bombs, along with unprecedented survival rates due to progress in battlefield medicine, has resulted in approximately 92 percent of soldiers wounded in Iraq and Afghanistan returning safely home, according to the Army Surgeon General (Vergun, 2016). This is a sweeping increase from survival rates in WWI (4%) and WWII (50%) (Vergun, 2020). However, these injuries indicate significant numbers of service members and veterans impacted by TBI and psychological injuries, including PTSD, and treating these complex conditions, especially when they co-occur, continues to be a challenge. Traditional approaches of healthcare were not achieving the desired results and thus a new, integrated approach to care was warranted.

Creating an integrated model of care

The NICoE is a clinical research center that treats TBI and psychological health conditions through an integrative and patient-centered approach. It was created with the intent to bring various clinical specialties and services needed to care for complex patients into one physical space. This "one-stop-shop" approach improves the patient experience because rather than patients having to navigate complicated healthcare systems to obtain laboratory tests, diagnostic imaging, and specialty consultation, the relevant services were collocated in one space. This concept of treatment has generated an overwhelmingly positive response, and testimonials from patients highlight the benefits of having an interdisciplinary team work together to meet their needs. NICoE patients have consistently reported that rather than retelling their history repeatedly to different providers, the quality of collaborative care of the NICoE interdisciplinary treatment team was beneficial to their rehabilitation process from commencement to conclusion. Figure 4.2 is an example of the type of interdisciplinary model of care implemented at the NICoE and satellite Intrepid Spirit Centers (ISCs) located at military treatment facilities across the U.S.

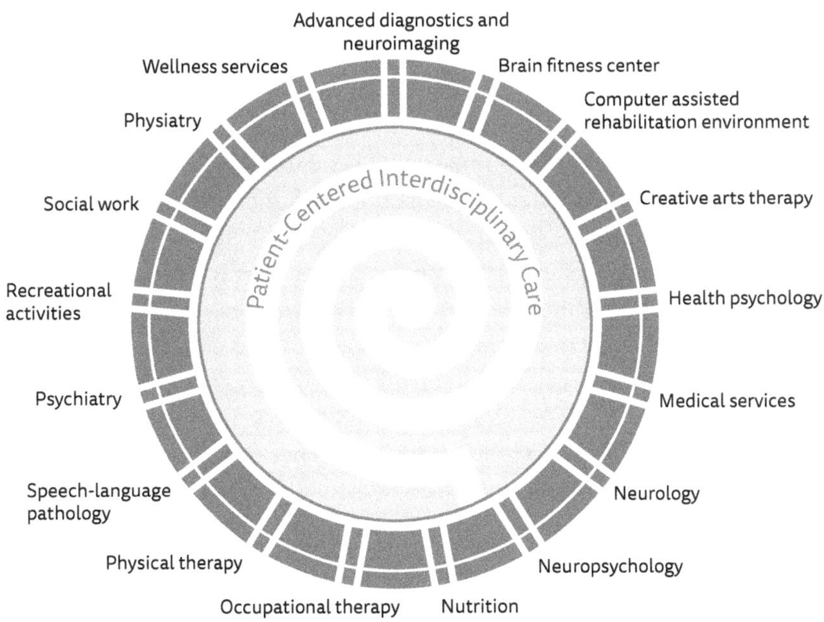

Figure 4.2: Integrated Care Model (Note: This diagram does not include all embedded disciplines at the NICoE and ISCs, and disciplines listed may not be present at all sites.)

Sustained integration and clear impact

Creative arts therapies are included in the NICoE and ISC interdisciplinary program models as a core element of treatment and are a critical component to the success of this integrative approach. In addition to being efficacious, the integrated care approach is economically effective and can be delivered at a fraction of the cost of traditional treatment. CATs, specifically, are one of the less expensive clinical disciplines, costing less than 1 percent of the overall operational budget of a facility such as the NICoE and ISCs. As part of the interdisciplinary team, CATs assist in assessing patient needs, establishing treatment goals, and implementing clinical interventions to advance those goals. Furthermore, they attend team meetings to inform treatment planning for patients. In that way, CATs can provide insight regarding the benefits directly achieved in creative arts therapies sessions and support increased effectiveness across the entire interdisciplinary treatment team.

Additionally, creative arts therapies have appeared to motivate patients to engage more completely in all their therapies. Clinical directors at Creative Forces sites within the DoD and VA often refer patients to creative arts therapies who experience barriers in traditional treatments, such as physical therapy or behavior health services. This has shown to help patients become "unstuck" and holistically engaged in their overall rehabilitation processes, demonstrating that the creative arts therapies are an essential component of this comprehensive treatment approach, rather than simply "nice to have" (Vaudreuil *et al.*, 2019a). There are, however, a limited number of CATs currently working within the DoD and VA healthcare systems. As a possible adjunct, recreational arts and Arts in Health programs offer arts engagement opportunities to interested patients, which can help support the process of transitioning from the clinical space and into the community, when appropriate. Furthermore, there is a clear delineation between recreational arts engagement and clinical creative arts therapies. Creative Forces has done foundational work regarding the appropriate positioning of CATs, and research about the impact of their work in military and veteran healthcare systems. To provide consistency of care and to support patient reintegration, Creative Forces builds networks that support arts engagement on a clinic to community continuum (Vaudreuil *et al.*, 2019b).

Creative Forces' operational growth

Clinical operations

Creative Forces operates with three main mission elements: clinical treatment, community engagement, and capacity building, as shown in Figure 4.3. Although the clinical component was the initial and foundational element of this initiative, the other two elements are of equal importance. Establishing a strong clinic to community continuum is critical in supporting transition as patients leave treatment and addresses the needs of individuals who may not seek access to traditional clinical care. This continuum is based on the development of local ecosystems that support arts engagement for veterans, service members, and military families. In these community models across the Creative Forces network, CATs engage with local artists, arts organizations, and state and local arts agencies to share information about their respective missions, build reciprocally purposeful relationships, and refine programming to offer impactful and informed experiences to the military populations served.

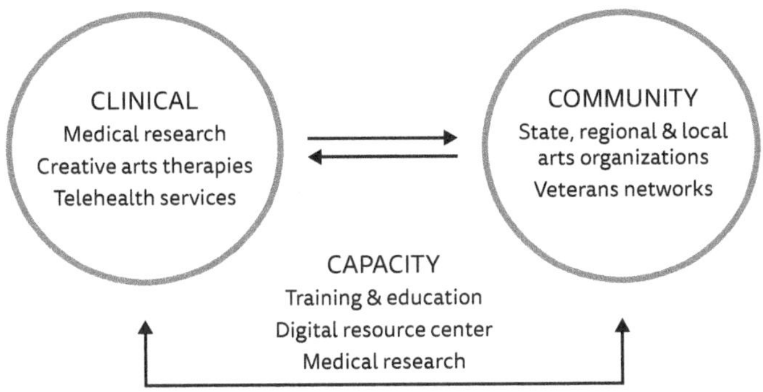

Figure 4.3: Creative Forces' pillars of operation (image credit: National Endowment for the Arts, 2020a)[1]

Community engagement

Many patients who benefit from the creative arts therapies seek to continue treatment after they have reached their goals. In some circumstances, continued engagement with therapy is possible and clinically indicated. However, with the growing demand for services, CATs find themselves needing to evaluate the individual benefit of continuing a patient's clinical care against taking referrals for new patients, who also have an identified need for treatment. The clinic to community continuum supports a smoother transition for continued creative expression through arts engagement by providing a warm handoff to community partners that can assist in the maintenance of health and wellness after treatment is terminated. Additionally, community artists and arts organizations play a significant role in supporting service members and veterans who may be reluctant to access clinical care or who do not believe they need formal treatment.

1 https://www.arts.gov/initiatives/creative-forces

Military-focused community arts opportunities forged through established community connections projects between Creative Forces and local artists and arts organizations include open mics, Community Creative Arts Cafés, bronze-pouring and glassblowing classes, writing workshops, mindfulness training, and guided dance/movement experiences. These may be the first places some veterans or service members interface with the arts; therefore, collaboration between CATs and local arts communities and agencies allows Creative Forces to operate as an inclusive network that serves as a resource in impacting the wellbeing of the military population on micro, mezzo, and macro levels. Creative Forces empowers its constituents by serving individuals and families, developing networks, and creating replicable models to implement in communities nationwide.

Capacity building

Capacity building is crucial, as with continued growth, the demand for creative arts therapies services will far exceed the ability for Creative Forces to meet the increasing need. By conducting research to expand our knowledge of the impact, outcomes, and mechanisms of action of creative arts therapies, Creative Forces advances the effort to make these treatments more widely accessible in healthcare systems and eventually to become a covered benefit. However, it is not enough to conduct and publish research, as disseminating findings and lessons learned is of equal importance. Information must be made readily accessible to military leadership, clinical directors, other researchers, and funders of clinical programming and research. To that end, Creative Forces has established the National Resource Center (NRC), an online portal that supports easy access and engagement with research, discovery, and data. The NRC houses resources that support CATs, community artists, researchers, funders, and other stakeholders to expand on the work of Creative Forces to reach wider audiences and further enhance impact (National Endowment for the Arts, 2020a).

Creative Forces: a learning endeavor

Throughout 2016, Creative Forces engaged in a multifaceted discovery process aligned with its mission of being a learning venture. The stages of discovery included clinical site visits, meetings with site leadership teams, and community gatherings to learn about how local organizations engage with military populations. These efforts provided networking opportunities between the military installation and the community, hence strengthening their connections.

Additionally, fostering connections between military leadership and community artists and organizations was imperative in establishing programs that were positioned for success and able to be replicated to increase access for service members, veterans, and their families and caregivers.

Creative standardization

Creative Forces' methodology for program expansion includes creating clinical models of art therapy, dance/movement therapy, and music therapy, which can be replicated across multiple sites in the DoD and VA. Over time, Creative Forces has developed and applied standardization processes across the disciplines and at various sites which have yielded meaningful information for program evaluation. Creative Forces provides support and clinical resources such as assessment and treatment protocols, documentation templates, and provider referral guides, throughout the replication and program expansion processes. This allows CATs to make customized and informed recommendations for patient care while allowing for adaptability to meet patient needs in the moment. This clinical standardization has set the foundation for multisite research in the future. The following discipline-specific case examples show the growth, replication, and standardization of each of the creative arts therapies represented in Creative Forces.

Creative Forces: art therapy

Art therapy existed within the NICoE Healing Arts Program model prior to the partnership with the NEA, but creative arts therapies programming evolved due to what eventually became known as Creative Forces. Operation Homecoming, an NEA initiative that supported a writing program, was originally brought to the NICoE in 2012 under the supervision of the Healing Arts Program coordinator, who is an art therapist. Based on positive patient feedback and high-level official suggestions, a music therapist was embedded by Creative Forces at the NICoE alongside the art therapist, and shortly afterwards the art therapy program was replicated at the first ISC at Fort Belvoir. The program was replicated by an art therapy graduate program intern of the NICoE—which has been repeated by graduating interns at three sites since. Patient and staff feedback at the ISC provided proof-of-concept for the replication of these efforts within art therapy and across the creative arts therapies disciplines (Jones *et al.*, 2018). When the ISC Fort Belvoir art therapist became a full-time permanent position, similar replicative modeling ensued, with Creative Forces supporting the addition of a music therapist to work alongside the art therapist as part of the interdisciplinary care team at that location.

Creative Forces: music therapy

Music therapy was integrated into Creative Forces in 2012, starting with a program at the NICoE. Learning from the expansion of art therapy programming, music therapy created a foundational program model designed with the intention of multi-site replication, which is detailed further in Chapter 6. In 2015, music therapy was successfully piloted at ISC Fort Belvoir in Virginia. Much like art therapy, music therapy was found to be a beneficial part of the interdisciplinary care model and was integrated as a standard of care in the longitudinal treatment model at ISC Fort Belvoir (Bronson *et al.*, 2018). In the years that followed, music therapy programs were requested at many more Creative Forces sites. With consideration to working with military populations, Creative Forces music therapists implemented: coordinated approaches to intervention facilitation (Bradt *et al.*, 2019; Vaudreuil *et al.*, 2019a); clinical group protocols (Vaudreuil *et al.*, 2020a); informed technological innovation in music therapy telehealth (Spooner *et al.*, 2019; Vaudreuil *et al.*, 2020b); and standardized assessment and documentation templates (Hogue *et al.*, 2020). To date, Creative Forces music therapy programs have been established at six DoD and four VA sites, with further expansion planned.

Creative Forces: dance/movement therapy

Dance/movement therapy was piloted through Creative Forces at the NICoE in 2017 and integrated into both the Healing Arts Program and Wellness and Rehab programming. This positioning was designed to support increasing awareness of the mind–body connection, build mind–body skills through practice, and develop the confidence to continue engaging in breath and movement practices for ongoing self-care. Working with patients both individually and collaboratively in groups, dance/movement therapy leverages embodied cognition in treatment, recognizing the connection between mind and body as bi-directional and movement as developmental, expressive, communicative, and adaptive. Dance/movement therapists help patients to develop personally meaningful ways of utilizing breath, sensation, and movement to regulate the nervous system. As their skill level with managing autonomic arousal increases and social engagement processes are restored, patients are then able to connect with others through movement and verbal reflection. Patients reported that from engagement in dance/movement therapy, they experienced increases in mind–body awareness and self-confidence with mind–body practices (Winters-Fisher, 2019). Creative Forces dance/movement therapists work alongside art and music therapists in both DoD and VA treatment facilities.

Creative Forces: national expansion efforts

In October 2016, Creative Forces®: NEA Military Healing Arts Network officially launched at the Walter Reed National Military Medical Center (WRNMMC) in Bethesda, MD. The then Chairman of the NEA, Dr. Jane Chu, joined with senior leaders from WRNMMC to announce the intent of network expansion to include ten additional clinical sites beyond WRNMMC and the first ISC to open at U.S. Army Fort Belvoir in Virginia. Dr. Chu shared her thoughts about the impact and importance of Creative Forces, which is currently the NEA's largest initiative:

> We are seeing such transformational results in our service members and our expansion plans have come as a result of them saying that they want this program to be closer to their communities as they make a transition back into civilian life. This is a way to help service members and veterans [and their families] understand the dignity that they already have and so much deserve. (U.S. Department of Defense, 2016)

Key elements involved in the decision-making process of expanding Creative Forces programming to a new location included:

- Degree of program support from medical center leadership.
- Community arts organization enthusiasm, support, and capacity.
- Local military and veteran population that would be served.
- Geographic location(s).

Additionally, ensuring that the local clinical site would commit to providing space and support of the creative arts therapies in the integrated care programs was paramount.

Figure 4.4 is a visual depiction of the expansion of Creative Forces, which started at a DoD facility in the National Capital Region and grew nationally in both the DoD and VA.

Furthermore, the coordinated efforts of Creative Forces broadened access to community arts engagement and services provided to remote locations through distance delivery via creative arts therapies telehealth and tele-arts engagement opportunities.

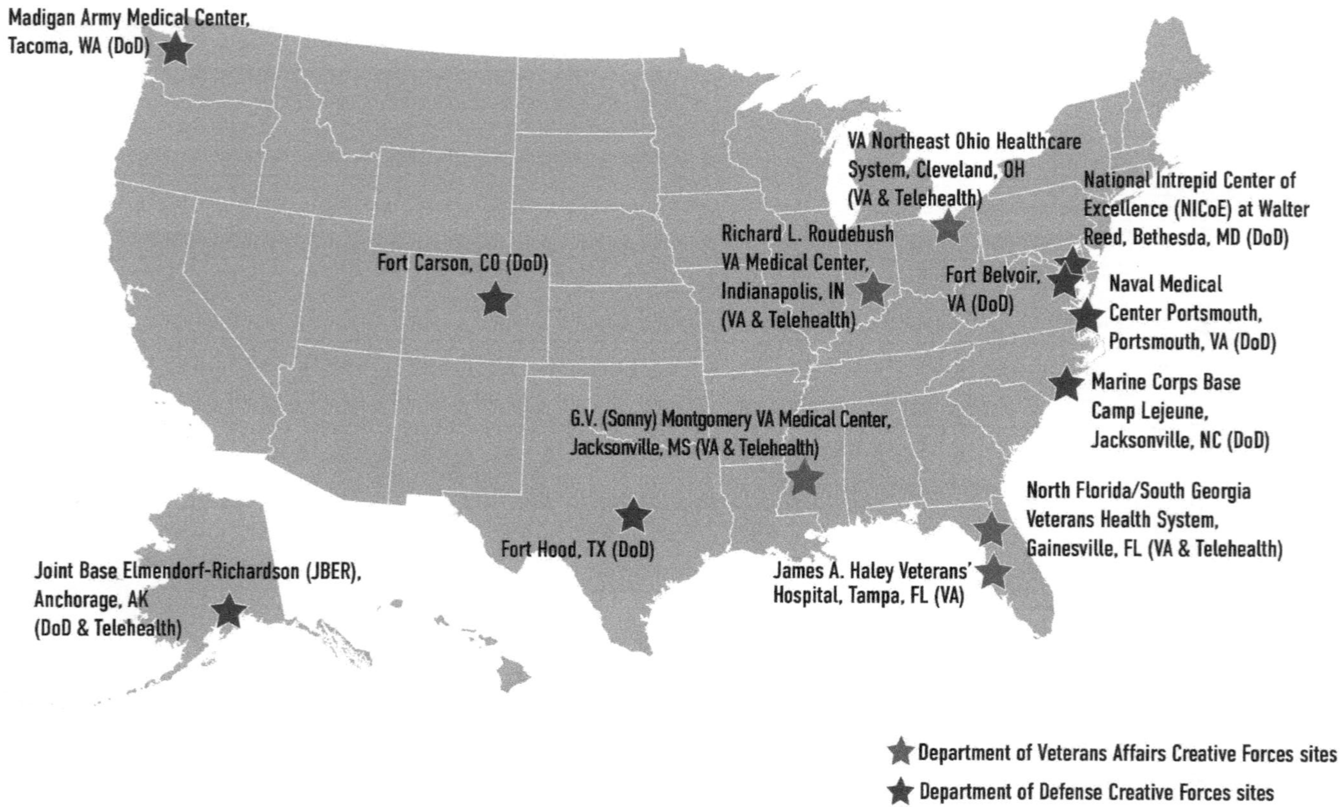

Figure 4.4: Locations of Creative Forces (image credit: National Endowment for the Arts, 2021)

Building a network of consistent high-quality care

By 2017, Creative Forces had further refined its implementation processes, starting with educating site leaders who had limited knowledge of the creative arts therapies, but had learned about their impact. Clinic directors were eager to learn that there was a way to access and integrate creative arts therapies treatment into their interdisciplinary programs. This initiative funded the placement of CATs and provided resourcing support for sustainability and success. Additionally, Creative Forces implemented infrastructure to guide site leaders through this process and created discipline-specific lead positions to provide support to the network of CATs as they built and adapted programming to meet the needs of their specific clinic's design. The infrastructure support, clinical and research mentorship, and ongoing professional development opportunities that Creative Forces provides have been instrumental in ensuring consistent delivery of high-quality care across the network (Vaudreuil *et al.*, 2020c).

Supporting the expansion of CATs within the DoD/VA healthcare system

These targeted efforts have supported the generation of employment opportunities for CATs within the DoD and VA medical systems. For example, at the outset of Creative Forces, there was one general schedule (GS) art therapist position in the network. Between 2014 and 2020, the number of Creative Forces-networked art therapists has grown to over a dozen, including four GS art therapists. As of March 2021, there are currently 14 music therapists in the Creative Forces network, five of whom are GS music therapists; two work in the DoD and three work in the VA. There are two Creative Forces dance/movement therapists supported by the clinical cooperator, one working in the DoD and one working in the VA. Creative Forces and GS-employed CATs use discipline-specific interventions as well as co-treat to generate cross-discipline clinical practice and research collaborations. Creative Forces has worked to build and leverage network strength to support and inform clinical standardization of practice for both in-person and telehealth services. The early integration of telehealth as a platform for delivery of creative arts therapies services proved especially beneficial during the global pandemic in 2020. This allowed the network to swiftly shift to virtual care to meet the ongoing needs of patients. The network of CATs is critical to achieving the two-pronged mission of the Creative Forces program:

1. To increase access to creative arts therapies and arts engagement for health and wellness.
2. To deepen our understanding of the value and the impact of the arts.

Music therapy in Creative Forces

As indicated throughout the chapter, music therapy programming, alongside art and dance/movement therapy, was an integral part of the Creative Forces expansion process from the early stages of site visits to on-site training of new music therapists across the network. Similar to a military structure, Creative Forces operates using a chain of command. For example, the Lead Music Therapist provides mentorship for the music therapy team in the realms of clinical programming, community outreach, and research support. In turn, the music therapy team has an open line of communication to the Lead Music Therapist. Continuous peer support and resources are provided during training and on-board processes, many of which have been converted to digital files (e.g., documents, training videos) and are housed on the Creative Forces NRC. The music therapy team meets regularly and individual consultations, as needed by the music therapists, are accommodated. As part of programmatic growth of Creative Forces music therapy, clinical competencies and standardization resources (e.g., referral criteria, assessment tools, intervention protocols, session materials, and documentation templates) are disseminated for use across the music therapy team.

Clinical competencies

Clinical competencies have been identified for CATs to successfully work with military populations. For Creative Forces music therapists, these are a combination of the American Music Therapy Association's professional competencies (American Music Therapy Association, 2013), military-specific cultural competencies, and clinical practice competencies that Creative Forces has developed over time. Competency areas include: assessment and treatment planning; clinical proficiency; implementation and documentation; therapeutic communication with patients and families; patient education; interdisciplinary collaboration; professional development and continuing education; and cultural humility in practice. Table 4.1 provides the Creative Forces music therapy competencies as of 2020.

Table 4.1: Creative Forces clinical music therapy competencies

Competency area	Competencies
1. Assessment and treatment planning	1.1 Provide music therapy (MT) evaluation session for referred patients to identify and prioritize their needs and set treatment goals. 1.2 Assesses patients' needs based on physical, cultural, religious, educational, language and age-specific criteria. 1.3 Identify patients' functioning level, strengths, and areas of need in the following domains: Cognition, Communication, Physiological, Sensorimotor, Socioemotional, Spiritual. 1.4 Provide trauma-informed care through MT treatment. 1.5 Maintain patient confidentiality.
2. Clinical proficiency	2.1 Provide care in a safe and therapeutic environment and engage patients in individual and group treatment conducive to rehabilitation as indicated in the American Music Therapy Association Code of Ethics (2019) and Standards of Practice. 2.2 Demonstrate basic knowledge of the psychological and physiological aspects of musical behavior and experience (e.g., affect; physiological responses; perception and cognition; preference; creativity). 2.3 Adequately supervise patient and family use of the MT spaces. 2.4 Maintain MT cleanliness and organization of MT spaces and reconcile MT supplies and budgetary needs. 2.5 Demonstrate basic knowledge of the use of current technologies in MT assessment, treatment, and evaluation. 2.6 Develop metrics to evaluate the therapeutic effects of music with military populations. 2.7 Telehealth 2.7.1 Deliver MT via telehealth in accordance with facility mandated regulations and guidelines to include: utilization of appropriate connectivity platforms, acquiring patients' written or verbal consent and confirmation of patients' contact information and physical address/location in the event of an emergency. 2.8 Research 2.8.1 Ensure basic knowledge/familiarity of research procedures and protocols. 2.8.2 Complete site-specific research training as required. 2.8.3 Collaborate in research studies on the definition, execution, and efficacy of MT and creative arts therapies treatment with military-connected populations.

cont.

Competency area	Competencies
3. Implementation/ Documentation	3.1 Produce documentation that accurately reflects patient outcomes and meets the requirements of internal and external legal, regulatory, and reimbursement bodies. 3.2 Document and revise the treatment plan and document changes to the treatment plan. 3.3 Observe, record, and report: 3.3.1 Patients' physical condition, emotional state, and/or behavioral patterns 3.3.2 Changes in above 3.3.3 Patients' non-compliance with treatment plan 3.4 Use standardized note templates, if applicable, for documenting on patients' electronic medical records.
4. Therapeutic communication with patients and families	4.1 Use oneself effectively in the therapist role in both individual and group therapy (e.g., appropriate self-disclosure, authenticity, empathy, etc.) towards affecting desired behavioral outcomes. 4.2 Provide verbal and non-verbal communication and cues necessary for patient participation. 4.3 Communicate to the patients expectations of their behavior and provide feedback on their communications. 4.4 Be proficient in using MT techniques to enable patients and families to manage physical, emotional, and psychological stress. 4.5 Recognize, interpret, and respond appropriately to significant events in the MT session as they occur. 4.6 Identify environmental, cultural, and other variables that could potentially affect communication. 4.7 Actively seek feedback from patients and families regarding effectiveness of MT treatment. 4.8 Demonstrate behaviors within appropriate professional boundaries: consistency, caring, confidentiality, credibility, genuineness, empathy, respect. 4.9 Show comprehensive understanding of military culture and ability to engage with military populations.

5. Patient education	5.1 Assess learning needs of patients and families and identify barriers to learning. 5.2 Assess patient education needs based on physical, cultural, religious, educational, language and age-specific criteria. 5.3 Communicate patient education effectively to patients and family members. 5.4 Communicate with patients, families, and team members regarding treatment progress. 5.5 Encourage patients to become active members in their MT treatment plans. 5.6 Appropriately answer patient and family questions or consult with other team members to obtain information. 5.7 Make recommendations for use of music in daily routine, where appropriate. 5.8 Identify community-based arts engagement that represents best practices for supporting a continuum of healing arts—from clinical intervention to community reintegration.
6. Interdisciplinary collaboration	6.1 Participate in interdisciplinary team evaluations of patients and provide recommendations for treatment. 6.2 Demonstrate effective interpersonal skills with colleagues and other members of the medical facility. 6.3 Convey music therapy practice, goals and outcomes, and inclusion/exclusion criteria during team meetings, in services effectively. Convey Creative Forces mission, structure, and history when appropriate. 6.4 Communicate all pertinent data to the interdisciplinary team, especially the rationale for MT services and the role of the MT. 6.5 Identify situations requiring a call for emergency assistance. 6.6 Exchange information with patients, family members, treatment team and clinics for the purpose of planning and facilitating patients' and families' evaluation and treatment. 6.7 Work with supervisors and leadership to continually improve MT programming.
7. Professional development and continuing education	7.1 Participate in continuing education (as required for maintenance of professional licensure and/or credentials). 7.2 Seek out and utilize Creative Forces MT team for peer support and discipline-specific consultation. 7.3 Develop and maintain a repertoire of music for age, culture, and stylistic differences.
8. Cultural humility in practice	8.1 Demonstrate knowledge of and respect for diverse cultural backgrounds. 8.2 Treat all people with dignity and respect, regardless of differences in race, ethnicity, nationality, language, religion, marital status, gender, gender identity or expression, sexual orientation, age, ability, socioeconomic status, or political affiliation.

Key components of music therapy competencies include population and therapeutic awareness, authentic engagement with patients and families, musicianship, and the foundational knowledge of innovative programs and pioneering research pertaining to music therapy with military populations. In addition to the Creative Forces comprehensive training that networked music therapists receive, resources to support these competencies for all music therapists include online trainings (e.g., PsychArmor), published research on the topics of TBI and PTSD, published research about music therapy and military populations, the *Diagnostic and Statistical Manual of Mental Disorders* (fifth edition, American Psychiatric Association, 2013), and the Creative Forces National Resource Center (2020).

Standardization efforts of Creative Forces music therapy clinical programming and research

Music therapy has been shown to be an effective treatment for military-connected populations in the U.S. and abroad (Gooding & Langston, 2019). The Creative Forces music therapy program developed a clinic practice model that meets the myriad of needs specific to military populations, including active-duty service members, veterans, and their families in both intensive outpatient program (IOP) and longitudinal care models (Bronson *et al.*, 2018). This process has informed a clinical treatment trajectory aligned with traditional rehabilitation disciplines that supports patients from assessment to termination. This clinical process is implemented across Creative Forces creative arts therapies programming, as shown in Figure 4.5. Creative Forces adds the community reintegration component, which supports patients' continued engagement in the arts after termination from formal treatment.

Through standardized goal setting and intervention facilitation, Creative Forces music therapists have identified common music therapy interventions that have shown to be impactful with military populations. These include: songwriting for emotional expressivity (Bradt *et al.*, 2019); performance integration for socialization (Vaudreuil *et al.*, 2019b); active, intentional music listening and group drumming (Vaudreuil *et al.*, 2020a); and the use of neurologic music therapy techniques for co-treatment with traditional rehabilitative disciplines (Vaudreuil *et al.*, 2019a). In addition, Creative Forces has published findings related to the integration of music therapy and telehealth practices (Spooner *et al.*, 2019; Vaudreuil *et al.*, 2020b). Detailed examples of individual and group music therapy interventions can be found in Chapters 5 and 6.

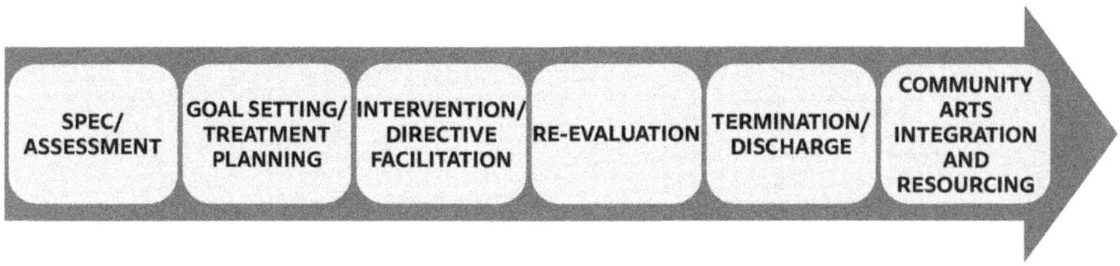

Figure 4.5: Music therapy treatment trajectory

While acknowledging and appreciating the unique artistry and clinical approaches of CATs, Creative Forces has made significant efforts to achieve standardization of clinical operations across the creative arts therapies. Music therapy helped pioneer Creative Forces' standardization in the realms of clinical intervention facilitation, treatment trajectories for IOP and longitudinal care models, and documentation templates (Hogue *et al.*, 2020). To achieve this level of standardization across the creative arts therapies, Creative Forces supports the development of clinical resources such as referral tools, playbooks, training videos, and assessment and intervention protocols. For example, an Introduction to Music Therapy group protocol has been used by Creative Forces at multiple sites that employ both IOP and longitudinal programming to inform treatment planning for patients receiving care in integrated health models (Vaudreuil *et al.*, 2020a).

The future of Creative Forces: what's ahead?

As a continuous learning endeavor, Creative Forces must grow to increase access to services, but the Creative Forces mission is clearly rooted in exploration to understand the value and impact of the arts—clinically and otherwise. As Creative Forces learns more about the core foundation and impact of creative arts therapies practices, it can better understand emerging needs and then expand target populations to inform future endeavors that are refined and focused around priority research areas. For Creative Forces-supported creative arts therapies disciplines, conceptual frameworks were developed to inform clinical practice standardization and research aims, which have yielded 19 scholarly publications to date as well as identified priority areas and specific lines of inquiry for continued research efforts. Creative Forces' research efforts, which include a systematic approach to examining existing literature, identifying gaps and need, and determining how to address them, are elaborated on in Chapter 11. Furthermore, the development of new target populations is informed by a phased development sequence, which includes discovery, pilot and logic model development, model implementation and evaluation, and revision and replication. This is demonstrated in Figure 4.6.

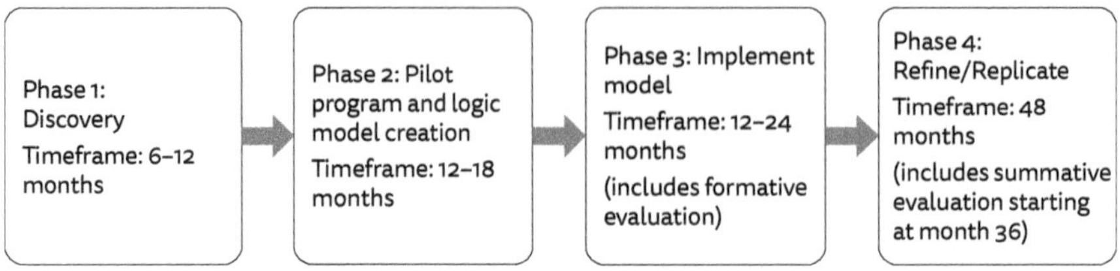

Figure 4.6: Creative Forces phased development sequence

In addition to in-person creative arts therapies and community arts engagement, Creative Forces has pivoted its practices across the continuum to include clinical telehealth and virtual arts engagement, including workshops focused on resilience and self-care for providers. This was an initial response to COVID-19, which has impacted the provision of healthcare on a global scale. However, technology has demonstrated efficacy in bolstering clinical care and community engagement; therefore, Creative Forces will continue to explore ways to leverage technology to create best practices that optimize patient outcomes and consistency of care across the clinic to community continuum.

Summary

The inception of the NICoE Healing Arts program in 2010 laid the groundwork through replication and expansion for a network of CATs to be embedded within DoD and VA facilities across the nation in support of the advancement of military healthcare. The focus that Creative Forces has maintained on research, capacity building, and community engagement, while providing high-quality clinical care, has allowed the impact of this initiative to grow beyond the healing of the individual patient to a macro level within the military medical system. As the Creative Forces network remains relevant and responsive, and maintains its mission of being a learning endeavor, it will continue to develop innovative ways to strengthen clinical best practices, nurture valued partnerships, and use technology to improve the health, wellbeing, and quality of life for military-connected populations.

SECTION II

Music Therapy Clinical Application and Community Integration

Chapter 5

Military Music Therapy in Individual Settings

MEGAN WONG AND NATALIE QUINTANA

Introduction

Individual music therapy sessions are an important component of the treatment process, as they allow patients to focus on personalized goals with the direct support of a music therapist. Patients can gain insight on their unique needs (e.g., coping strategies, emotional regulation, functional skills) and benefit from music therapy interventions to address goal areas (Erkkilä *et al.*, 2011). Additionally, patients who are not appropriate for group music therapy can receive treatment in an individual setting as a means of building rapport with the provider and acquiring skills that may later enable them to participate in group music therapy as well as more diverse rehabilitation settings during treatment and on discharge from music therapy and their overall treatment program (Gold *et al.*, 2013).

This chapter details individual music therapy sessions facilitated with two military populations: 1) active-duty service members treated within the Department of Defense (DoD); and 2) veterans receiving care through the Department of Veterans Affairs (VA). This chapter will detail the similarities and unique distinctions of integrating individual music therapy treatment into DoD and VA settings, with considerations to stand-alone care and co-treatment.

Individual music therapy in the DoD and VA

Individual music therapy is offered to service members and veterans as part of treatment at military installations and VA medical centers (VAMCs) across the United States (U.S.). Individual music therapy sessions have assisted military-connected patients in their rehabilitation processes by: addressing symptomatology specific to the signature wounds of war, namely, traumatic brain injury (TBI) and post-traumatic stress disorder (PTSD), through receptive and expressive music therapy interventions (Bronson *et al.*, 2018); achieving continued gains in traditional therapies through co-treatment with interdisciplinary team members (Vaudreuil *et al.*, 2019a); assisting with emotional expression through songwriting (Bradt *et al.*, 2019); and supporting community reintegration and social transformation through performance (Vaudreuil *et al.*, 2019b).

Department of Defense

The music therapy program with active-duty service members in the DoD described in this chapter refers to treatment that takes place at the Intrepid Spirit Center (ISC-7) located at Marine Corps Base Camp Pendleton. This ISC the seventh of eight (as indicated by -7), with two more future locations planned, to total ten ISCs. These specialty clinics were constructed by the Intrepid Fallen Heroes Fund to provide care for service members suffering from TBI and PTSD. Each ISC is approximately 25,000 square feet and costs approximately $14 million to build and equip. They are designed according to an interdisciplinary treatment model that provides patients with comprehensive and holistic diagnostic and rehabilitative services.

ISC-7 Intensive outpatient program

Models of care at ISC-7 consist of an intensive outpatient program (IOP) and a longitudinal outpatient program. All patients who receive treatment at ISC-7 must have a primary diagnosis of TBI/concussion to be eligible for services in either of the programs. The IOP, called ACHIEVE, is five weeks in length. Participating service members receive command approval for a temporary duty assignment of engagement in TBI rehabilitation. Treatment consists primarily of group sessions; however, individual sessions specific to patients' highest areas of need are provided. Patients are referred to ACHIEVE by a medical provider within the patient's command, usually the primary care manager (PCM) or mental health provider. The referring provider completes an "ACHIEVE Referral Form," which examines legal issues, substance abuse, and suicidal or homicidal ideation history to determine if the patient meets inclusion criteria for the ACHIEVE program. Additionally, the patient completes a Warrior Administered Retrospective Casualty Assessment Tool (WARCAT), which includes supplementary details that further inform screening, such as combat deployments, a neurobehavioral symptom inventory, demographics form, sleep index, other reported mental health symptoms, and resiliency assessment. Other requirements for a service member to participate in ACHIEVE are that they must be able to complete all five weeks of the program, be more than 30 days away from their End of Active Service (EAS) date, and complete labs and drug screens before beginning treatment. The stringent processes (i.e., referral, assessment, screening) ensure that patients are able to perform the rehabilitative tasks required to accomplish the primary goals of ACHIEVE, which are to help patients return to duty and gain a higher level of functioning.

ISC-7 longitudinal outpatient treatment

The longitudinal outpatient program is for service members who reside locally (either on base or in the community), many of whom are on light or limited duty. Patients who receive ongoing treatment at ISC-7 have a diagnosis of mild, moderate, or severe TBI with possible co-occurring psychological health disorders. Referrals come from a patient's command medical officer or as a direct transfer from another TBI clinic. Prior to admittance to ISC-7's longitudinal outpatient program, the patient must complete certain labs and answer screening questions (e.g., details of injury, persisting symptoms) that are confirmed by the referring medical officer. The ISC-7 medical and clinic directors review all consults, determine appropriateness for an intake, or order a complete neuropsychological evaluation prior to enrollment. Exclusion criteria include patients: 1) with acute injury, for example, within the first 30 days of a mild TBI; 2) with active substance use/abuse; and/or 3) within three months of a permanent change of station (PCS) or EAS. A WARCAT must be completed by the patient prior to an intake session, which is facilitated by a nurse and licensed clinical social worker (LCSW). The nurse documents the patient's physical symptoms and TBI history, and the LCSW documents cognition and mental health related symptoms, risk assessment, and substance use/abuse history, while also providing patients with psychoeducation about the ISC-7 treatment process and clinical expectations and guidelines.

After the intake session, the patient meets with the ISC-7 PCM, who makes referrals to specialists based on assessment results and identified patient needs. The patient works with the PCM to develop a treatment plan that consists of individual and/or group therapies. The patient follows up with the intake team after three months of treatment to determine progress. Generally, patients are discharged from the clinic within six to nine months of enrollment. Although the primary goal of the clinic is to help patients return to duty, some patients are unable to do so. In these situations, courses of action are taken to assist the patient in ending their service through a process determined by their military status, rehabilitation progress, injury, and other factors such as service-connectedness of injuries. These considerations will be addressed later in this chapter.

ISC-7: setting the stage for success

ISC-7 is unique because it was the first clinic of its kind to be constructed with the intention of including a music therapist as part of the interdisciplinary team. A space was specifically designed as a music therapy clinic, with extra insulation in the walls to add sound-proofing, and built-in shelving units to display and store instruments. It is located on the opposite side of the building from mental health and neuropsychology testing rooms, which minimizes sound distraction as patients are engaging in testing, assessment, or mental health treatment. This exemplifies how the integration of music therapy as a standard of care into an interdisciplinary team was executed in an intentional and considerate way, ultimately setting the stage for programmatic success.

Department of Veterans Affairs

As described in the first four chapters of this book, music therapy originated in the VA through innovative programs enacted during World Wars I and II, which used recorded music to soothe convalescing Soldiers, and community musicians to engage those experiencing combat fatigue or shellshock—what we recognize today as PTSD—though live music performances. Since then, music therapy has been positioned as part of recreation therapy in the VA, providing care for veterans.

The Creative Arts Therapy program at James A. Haley Veterans' Hospital in Tampa, FL, serves active-duty service members and veterans as part of innovative programming for the comprehensive treatment of TBI and PTSD. This

VA houses over 500 inpatient beds treating medical, geriatric, and mental health concerns. Outpatient programs targeting homelessness, community living for those with psychiatric diagnoses, cancer, and other health issues are also provided at VA-affiliated locations throughout the greater Tampa Bay area. Furthermore, James A. Haley VA is recognized for innovative treatment programs and specialized medical and rehabilitative units for service members and veterans with spinal cord injury, TBI, and stroke. Music therapy treatment pertaining to the VA discussed throughout the remainder of this chapter refers to three specialized TBI models of care that include evaluation with treatment arm, inpatient, and transitional treatment programs.

Post-Deployment Rehabilitation and Evaluation Program

The first of these programs is the Post-Deployment Rehabilitation and Evaluation Program (PREP). Similar to the ISC-7 ACHIEVE IOP, PREP is a three-week program that treats active-duty service members and veterans with mild TBI or persistent post-concussive symptoms with possible co-occurring psychological health disorders. Further rehabilitation is offered to the patients if indicated at the completion of PREP. Veterans are referred to PREP through their VA physician, and active-duty service members are referred to PREP by a medical provider within their command. The initial evaluations address physical, cognitive, and mental health concerns through an interdisciplinary team approach. Goals for PREP include improving functional abilities, reducing symptom complaints, stabilizing psychological distress, enhancing family relationships, and assisting patients with ongoing recovery.

Inpatient and transitional programming

The second program, the Acute Brain Injury Inpatient Program, is an inpatient medical and rehabilitation unit that provides care to active-duty service members and veterans with moderate/severe TBI and disorders of consciousness. This unit offers comprehensive care for these patients and families adjusting to new routines. Lastly, a transitional program, Polytrauma Transitional Rehabilitation Program (PTRP), assists patients with TBI/stroke in community, supported, or independent living. Table 5.1 indicates the ISC-7 and Tampa VA music therapy programs' descriptions, clinical space considerations, diagnoses treated, referral processes, assessments used, goal areas, music therapy approaches, treatment durations, and examples of interdisciplinary care and co-treatment.

Table 5.1: ISC-7 and Tampa VA program models

	Intrepid Spirit Center-7, Camp Pendleton	James A. Haley Veterans' Hospital
Program description	• Intensive Outpatient Program (IOP) • Longitudinal Outpatient Care	• Inpatient rehabilitation programs • Inpatient evaluation and treatment programs • Transitional program • Treating active-duty service members and veterans
Clinical space	• Intentionally constructed music therapy clinic in a building specifically designed for outpatient interdisciplinary treatment for TBI	• Designated music therapy clinic for individual sessions • Shared spaces for group sessions
Diagnoses treated	• Mild/moderate/severe TBI	• Mild TBI and post-concussion syndrome • Moderate TBI and stroke • Severe TBI and emerging consciousness
Referral process	• Referred through doctors/case managers for evaluation by ISC-7 team	• Referred through physiatrists for evaluation by unit • Interdisciplinary treatment team
Assessments used	• Individual assessment session • Interview-based assessment	• Individual assessment session • Interview-based assessment • Standardized assessments based on diagnoses or treatment areas
Goal areas	• Cognition • Psychosocial skills • Fine/Gross motor skills • Vestibular function	• Cognition • Psychosocial skills • Fine/Gross motor skills • Sensory stimulation
Music therapy approaches	• Neurologic music therapy (NMT)	• NMT • Music therapy in behavioral health
Treatment durations	• Five weeks for ACHIEVE IOP • Six to nine months for longitudinal outpatient program	• Three-week evaluation period, rolling into extended treatment period if indicated • Six to twelve months for inpatient rehabilitation
Interdisciplinary care and co-treatment	• Occupational therapy • Speech therapy • Vestibular therapy	• Occupational therapy • Speech therapy • Mental health

Individual music therapy treatment process

The music therapy treatment process follows a standardized trajectory from referral to termination, as shown in Figure 5.1. These steps include referral, assessment, treatment through the delivery of music therapy interventions, reassessment, and termination/discharge. Music therapists may benefit by frequently referring back to this treatment trajectory during treatment processes to ensure that the patient is on a pathway to maximum benefit from individual music therapy. In preparation for the end of treatment, the patient is provided with non-clinical resources and referral to community arts engagement, as applicable and available.

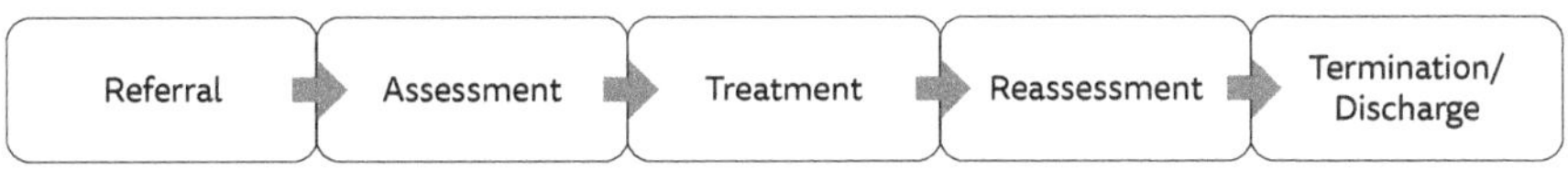

Figure 5.1: Music therapy treatment process

Referral

The referral process varies based on the protocol of the specific treatment facility. Generally, patients are referred to individual music therapy by a PCM or case manager. At interdisciplinary care clinics, there might be a higher number of internal referrals from providers within the treatment team. For example, if a patient is struggling to meet fine motor control goals in occupational therapy treatment, the occupational therapist might refer the patient to music therapy to incorporate therapeutic instrumental music performance (TIMP) to support functional motor skills.

It is imperative that music therapists consistently educate referring providers about criteria for appropriate patient referrals. This minimizes the number of patients who are referred to music therapy for reasons such as: "they used to play in a band" or "they are interested in learning to play guitar." Additionally, it is helpful for the referring providers to have a specific list of goal areas that music therapy can address. This is also beneficial for the patient because it gives them a better understanding of what to expect in their individual music therapy sessions. Examples of music therapy goal areas and interventions extracted from a referral resource created by Creative Forces®: NEA Military Healing Arts Network are provided in the box below.

Music therapy goal areas and intervention examples

Patient must have a non-musical goal in one of more of the following areas:

- Motor skills (e.g., gross, fine) and/or bilateral coordination. Patient may benefit from playing an instrument.
- Cognitive skill development. Patient may benefit from learning how to use music to support attention and memory.
- Healthy coping mechanisms and leisure activity development. Patient may benefit from engagement in music-guided relaxation, music-making, singing, and music and mindfulness exercises.
- Developing communication skills. Patient may benefit from self-expression and social interaction with others through songwriting, performance, and music production projects.
- Emotional processing and reminiscence of military experiences and general life conditions. Patient may gain self-insight and optimize interpersonal relationships though music listening and lyric discussion.

In the context of interdisciplinary care, patients are referred to music therapy by caseworkers and PCMs (e.g., doctors, nurse practitioners). In the process of creating effective and beneficial treatment plans with patients, it is helpful for referring providers to be educated on the criteria that help them determine whether or not a patient may benefit from music therapy services. Examples of these criteria include:

- The patient benefits from music engagement (e.g., is calmed by or can emote through music).
- The patient has received treatment from other disciplines but could benefit from additional support (e.g., co-treatment or consultation with other providers such as music therapy).
- The patient is motivated and interested in trying new or different forms of treatment.

Examples of exclusion criteria include if a patient has significant comorbid substance use/abuse issues or requires a higher level of care, experiences extreme auditory sensitivity (e.g., migraine triggers), or lacks interest in music therapy.

Assessment

Individual music therapy treatment begins with an assessment session to evaluate the patient's appropriateness for music therapy. In preparation for this, it is important for the music therapist to familiarize themselves with the patient's case. This may include a chart review of the patient's medical history, discussing the patient's needs with the referring provider, and/or meeting with the patient's treatment team. These preparatory actions support rapport building with the patient and maximize efficiency of the assessment session. During this session, it is important to assess the origin of the patient's injury or injuries, current presenting symptoms, and if they have been combat-deployed.

During assessment, the music therapist collects information about the patient's need areas, current treatment plan, medical history, current substance use, and relevant personal and social history. Additionally, the patient's music history and preferences are discussed to glean past and current interest in, engagement with, or use of music. This information helps to develop an understanding of the patient's personality and coping strategies. During the assessment session, the music therapist and patient determine the treatment path for the patient.

Additionally, the assessment session is an opportunity to provide patient education. Many patients have misunderstandings or misconceptions about what music therapy is, and therefore have uninformed expectations of treatment. An example of this was when a PCM referred a Marine Gunnery Sergeant (GySgt) to music therapy because during his intake session, he disclosed that he was independently learning the ukulele. Due to this referral rationale, the GySgt expected to receive music lessons. During the evaluation session, the music therapist informed him of the various ways that music could be used as a therapeutic tool to address clinical goals. The GySgt had many goals he was working on with a mental health provider. On learning that music therapy incorporated interventions such as lyric analysis and songwriting for emotional processing and expression, the GySgt stated, "I never thought of using song lyrics to discuss my thoughts and feelings. That would have made so much difference through all those appointments with my psychologist." Equipped with the knowledge of how to integrate music therapy interventions into other facets of his treatment, the GySgt processed the music therapy experiences, developed a clinical goal and objective, and created a customized treatment plan with the music therapist that incorporated strategies for emotion identification and expression through lyric analysis and songwriting.

Developing treatment goals

The development of individual treatment goals begins with the initial referral, includes the information gathered in the chart review, and is formalized with the input of the patient and their caregiver, if applicable, through the assessment process. The music therapist maximizes these avenues to map out the plan of care. Based on the knowledge gleaned from these processes, the music therapist first sets the specific treatment goal(s). The music therapist then determines the evidence-based intervention(s) to best achieve the goal(s), while being mindful of length of treatment, access to services, frequency of sessions, and scheduling availability. Interventions should be appropriate for the goal areas, abilities, and preferences of the patient.

The development of a treatment goal would be incomplete without choosing a method to measure progress. The music therapist is responsible for tracking progress and determining appropriate evaluation methods. This could include subjective domains such as patient self-report, and objective domains such as biofeedback (e.g., emWave®, bioDOTs™, Fitbit®), behavioral dimensions, or reassessment of target objectives. An appropriate system of progress measurement is vital to calculating effectiveness of the treatment plan. Conversely, if data indicates that the intervention is not effective to meet the goal, the music therapist may adjust the treatment plan.

Implementing music therapy treatment

Active-duty service members and veterans often require rehabilitation for both physical and behavioral reasons due to their military experiences. Fortunately, music therapy is comprehensive and is utilized to meet a variety of goals. Different approaches can be taken when considering the consulting referral and treatment goal for individual patients. Table 5.2 indicates the distinctions of music therapy approaches for rehabilitation (e.g., NMT) and behavioral health. Realistic expectations, boundaries, and adherence to the plan of care allows for healthy rapport between the music therapist and the patient. The music therapist should consistently communicate progress to the patient to support self-efficacy; this can also be achieved through reassessment and pre-emptively supporting appropriate termination of services, which will be further discussed. Additionally, preparing for the provision of resources encourages the patient or family to continue their newly acquired skills through self-guided engagement both during treatment and thereafter.

Table 5.2: Music therapy approaches

Neurologic Music Therapy	Music therapy in behavioral health
Cognition • Auditory Perception Training (APT) • Musical Attention Control Training (MACT) • Musical Mnemonics Training (MMT) • Musical Executive Function Training (MEFT)	Adjustment • Lyric analysis to support validation, perspective, recognizing and challenging maladaptive cognitive distortions • Songwriting for expression and reflection Social support • Group musical interventions, such as song sharing and active music-making, for decreased isolation and increased cohesion
Motor • Patterned Sensory Enhancement (PSE) • Therapeutic Instrumental Music Performance (TIMP)	Trauma • Breathing, grounding, and body scan through music-based relaxation interventions • Processing trauma through lyric analysis and songwriting
Psychosocial • Music in Psychosocial training and Counseling (MPC) • Associative Mood and Memory Training (AMMT)	Coping mechanisms • Leisure education through active music-making • Symptom management through self-care and musical interventions

Co-treatment

Music in and of itself is motivating and humanizing, making it a dynamic and potent tool for rehabilitation when utilized correctly. Music therapists have the ability and responsibility of treating patients using music interventions appropriately in an evidence-based manner. Often, other disciplines are curious about music therapists and their work, and providers may ask about scope of practice, request to observe a session, and, perhaps, engage in co-treatment. Music therapists can advocate for themselves by providing education on music therapy scope of practice, formal training, and professional credentials. Ensuring a clear understanding of what music therapy is and is not, communication and consistency are the foundations to appropriate and beneficial co-treatment. Reasons for co-treatment could include to streamline a patient's schedule, to best generalize a therapeutic goal in a novel environment, or to provide the therapists with optimized opportunities for behavioral observation and documentation when treating a high-needs patient. Table 5.3 displays goals and music therapy interventions commonly used in co-treatment with various disciplines.

Table 5.3: Common co-treatment goals

Discipline	Shared goals	NMT techniques & music therapy interventions
Speech and language pathology	Improve cognition	• Auditory Perception Training (APT) • Musical Attention Control Training (MACT) • Musical Mnemonics Training (MMT) • Musical Executive Function Training (MEFT)
	Improve communication	• Oral Motor and Respiratory Exercises (OMREX) • Melodic Intonation Therapy (MIT) • Vocal Intonation Therapy (VIT)
Physical therapy	Improve range of motion or improve endurance and stamina	• Patterned Sensory Enhancement (PSE) • Therapeutic Instrumental Music Performance (TIMP)
Occupational therapy	Improve dexterity	• Therapeutic Instrumental Music Performance (TIMP)
	Improve response to sensory stimulation	• Music Sensory Orientation Training (MSOT)
Mental health	Improve adjustment to disorder	• Lyric analysis • Songwriting
	Increase healthy coping mechanisms	• Music and mindfulness for emotional regulation • Active music-making
	Process trauma	• Music and mindfulness • Lyric analysis • Songwriting

Interdisciplinary team meetings

As allied health professionals, music therapists have important insights to offer the interdisciplinary care team and often work towards similar goals as other disciplines, or on a specific goal that has been delegated to them. Because of these reasons, it is imperative that music therapists attend team meetings to report on their patients' progress. Interdisciplinary care team meetings typically consist of the lead physician, rehabilitation therapists such as physical therapists, speech and language pathologists, occupational therapists, mental health specialists such as psychiatrists and psychologists, other medical professionals such as dietitians, nurses, sleep specialists, case managers, and social workers. Other healthcare providers in specialized areas may be included, dependent on the patient case. A music therapist's role includes understanding the verbiage of other disciplines and disseminating music therapy progress in similar terms and in a time-sensitive manner.

In addition to consistent formal meetings, the music therapist should maintain direct lines of communication with individual healthcare providers. Music therapists should be open to ongoing consultation and informal case management discussions for greater consistency of care and reduction of treatment redundancy.

Reassessment

After a pre-determined amount of time in music therapy treatment, it is essential that the music therapist re-evaluates the patient to determine progress towards the treatment goals. If the patient is making progress towards their goal(s), the music therapist may schedule the patient for more individual sessions to reach goal completion. If the patient is not making progress towards the treatment goals or progress has stagnated, the music therapist must explore possible causes and solutions. Some hindrances to patient progress may include the patient being engaged in too many therapies simultaneously and experiencing difficulty with managing appointments, lack of understanding the purpose of engagement in music therapy, and lack of interest or motivation.

If the patient is overwhelmed with balancing appointments with multiple providers, the music therapist may consider delaying individual music therapy sessions until the patient has been discharged from other therapies. This will benefit the patient by allowing them to be more fully engaged in the treatments they are currently enrolled in, as well as create a smooth continuum of care.

When patients do not understand the purpose of music therapy, they will often treat their appointments as music lessons. While music learning and playing have many benefits, they alone will not necessarily assist the patient in accomplishing specific goals and objectives related to their rehabilitation process. It is important that the music therapist provides further education and reiterates how the patient can engage with the music in an increasingly intentional way that targets distinct functions and behaviors to improve the patient's health and wellbeing in their goal areas.

If a patient is not making progress towards their goals due to lack of interest or motivation, the music therapist should explore why the patient did not feel compelled to engage. Perhaps the patient is displaying the same patterns of behavior with all of their therapies and is therefore not benefitting as much as they could be across all therapies. If the music therapist is experienced with motivational interviewing techniques, they can use these methods to help the patient discover why they are disinterested or unmotivated to make necessary changes. If the patient continues to resist complying with their plan of care, the music therapist should discharge the patient.

Termination

Termination is a vital component of music therapy that requires sensitivity; therefore, throughout the treatment process, it is important to keep in mind a plan for termination. This will occur when the patient has reached their clinical goals and objectives or if a patient is not benefitting from treatment. Termination may occur organically, for example if a patient's commitments prevent them from consistently attending music therapy sessions and engaging in independent treatment-related tasks, or if they are unmotivated or non-compliant with treatment. It is important for the music therapist to incorporate creative treatment approaches to encourage engagement and motivation with a patient before considering termination, especially if the music therapist observes that the patient is struggling with engagement in other therapies as well.

The music therapist can prepare the patient for termination of services by keeping the clinical goal as the main focal point of treatment. Especially when the patient was involved in the development of their goals, they may feel an increased sense of accomplishment and empowerment when they reach their objectives. During the discharge session, the music therapist will reiterate what the service member gained in their treatment process and discuss a plan for continued use of music as an independent coping strategy, leisure activity, or tool for family bonding or community engagement.

Resourcing/referral to community arts engagement

The availability and awareness of community resources is a crucial component in the continued health and wellbeing of the service members, veterans, and their families on termination of treatment. It provides for a smooth transition from the patient role to a supportive community. Additional information about community resourcing can be found in Chapter 9 of this book.

Individual music therapy case examples

Common goals of individual music therapy treatment with service members and veterans with TBI, PTSD, and other physical and psychological health concerns include increase in functioning across multiple rehabilitation and behavioral health domains, such as cognition, motor, speech/language, occupational, familial, social, emotional, and spiritual.

The balance of these domains is essential for service members' success in their duties, mission readiness, and being deployable for combat. It is also essential for veterans to maximize independence within their own lives and in their communities. Rather than enabling a return to full duty or deployment, treatment of veterans can positively impact their ability to transition to civilian life, cohesion within their family unit, or attainment of the highest possible level of physical, cognitive, or emotional autonomy. The following cases are examples of individual music therapy sessions with service members and veterans.

Case 1: Individual music therapy for executive functioning, motor control, and relational support

"John" was a 58-year-old retired Lieutenant in the U.S. Navy. He had a stroke 11 months prior to music therapy treatment. He had previously been receiving care in an acute inpatient neurorehabilitation setting before transitioning to longitudinal outpatient care at ISC-7. John was referred to individual music therapy for cognitive deficits and difficulty with fine motor mobility and control of his right upper extremity. He had previous music experience playing the saxophone and guitar but expressed interest in incorporating the piano into his music therapy treatment plan. John was seen once a week for 60-minute sessions over a period of six months. The music therapist integrated piano and music theory with neurologic music therapy (NMT) interventions including: Musical Executive Functioning Training (MEFT) to practice skills such as reasoning, comprehension, and decision making (Thaut *et al.*, 2009); Musical Attention Control Training (MACT) to practice sustained, divided, and alternating attention (Knox *et al.*, 2003); and Therapeutic Instrumental Music Performance (TIMP) to exercise functional movement patterns (Lim *et al.*, 2011).

In the first session, John was challenged with memory and attention skills by memorizing scales, chord patterns, and chord progressions from his selected songs. He employed memorization strategies such as pattern recognition and information chunking. Throughout his first seven sessions, he worked on improving his digit dexterity, physical endurance, and fine motor control of his right hand through the gradual increase of playing time and complexity of motor tasks.

In the eighth session, John further challenged his executive functioning skills by beginning to write an original instrumental composition. After he had completed the full song in session 12, John and the music therapist processed the songwriting experience and he shared, "I didn't realize what my song was about until I was in the middle of writing it, but it makes sense. The song is about my stroke."

The patient's wife attended one of his final sessions, during which he played the song for her. She expressed that he had not let her hear him play before, because he always used headphones with his keyboard when he played at home. When John finished playing the song and shared its meaning with her, she started crying and spoke about the impact that the challenges of his recovery process had on both of them. The music therapist validated the spouses' feelings and facilitated a discussion between John and his wife to process their shared and unique experiences throughout his recovery.

In his final individual music therapy session, John recorded his original song with the music therapist. After completing the recording, he shared:

> Putting my experiences to music helped me to process my recovery in a way that was manageable and in which I could do something creative. Music therapy was one of the most effective and comprehensive of all my treatments. I worked on my cognitive processing in speech therapy, my fine motor skills in occupational therapy, and talked through my feelings with my [psycho]therapist. Music therapy brought all of these together and helped me express what I wasn't able to put into words.

Individual music therapy was impactful for John because he was able to take control of his treatment process and creatively engage in his own recovery. He independently decided to combine all the skills he was working on in music therapy to compose an original song on the piano. He selected the theme of the song as his healing process from his stroke. He used the song to connect with his wife and share with her through music the emotions he had not yet been able to put into words. John was a perfect example of how a person can transition from the patient role into a position of creative self-fulfillment.

Case 2: Lyric analysis, songwriting, and performance for treatment of PTSD

"Daniel" was a 41-year-old GySgt in the U.S. Marine Corps. His military occupational specialty (MOS) was Parachute Jumper and Combat Engineer. He experienced multiple blast exposures and over 100 free-fall and static jumps. His primary injury occurred during a mid-air entanglement with another parachute jumper, which resulted in him hitting a tree during landing, traveling at 31 miles per hour. He was diagnosed with TBI and also had a diagnosis of PTSD. Daniel had multiple symptom complaints, including impaired cognitive functioning (memory, attention/concentration) and mood/emotion dysregulation, all of which initiated a referral to individual music therapy. Daniel and the music therapist created a customized and comprehensive treatment plan to address all of his aforementioned complaints; however, as he progressed in individual treatment, the focus shifted to mainly address his PTSD-related mental health symptoms. Daniel was seen once a week for 60-minute sessions over the course of ten months in the context of longitudinal outpatient treatment at ISC-7.

During the music therapy assessment session, Daniel reported that he consistently engaged in trauma processing with a mental health provider who facilitated therapeutic intervention focused on treating moral injury, survivor's guilt, and suicidal ideation. He incorporated topics from psychotherapy into his music therapy goals, and the music therapist facilitated Associative Mood and Memory Training (AMMT) to induce a positive emotional state in the learning and recall process (Guétin *et al.*, 2009), and Music in Psychosocial training and Counseling (MPC) for self-awareness and expression (Wheeler, 2014).

In the sixth session, Daniel engaged in songwriting using the piggybacking technique. A video of his parachuting accident had been captured and put to music using the song "Don't Stop Believin'" by Journey as background music. This inspired him to use the basic framework of the song, and he modified key words and phrases by integrating his own thoughts, emotions, and experiences. Daniel included lyrics that expressed the support of a fellow Marine who was with him during the fall and portrayed his desire to get back to jumping. He wrote, "Some will tap, some will cry, some were born to get back up and fly again. Oh, the jumping never ends, it goes on and on and on and on."

Throughout treatment, Daniel continued to focus on lyric analysis and songwriting to treat his symptoms and chief complaints. He stated, "I have trouble putting into words what I'm thinking and feeling, but I can always get it out with music." During the eighth session, he engaged in lyric analysis to the song "Sleepwalker" by Santo and Johnny to work on emotion identification. He stated that this song symbolized challenging memories and reported that he had not listened to the song in its entirety for years, due to emotional triggers. When he finished listening to the song while following the lyric sheet, the music therapist checked in with him. He endorsed feeling stable and proceeded with the lyric analysis, discussing the personal significance of the song as associated with specific lyrics that he identified during the process.

During Daniel's ninth session, his affect was significantly more positive than in his prior eight appointments. He reported that in the time between sessions he and his wife listened to the song together and discussed the importance of creating corrective experiences with triggers. To achieve this, the patient and music therapist identified songwriting as a way to improve self-expression, which could be a positive catalyst for enacting corrective experiences and working towards the main goals of cognitive functioning and emotional dysregulation.

In the following sessions, Daniel began to write an original song. He selected the topic of his military career and included experiences of combat deployments, deaths of fellow service members, separation from his family through most of his service, and his struggles with PTSD and TBI. He wrote the song in the form of a rap, and the music therapist helped him to create beats to accompany his lyrics using the music software, *GarageBand*. He completed the song and performed it in the clinic's Creative Arts Café to an audience comprising his providers and fellow service members. The Creative Arts Café, a performance platform where patients can highlight certain aspects of their treatment processes, was developed at the National Intrepid Center of Excellence (NICoE) in 2016 and replicated across DoD and VA clinical sites (Bronson *et al.*, 2018). This performance was an integral part of Daniel's creative and therapeutic process, as it empowered structured risk-taking and provided an experience that supported transition to community-based opportunities (Vaudreuil *et al.*, 2019b). Daniel was able to see how his lyrics impacted his fellow service members in the audience and told a story that they could understand and relate to. It created an environment where Daniel felt supported by his community, took pride in his work, and turned his dark memories into a catalyst for connection.

Case 3: Neurologic music therapy to support functional communication goals

"Fred" was an active-duty Staff Sergeant in the U.S. Army. He suffered a severe TBI while overseas that resulted in moderate cognitive and communication deficits, for which he was receiving polytrauma treatment at James A. Haley VA Hospital. On initial assessment, the music therapist utilized augmentative and alternative communication devices (e.g., a tangible list of musical genres, basic binary questions about past musical experiences) to identify the patient's musical history and preferences through verbal discussion. Due to limitations in verbal communication, the music therapist also worked closely with the interdisciplinary treatment team and Fred's family to gather information regarding current concerns and progress in other therapies. He received speech therapy and, in addition, the team referred him to individual music therapy to address articulation, improve vocal strength and endurance, support word finding, and aid concerns regarding expressive communication.

The initial treatment plan focused on oral motor and respiratory concerns supported through the NMT technique of Oral Motor and Respiratory Exercises (OMREX). Fred engaged in diaphragmatic breath training and basic harmonica playing to promote respiration, and in articulation exercises to assist in rehabilitating his speaking voice to a functional status. He was further challenged through various interventions that addressed word-finding and language-based concerns through interventions such as lyric discussion, musical mad-libs (shown in Figure 5.2), and simple songwriting exercises for expression. In addition to the music therapy supporting Fred's main goals of communication, the inclusion of his preferred music interventions provided him with valuable tools to identify, process, and communicate his experiences and complex reactions to adjustment to injury, rehabilitation, and goals for the future.

Music therapy was an effective clinical approach to help rehabilitate Fred's vocal quality and promote his return to a functional level of communication. The interdisciplinary treatment team regarded music therapy as instrumental in providing care that allowed the speech therapist to focus solely on addressing swallowing concerns. Through this integrated treatment approach, Fred was able to eat solid foods sooner than anticipated.

"We Will Rock You"
By: Queen

Buddy you're a ________ (noun) make a big ________ (noun)

________ (verb) in the ________ (noun)

Gonna be a big ________ (noun) some day

You got ________ (noun) on yo' ________ (noun) You ________ (adjective)

________ (verb) your ________ (noun) all over the ________ (noun)

Figure 5.2: Musical mad-lib example

Challenges and limitations

Working with military populations presents music therapists with a unique set of challenges. For example, the military has its own culture that the provider must learn and become familiar with, including rank structure, language (e.g., significance of various acronyms), and occupational roles within the military (e.g., infantry, intelligence, special operations). Additionally, each branch of the U.S. armed forces (Army, Air Force, Navy, Marine Corps, Coast Guard) has a subculture with different ranks such as enlisted personnel and commissioned officers, which have various MOS. Similar to service members, veterans face challenges related to the specificity of military culture, and their experiences can have lasting impact during the transition from active duty to veteran status and beyond. Veterans can face an exceptional hurdle when professionally establishing themselves outside their military career due to transfer of occupational skills and change in routine, structure, punctuality, and chain of command. They may experience a loss of camaraderie and cohesion naturally fostered by military values, or feelings of estrangement and isolation from their civilian counterparts (Kintzle *et al.*, 2018). It is imperative for music therapists to be aware of these particular obstacles when working with military populations. Openness to learning about military culture and its divergence from civilian life is important and provides an effective way to gain understanding and build lasting rapport.

A unique challenge that patients face is the medical separation process. If a service member suffers from an injury or illness that prevents them from successfully performing their MOS, they will have to file a physical evaluation board (PEB). If they are found unfit for duty due to an injury or illness acquired during their military service, the patient is eligible for medical separation. A service member who wants to remain on active duty may downplay their medical issues to be able to maintain their MOS and remain in service. In contrast, a service member who is hoping to be separated and receive continued benefits may exaggerate their symptoms. In both cases, it is important for the music therapist to be in communication and collaboration with the interdisciplinary care team in order to identify potential for secondary gains and better inform the medical separation process. The struggle to enroll in benefits may not end at the medical separation process. Many veterans and their caregivers, especially those with moderate to severe TBI, may feel overwhelmed by the changes that accompany military separation. Finding additional resources for patients, respite opportunities for caregivers, and support for familial cohesion and coping with change, will aid patients and their families in establishing and maintaining new routines. The music therapist should be aware of, and accommodating to, the particular obstacles of service members, veterans, and their families.

Additionally, the therapeutic relationship, which is vitally important in creating an environment conducive to wellness and recovery, can present with a distinct set of challenges. Immediate buy-in of the patients is important, as first impressions often inform the final opinion with military populations. It may be difficult to build rapport; patients may be unaware of how music therapy is integrated with traditional medicine as a valued treatment to help treat warfighters. Providing the bottom line up front (BLUF) is critical to help establish understanding and build rapport (Vaudreuil *et al.*, 2020a). From another angle, patients who benefit from music therapy may associate their treatment success with their music therapist. Because engaging in music playing, songwriting, and sharing and discussing personally significant songs can cause the patient to feel a profound sense of vulnerability, it may be difficult for them to accept closure of the therapeutic relationship. Moreover, a patient might delude themselves into thinking of the therapeutic relationship with the provider as more of a friendship, as playing an instrument and songwriting are often done with friends and loved ones. Therefore, it is important for the music therapist to establish their role as a provider early in the treatment process and continue to enforce strong boundaries, maintain a focus of treatment on the non-musical goals, and terminate treatment at the appropriate time.

Summary

Individual music therapy sessions can be a meaningful addition in the rehabilitation of military populations, especially for patients who are not appropriate for group music therapy. Personalized goals and necessary treatment accommodations can be achieved through individualized care. It is the music therapist's responsibility to be aware of these considerations through the referral and assessment processes and develop and enact a specified treatment plan that leads to an informed transition during termination. The music therapist must further support individualized sessions through communication with other providers, attend interdisciplinary meetings, enforce clear boundaries dictated by scope of practice, and advocate for co-treatment when indicated. Lastly, music therapists must be cognizant of the particular cultural experiences and challenges faced by military populations so that they can provide potent and robust methods to meet the unique needs of active-duty service members and veterans.

Chapter 6

Military Music Therapy in Group Contexts

NATHANIEL MCLAUGHLAN AND
DANIELLE VETRO-KALSETH

Disclaimer: The opinions contained in this chapter represent the private views of the authors and are not to be construed as official or as reflecting the views, opinions, or policies of the Henry M. Jackson Foundation for the Advancement of Military Medicine, Inc., the Department of Defense, the National Endowment for the Arts, or the U.S. Government. Mention of trade names, commercial products, or organizations does not imply endorsement by the U.S. Government. This document was created free of branding or market affiliation. The authors are operating solely as contributors.

Introduction

Working in a group dynamic is commonplace within military culture. During indoctrination, training, and early in their military careers, service members are assigned to units, squadrons, flights, companies, teams, or platoons. Group music therapy is uniquely positioned to promote camaraderie and resiliency, as it offers service members opportunities to collectively engage in creative ways while learning about the effects of traumatic brain injury (TBI) and post-traumatic stress disorder (PTSD) through sharing lived experiences and personal stories (Bronson *et al.*, 2018). Group discussion allows for further processing of traumatic events and can deepen the impact of rehabilitation. Group music therapy provides the environment for service members to generate cohesion, learn self-regulatory strategies, improve communication, enact self-expression skills, foster resilience, and practically apply newly acquired information as a team. Working with service members in a group setting provides music therapists with unique opportunities to observe social interaction and offer techniques for cultivating camaraderie within a musical structure that can generalize to harmonious personal, occupational, and social relationships. This chapter highlights music therapy group programming with service members and veterans in intensive outpatient (IOP) and longitudinal care programs at two clinical sites. Music therapists providing care within each of their respective programs offer feedback on their experiences.

Background

Group therapy was first recorded in the United States (U.S.) in 1906 by Boston physician, Dr. J.H. Pratt. Group therapy served as a cost-effective treatment compared with individual therapy for patients with tuberculosis. Pratt found benefits in the development of emotional connection, which stemmed from shared experiences among group members (De Schill & Lebovici, 1999). Group therapy gained momentum after World War II when combat veterans received group treatment and similar findings of effectiveness were observed. In 1944, a War Department Technical Bulletin from the U.S. Army stated, "The favorable response of patients to comparatively brief treatments in groups warrants widespread adoption of this method of therapy" (Marshall, 1944, p.6).

Group cohesion, sometimes also referred to as cohesiveness, is "a function of the extent to which group members perceive the group as an effective means for satisfying their needs" (Capuzzi & Gross, 1998, p.226). From this lens, patients often perceive cohesion as a powerful factor for engagement in treatment because it supports them in lowering their customary inhibitions of expressing authentic emotions in the presence of others (Singer, 1983). In music therapy studies, group cohesion has been identified as an important factor in the effectiveness of music-based intervention. Although these studies were not specific to military-connected populations, nor addressed specific trauma diagnoses (e.g., TBI, PTSD), they examined associations between emotional stressors and medical trauma in adults undergoing cancer treatment (Waldon, 2001) and those with HIV-positive diagnoses (Cordobés, 1997).

Waldon (2001) measured mood states and cohesiveness among patients with various cancer diagnoses over ten weekly music-making or music-listening group sessions. This study found that increased group cohesion as a survey-quantified variable was not significantly associated with the music therapy interventions themselves. However, the group of participants who started their first music therapy session with a music-making intervention did not experience any "non-cohesive absences" throughout the remainder of the study. The group condition that began with music listening experienced challenges with attendance retention. Members of both groups reported improvement in mood states.

Although confounding factors were acknowledged, which affected objective measurements (e.g., lack of a pre-test/post-test procedure, side effects of cancer treatment), the experimenter observed that the tasks in the music-making group, which required members to work together and communicate, likely contributed to the members' more consistent attendance and perceived usefulness of the group. Increased group connectivity appears to motivate continued participation and enhance engagement, therefore elevating potential benefits.

In a study with HIV-positive participants, Cordobés (1997) compared a songwriting group with a non-musical game-playing group and a control group and measured group cohesion through a post-test questionnaire. Participants' use of emotion words was also analysed by coding transcriptions of each session. Data indicated that cohesion scores were not significantly different between the two activity groups; however, both groups yielded high ratings of cohesion indicated by post-test evaluation. The thematic analysis of session transcripts showed significantly higher usage of emotion-focused dialogue in the songwriting intervention group compared with the game-playing group. These findings validate that creative and productive group activities can boost group members' experience of trust and closeness with others. They also indicate the role of music-centered creative experiences in encouraging treatment-relevant dialogue, contributing to mood enhancement, and activating emotion-regulation coping skills.

Engaging in group music-making offers a unique approach to achieving a sense of togetherness by synchronizing through harmony and rhythm. This is distinct from group discussion, in which isolated speech is required for intelligibility. Group music-making involves the simultaneous engagement of participants, and therefore opens possibilities to process sounds and experience music in a social context by: 1) actively listening to the music created as a group; 2) being aware of music that other participants create; and 3) engaging in teamwork to create a group musical product (Vaudreuil *et al.*, 2020a). These events can occur as stand-alone or simultaneous interactions and may involve eye contact and other prosocial body language beyond verbal communication. While creating music together, people tend to experience their group as something outside themselves of which they are an integral part (Bensimon *et al.*, 2008).

Music therapy literature for group-based TBI recovery is sparse, due to the fact that most neurologic music therapy (NMT) interventions are focused on rehabilitation with individual patients (Thaut & Hoemberg, 2014). Several studies have identified the relevance of music therapy to treat PTSD, a common comorbidity for patients in military populations diagnosed with TBI. In a study by Carr *et al.* (2012), group music therapy was effective in reducing the occurrence of PTSD symptoms, namely hyperarousal, avoidance, and re-experiencing of traumatic events. Furthermore, music-making encouraged socialization through positive shared experiences, increased focus and attention during active music-making, a structured environment for building tolerance to potentially triggering sounds, and development of non-intimidating means of habituation that supported arousal reduction and emotion regulation. It has been found that the therapeutic gains of group music therapy for patients with PTSD include improved interpersonal communication and an increased sense of belonging (Bensimon *et al.*, 2012).

Description of clinical models

The music therapy programs presented in this chapter are part of an initiative of the National Endowment for the Arts (NEA), Creative Forces®: NEA Military Healing Arts Network. Creative Forces is a partnership with the U.S. Departments of Defense (DoD) and Veterans Affairs (VA), and state and local arts agencies that seeks to improve the health, wellness, and quality of life for military and veteran populations exposed to trauma, as well as their families and caregivers. Creative Forces is managed in partnership with Americans for the Arts and the Henry M. Jackson Foundation for the Advancement of Military Medicine.

Creative Forces programs are located in the National Intrepid Center of Excellence (NICoE), Intrepid Spirit Center (ISC) satellite clinics, military treatment facilities, and VA hospitals, and include a telehealth program. This programming addresses the needs of patients with TBI/concussion, PTSD, and associated psychological symptoms using a patient-centered, interdisciplinary approach delivered through intensive outpatient and longitudinal models of care.

Intensive outpatient (IOP) model

Service members and veterans receive treatment through interdisciplinary care models, which are implemented both in the DoD and VA. An example of this is the IOP program at the NICoE, a directorate of Walter Reed National Military Medical Center (WRNMMC) in Bethesda, MD, and ISC clinics located across the U.S. These clinics specialize in the treatment of service members with TBI, PTSD, and other psychological health concerns. This chapter will demonstrate music therapy integration into IOP programming, which serves as a framework for other Creative Forces music therapy programs, including longitudinal treatment models.

Music therapy is integrated into interdisciplinary treatment, and interventions are targeted at rehabilitation and behavioral health goals to address the physical, psychological, neurological, and moral injuries prevalently experienced by military populations. Patients receive four weeks of comprehensive rehabilitative care as part of a cohort, which consists of approximately four to six service members. Historically, cohorts began treatment on Mondays of each week and four cohorts occurred simultaneously, yielding about 16–24 service members engaged in IOP treatment at any given time. Program adaptations in response to COVID-19 safety protocols have shifted this to one cohort per month and can be adapted as warranted moving forward. Music therapy is provided as a standard of care in the IOP, both through individual and group sessions that span the duration of treatment. Cohorts receive weekly group music therapy sessions including stand-alone and co-treatment with other creative arts therapies, as well as individual and family sessions. The groups described in Table 6.1 are adapted from Bronson *et al.* (2018). Music therapy is also provided in longitudinal outpatient care through referrals by primary care managers and as part of a patient's continuation of care after discharge from the inpatient neurology unit at WRNMMC.

Table 6.1: NICoE IOP program model

	Group title	Session length	Description
Week 1	Movement, Music, and Meditation	60 min	Music therapy and wellness program co-facilitation using music and movement to inform mind–body connection through kinesthetic awareness.
Week 2	Introduction to Music Therapy	90 min	Music to evaluate and treat auditory perception, emotional regulation, relaxation, diaphragmatic breathing and entrainment via music listening. Sustained/divided/alternating attention and increased auditory tolerance is promoted through drumming.
Week 3	Music Therapy Songwriting/ Jam	60 min	Music to assist with social engagement, effective communication skills (verbal and non-verbal), and problem solving through active music-making and songwriting.
Week 4	Creativity and Closure	60 min	Music therapy and wellness program co-facilitation to process experiences in creative arts therapies, wellness programming, and overall treatment using improvisational music and creative writing to create final expressive works performed to improvised music.

Longitudinal outpatient treatment model

The mild traumatic brain injury (mTBI) clinic at Joint Base Elmendorf-Richardson (JBER) in Anchorage, Alaska, is an outpatient clinic providing long-term treatment to active-duty U.S. Air Force (Elmendorf), U.S. Army (Fort Richardson), and Alaska Air National Guard. Because JBER is a joint-venture base, it also serves veterans and eligible military-connected populations, such as dependents.

Patients are referred to music therapy by interdisciplinary team providers such as the neuropsychologist, occupational therapist, speech language pathologist, nurse case manager, and TBI educator during arena intakes. Patients initially engage in a Music Therapy Intake Group, which follows a group protocol, Introduction to Music Therapy Group, that was designed and evaluated by Vaudreuil and colleagues (2020a) in the NICoE IOP program. Based on observational assessment and patient self-evaluation of this group protocol, the music therapist gleans insight in determining patients' treatment plans and follow-up services. Patients are often scheduled for an individual follow-up session for further evaluation and to develop customized treatment aimed at supporting functional goals, including speech and language, motor coordination, social integration and engagement, and psychological health. Figure 6.1 illustrates a longitudinal treatment plan consisting of both individual and group sessions, referred to as hybrid treatment. Rather than exclusive individual or group treatment, the hybrid model is the most utilized treatment plan and averages four to six months in length.

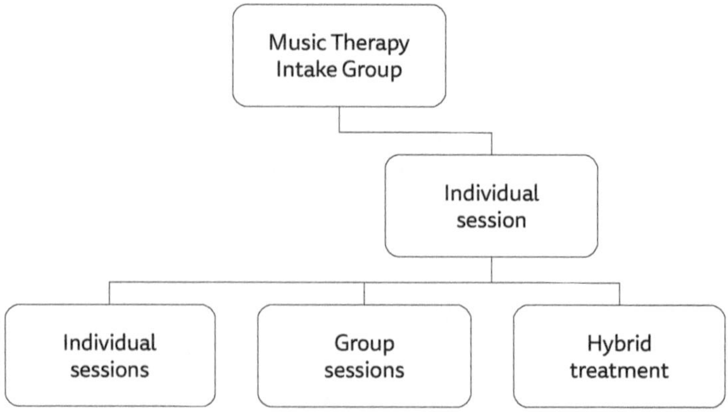

Figure 6.1: JBER longitudinal music therapy treatment model

Introduction to Music Therapy Group (IOP)/ Music Therapy Intake Group (longitudinal)

This group protocol consists of four parts: 1) rapport-building and group introductions/check-in; 2) intentional, active music listening; 3) group drumming; and 4) group processing/check-out (Vaudreuil *et al.*, 2020a). In part 1, the music therapist provides expectations of the group and shares information about music therapy, its historical connection to military healthcare, and how it can assist in rehabilitation of patients with TBI and PTSD. Patients provide and receive information, which has been found to foster an environment of non-judgmental listening and identifying areas of commonality among patients. This is accomplished through sharing music preferences, social engagement with music (e.g., concerts, open mics), prior music-making experience(s), use of music on deployment, and current use of music in daily life. The music therapist asks follow-up questions to prompt further processing, which models genuine interest and validation of unique and shared preferences and experiences that each patient contributes to the group dynamic.

In part 2, the music therapist facilitates receptive listening exercises during which patients can engage their senses, thoughts, and feelings, and identify music preferences while listening to a sequence of live improvisations, each approximately two to three minutes in length, played on various instruments. For patients with PTSD, being present, mindful, and gaining awareness of auditory responses can be a challenge, considering that many patients endorse hypervigilance and distractibility as chief symptoms. During this intervention, the music therapist observes non-verbal cues to identify which patients display difficulty relaxing. Indicators of stress response include leg shaking, open or fluttering eyes, fidgeting, and physical tension/spasticity. Patients displaying these behaviors may benefit from further exploration of intentional music listening and music-assisted relaxation. Part 2 concludes with processing the listening experience.

In part 3, the music therapist introduces group drumming to enhance group interaction, promote relaxation through physiological release of tension, reinforce intentional listening, engage different types of attention, and assess motor coordination. Patients with TBI may have difficulty sustaining attention on tasks, impaired motor functioning, and auditory issues (e.g., tinnitus, hearing loss). To accommodate the group, the music therapist introduces physical aspects of playing various hand drums (e.g., djembe, tubano, bongo, cajon) using reductive instruction. The music therapist facilitates synchronized playing using simple rhythmic patterns that gradually increase in complexity and tempo, which has shown to be positively associated with increased group entrainment. The music therapist may add rhythmic variations to further engage active listening and attention and reinforce the patients' experiences of successful mastery. Patients with sound-triggered headaches are given options to use earplugs or to opt out of the drumming intervention. Part 3 concludes by processing the group drumming experience.

In part 4, the music therapist prompts further processing of the patients' personal responses to the previous three parts of the group. Through considering the completed sequence of events, patients have the opportunity to reflect on the synergy, interrelatedness, helpfulness, and challenges of the different interventions. For example, patients may identify how the relaxation response from music listening in part 2 supported the activation of entrainment during group drumming in part 3. Additionally, patients typically endorse experiencing a physiological relaxation response associated with the sounds of individual instruments. This includes, notably, slowing or lengthening of breath cycles, extra-musical associations such as concepts outside the music characteristics (e.g., meditation practice, nature experiences, ceremonies), mental imagery inspired by sensory activation, and shifts in mood. Discussion of the drumming intervention often uncovers themes of overcoming an unfamiliar challenge, identifying reliable audio-visual cues and focal points, and comparison of expectations with outcomes. Part 4 concludes with the patients completing a standardized evaluation form. For additional information about this music therapy protocol please refer to the article, "Music Therapy with Active-Duty Service Members: Group Protocol Description and Secondary Analysis of Protocol Evaluations" (Vaudreuil *et al.*, 2020a).

Music therapist feedback: Nathaniel McLaughlan

In NICoE IOP, the majority of patients are career service members and often part of special forces units. Many patients have served multiple deployments, been assigned to missions with intense operational tempos, and have integrated particular coping methods to achieve optimal performance. An example of one such coping method is seeking to understand the bottom line up front (BLUF). The BLUF efficiently communicates the value of a novel proposition, which in this context is a new therapeutic mechanism. Thus, in the first part of the Introduction to Music Therapy Group, I aim to draw direct connections between concepts of music therapy and the patients' experiences throughout their military careers. Patients tend to respond more openly and expressively when I demonstrate an understanding of their mindset via the BLUF, which I gain increased awareness of the more I facilitate this group protocol. Initially, I thought it was important to quickly summarize the entirety of music therapy related to TBI and PTSD, but over time, I have noticed that this approach does not directly connect with most patients during the initial group experience. I have learned to utilize the interventions and outcomes of this group to build a structure of mutual understanding and trust that can be used to elicit sharing of information and resources.

Another concept I learned from experience with the Introduction to Music Therapy group protocol relates to the music-assisted intentional listening and relaxation intervention. Many patients experience symptoms of hyperarousal, which have been highlighted or even exacerbated by the direct suggestion to "relax." A patient in this group introduced me to the notion of the "quiet-alert state," comparing it to a mental skill used in teaching sharpshooting techniques. This indicates a slowing down (e.g., quieting) of physical activity, while remaining aware (e.g., alert) of external stimuli (e.g., music) and accompanying internal (e.g., mental) responses. I have continued to frame relaxation inductions this way and am always investigating different approaches to re-contextualize familiar knowledge and skills into new uses.

When I started facilitating this group, I was often met with uncomfortable silence from patients when prompting group discussion of their responses to the music listening intervention. Putting words to somatic and emotional experiences can be unfamiliar and challenging. Over time, I have modified the ways I phrase prompting questions, and also increasingly observed that there are frequent similarities between patients' experiences that are indicated non-verbally with a head nod or gesture. I received increased patient feedback when I stopped listening exclusively for words and started integrating their various non-verbal communications. This acknowledgement of differences and similarities seemed to bolster the sense of security and trust within the group.

A multitude of challenges and successes are discussed during the processing of group drumming. A highly recurring statement is that patients find that they aren't thinking of anything else and are solely focused on maintaining their rhythm. Patients usually find this to be a positive and helpful experience in the way that that they are not distracted by intrusive thoughts while drumming. This validates the concepts of how cognitive load and mindfulness overlap. Something that surprised me the first few times I heard this feedback was that patients found the drumming to be fun and engaging, and mutually agreed that they were "ready to take this act on the road." Also, patients with tinnitus have reported that their tinnitus symptoms were masked or distracted rather than exacerbated by the drumming experience.

Although most of my patients have been open to the often new and unfamiliar experiences in music therapy, this is not a universal response. I offer a "challenge by choice" mentality while introducing group interventions, which aims to emphasize informed consent to engagement and my acceptance without judgment of those unwilling to participate for any reason. If a patient decides something is not for them, I will suggest an opportunity for engagement at a safe distance from the group experience, such as observing or listening from outside the circle and describing their unique perspective afterwards. Patients are able to decline this as well, but in my experience, creating space for different levels of engagement has generally helped maintain the group's sense that each patient's presence and preference is valued.

Music therapist feedback: Danielle Vetro-Kalseth

In the longitudinal care model at JBER, the Music Therapy Intake Group is a patient's first experience of music therapy; therefore, it provides an opportunity to educate patients about the benefits of music therapy treatment and determine if a patient is appropriate for continued services, and if so, this experience helps to inform their treatment plan. When setting up the clinical space, I consider the needs of the patients by placing the chairs in a circle, keeping in mind that many individuals with PTSD do not like having their backs to a door, and ensuring the area surrounding the door is clear. I use soft lighting to create a warm atmosphere and be considerate to the fact that headaches, migraines, and light sensitivity are common symptoms of TBI (U.S. Departments of Defense and Veterans Affairs, 2016).

Patients often come in with preconceived ideas of music therapy; therefore, during check-in, I explain the components of the group and the non-musical rationale for the interventions. This direct communication can help negate any perceptions that patients are expected to perform in a certain way, which can reduce anxiety and reconcile any false expectations that may exist at the outset of the group. I also validate patients for attending the session, acknowledging that they may be extending past their comfort zone. For patients with TBI and/or PTSD, attending a group session and engaging in an unknown experience is a remarkable first step towards healing. Positive reinforcement is necessary to keep individuals feeling committed and confident.

When I started facilitating this group, I was nervous. I had to adjust the way I facilitated the live music-listening protocol to accommodate my comfortability and skill level. Voice is my principle instrument, and I had concerns about my ability to use varied instrumentation to facilitate active listening and accompanied relaxation strategies. Instruments that I had experience playing were the mini harp and steel tongue drums, as they can be easily tuned to a pentatonic scale and are player friendly. When facilitating active listening on the piano, I play pentatonic scales, often using the black keys. When facilitating with the guitar, I start by playing the verse and chorus of a familiar song, often in a minor key, on electric guitar and end with fingerpicking a major chord progression on acoustic guitar. I often add soft humming and vowel sounds to create a soft lullaby-esque melody. Often, patients have expressed increased anxiety in response to the electric guitar, and a relaxation response to the piano and humming/singing with acoustic guitar, which they state reminds them of their mother or other maternal figure singing a lullaby. The harmonic modes used for each instrument can influence potential outcomes. For example, I typically play in the key of A minor on electric guitar followed by the C major pentatonic scale. These modal shifts can elicit sensorial experiences for the patients, namely, tension and release.

In processing the music-listening intervention, patients identify individual sound preferences. Most patients enjoy sharing their thoughts and connections to the music. I inquire further as to how they might incorporate an intervention like this into everyday life. Most patients comment that they listen to harp music as part of their sleep hygiene routines, female vocalists to create a sense of comfort, or soft piano playing to increase relaxation. There have been instances where this intervention has caused negative emotions in patients. The connection between musical sounds and memory can evoke both pleasant and distressing past experiences. I have had patients become emotional and, during one group a patient asked to leave because the feelings connected to the sounds were too strong to continue at that moment. As a music therapist facilitating this intervention, it was important for me to validate all feelings and use them to inform the discussion.

During the drumming component, I offer patients the option to use sterile, disposable earplugs to dampen the sound, as patients may experience sound sensitivity or frequent headaches related to their diagnoses. Initially, I was concerned the sound of drumming might be triggering for patients with PTSD. To this day, I have not encountered a patient, even those who are initially most resistant, who has been triggered by group drumming. Most patients express that they enjoy it and are able to recognize their non-musical responses to the intervention. Patients have shared feedback including, "I'm really having to concentrate" and "I can feel my brain working." Patients have also expressed that drumming is a fun and effective distraction for pain, through feedback such as, "I forgot that I had a headache because I was enjoying myself" and "I was smiling the whole time." Additional feedback from the Music Therapy Intake Group is provided in the text box below.

Patient feedback: Music Therapy Intake Group

"The Music Therapy Intake Group was the best therapy I have done in a while. It gave me great insight as to what I am having difficulty with and it was also a fun way of interacting with other people."

"I definitely want continued music therapy services. What a wonderful experience. There should be more treatments like this!"

"I honestly can't thank you enough. I now have hope that something is going to help me. Thank you."

Songwriting/Jam Group

Songwriting/Jam Group is also facilitated in both IOP and longitudinal outpatient treatment models. It is intentionally flexible and largely patient-driven. Patients often quickly build rapport and, therefore, take on leadership roles in shaping the session such as identifying song repertoire, song elements, opportunities for solo/leading, areas of strengths and weaknesses, and overall group process. The music therapist's role in the group is to guide and manifest each patient's agency in group decision making. This type of session structure can allow for group dynamics including deepening personal insight, clarity in understanding others' perceptions, and opportunities for closer collaboration. The music therapist can model active music-making techniques that promote expressive and receptive communication, socialization, and cognitive reorganization goals. In this group, music-making can take many forms including: 1) recreating an existing song selected by patients; 2) music therapist suggesting song options that are appropriate for the group based on skill levels; 3) patients creating an original group song; 4) the group collectively recreating an individual patient's original song; and 5) using pre-existing song themes as inspiration to rewrite or create an original group composition. Common songs "jammed" and/or recreated in Songwriting/Jam Group are included in the text box below.

Common songs for Songwriting/Jam Group

"Don't Stop Believin'" by Journey

"Folsom Prison Blues" by Johnny Cash

"Lean on Me" by Bill Withers

"Ring of Fire" by Johnny Cash

"Simple Man" by Lynyrd Skynyrd

"Three Little Birds" by Bob Marley

"Wagon Wheel" by Bob Dylan and Ketch Secor (Old Crow Medicine Show)

"Walk the Line" by Johnny Cash

When preparing group resources, such as lead sheets, tablature, chord charts, or sheet music, it is important to consider the different experience levels and needs of each patient. Individuals with trauma can experience neurocognitive symptoms such as issues with working memory (e.g., retention, retrieval), comprehension, varying levels of attention, executive functioning, intrusive thoughts, and cognitive control (Boals & Banks, 2012). Therefore, the music therapist often needs to adapt resources and facilitation techniques while at the same time offering opportunities for all patients to challenge themselves. This can be done by utilizing three- or four-chord songs with relatively consistent structure, reviewing chord repertoire at the beginning of the music-making experience, and introducing a pentatonic scale in the appropriate key so that interested patients can practice lead guitar or play solos during the jam. Providing opportunities for solos allows patients to engage in enhanced self-expression through vocal or instrumental improvisation. The music therapist can add interludes into the song structure, to allow patients the musical space to improvise. To promote inclusivity for patients with cognitive limitations such as difficulty with dual tasking, retaining complex information, or coordinating visual and motor functions, the music therapist can suggest a variety of handheld percussion instruments (e.g., hand drums, shakers, claves, bells, wood blocks, tambourines) that patients can play to contribute to the group, creating a more robust ensemble sound.

Patient feedback: Songwriting/Jam Group

"At first, I didn't want to participate. I put off attending it because I was timid and shy. After my first session, I was hooked. I had such a great time making music with the other guys and felt like I had finally found my place. I was where I belonged."

"Through Jam Group, I found a new part of myself that I thought I had lost. I became happier, less angry and more connected to my wife and kids."

Music therapist feedback: Nathaniel McLaughlan

Songwriting/Jam Group is the second group encounter that NICoE IOP cohorts have with the music therapist. Its duality indicates the divergent paths the group may take with flexible consideration to patients' preferences and the limited number of music therapy groups that patients receive due to the condensed nature of the IOP treatment model. At the start of the group, I introduce the primary goal of exploring collective creative expression. There are two common directions this process takes, which include songwriting and music-making or "jamming." Often, I share a few examples of past cohorts' group processes and products (with permissions), such as listening to previously recorded songs that illustrate the pairing of lyrics and music to express a shared theme of the group. By considering each patient's experiences in music therapy up to this point, I can inform their decision making to help guide the group in a direction that minimizes any potential friction or confusion with the group goal. This maximizes morale in the process towards goal attainment of shared creativity and expression. Distractibility can be high in individuals with TBI and PTSD, and I have found that redirecting the group towards more simple and achievable objectives can help them reach their goal in the 60-minute session. The creative process of songwriting and group music-making further strengthens feelings of group cohesion, as patients work together to troubleshoot small problems and work through minor disagreements that may arise.

A technique that I facilitate to introduce the group to music-making is the use musical improvisation. I often piggyback on the drumming experience from their first group by adding new instruments and percussion elements. This provides a rhythmic foundation on which to write lyrics inspired by the mood and energy established by each patient's participation in music-making. Alternatively, the improvisation-based experience may become the main focus of the group and patients may opt to improvise lyrics rather than write them, or not incorporate lyrics at all. Overall, the process is dependent on collaboration among the patients that captures individual and group preferences. Collective decision making is a skill that military populations are trained to employ, often under stress in extreme circumstances, which determines the welfare of military units. In the same way, channeling this skill set and translating it into a creative, structured, and non-threatening environment encourages self-reflection and collaboration, which have observable effects on mood, communication, and motivation.

When the group decides to create a song, they may elect to record themselves performing it. This provides a product that patients are able to take away with them as a token of their shared experience of musical and/or lyrical expression. The song can be shared with families, either live during family sessions in the fourth week of treatment or as a recording to take home. I've observed that this process allows family members to gain a deeper perspective on the patient's experience in the program, and the impact of their injuries. I find that this sharing aspect can be either motivating or counter-motivating depending on whether patients are excited to have a creative product to share or if they prefer to keep their clinical creative processes private. For the majority of the cohorts, a songwriting effort appears to strengthen their relationships with one another, and often they are proud to share their creative accomplishments with others.

Just as with the Introduction to Music Therapy Group, I start with a general plan for what we do together, and also leave openness for change, for example in the event that any patients have difficulty tolerating the usual Songwriting/Jam Group interventions. Group improvisation and songwriting can be too open-ended or not straightforward enough for some patients. In addition, it might be more demanding on cognitive load or emotional bandwidth than patients are willing or able to endure. During this group, the IOP patients are often in the midst of a full day of consecutive appointments across multiple specialty services; therefore, fatigue and disinterest are understandable. In such cases, I have aimed to provide less strenuous alternatives such as music-assisted relaxation, lyric analysis, drumming along to recorded music, and other unforeseen options co-created in the moment with patient input. In my experience of facilitating, there have been very few patients who have abstained from or walked out of the Songwriting/Jam Group. When this has occurred, I have followed up with each of them individually, and they were each able to articulate why the prospect of being involved in the group at that time was intolerable for them.

Music therapist feedback: Danielle Vetro-Kalseth

The music therapy program at JBER focuses more on the "jam" part of the group, as it is structured as open group that recurs once a week for 60 minutes. Patients are scheduled into the Jam Group based on their availability. Typically, this group is for patients with prior music experience, such as those who have reached clinical goals in individual music therapy and progressed to group sessions. Although a patient's outcomes in individual treatment may clinically indicate progression to group sessions, the patient may find themselves overwhelmed in an initial group experience. The patient can become overwhelmed because this group tends to move at a faster pace and, depending on other group members, the dynamic may initially be perceived as intimidating. When this occurs, I use it as an opportunity to educate about the therapeutic gains of the group and to advocate for no self-judgment or judgment towards others in the music therapy space. I strive to create an atmosphere of equal acceptance through shared positive musical experiences, peer mentorship, and brother/sisterhood.

Depending on opportunities for community engagement, which occurs as a transitional step to support reintegration efforts, the group can learn a pre-composed song with the intent of community performance. As part of socialization and community integration goals, the group may perform in various locations on-base (e.g., hospital dining facility, clinic lobby) or at community-based locations such as VA domiciliaries, Vet Centers, assisted living facilities, and local hospitals. Patients often bond during shared community performances, as they help each other overcome barriers, such as performance anxiety. Sometimes patients are unable to work through these challenges enough to perform but are still interested in community outreach. I typically offer non-performance methods of involvement, such as event coordination and preparation (e.g., creating/organizing lead sheets, tuning instruments), carrying equipment, setting up and breaking down, peer support, and audience participation. Participation in Jam Group can lead to enhanced relationships between patients in treatment as well as outside the clinical environment, as indicated by the patient testimonial below.

Jam Group patient story

"I started playing guitar shortly after graduating high school and continued to play while serving in the Army. After multiple deployments, I wound up in a dark place and couldn't find my way out. I sold every piece of music equipment and accepted the idea that my life really didn't have any meaning. I began to drink a lot, trying to empty sorrows into whatever bottle I could. I just wanted to numb myself from the world. It wasn't until I was on orders to Alaska, I really slowed down my drinking. I had a job I really enjoyed, but it led to my injury. I had multiple blows to the head and even blacked out from some of them. Before I knew it, I started to have problems with anger and was experiencing fatigue, ringing in my ears, communication with my wife was failing, and at some points, I didn't think we were going to make it. We managed to fix our communication, but I was still having problems.

When I sought treatment for my TBI, I was referred to music therapy. At first, I laughed it off and thought, 'Whatever, this isn't going to work.' I have never been happier to be so completely wrong in my entire life. I attended the weekly Jam Group and started playing my guitar again. I started writing music again and created my own YouTube channel to help others who are struggling with things like survival guilt, depression, anger, anxiety, PTSD, and TBI. I want to give back to help people like me. My life has meaning again."

Unique music therapy groups

Due to variance in patient population (e.g., active duty, veteran, special forces), clinic focus (e.g., rehabilitation, behavioral health, pain), and patient need (e.g., TBI and PTSD-related symptoms), there are group sessions specific to the structure, procedure, and community assets and opportunities of each military treatment facility. There are similarities and distinctions between IOP and longitudinal models, therefore group protocols and music therapy group approaches are adaptable to meet unique systemic needs—from micro to macro levels. The following unique groups are briefly presented to capture the variety of services provided between IOP and longitudinal treatment programs.

Unique IOP group: Movement, Music, and Meditation

This group takes place at the end of the first week of the NICoE IOP and is co-treated with a dance/movement therapist. Primary objectives are to introduce patients to a variety of gentle movement practices and interoceptive (e.g., somatic self-awareness) strategies. The dance/movement therapist leads patients in restorative stretching and a range of motion exercises leading up to mindfulness practices, including a walking meditation, followed by a body scan. The music therapist's role is to support each phase of movement and stillness with a blend of live and recorded music by synchronizing musical elements with the rate, shape, and intensity of each movement. At the end of the group, patients are prompted to reflect and discuss their experiences with the mind–body connection and how they might incorporate components of the movement, music, and meditation into their personal self-care practices. Many patients find that the emergent customized music supports their intended mental focus during these practices and they report gaining awareness of what specific music and movements they can use in continued practice to meet their individual needs.

Unique IOP group: Creativity and Closure

This group takes place in the final week of the NICoE IOP and is also a co-treatment with a dance/movement therapist. The format is highly flexible, with the intention of holding space and time for patients of each outgoing cohort to achieve a sense of closure related to their treatment experiences. Due to the intensive structure and density of clinical appointments throughout the four-week program, it is often challenging for patients to fully process and reflect on their experiences during treatment. It can be helpful to offer a non-exhaustive, open-ended list of potential ways to maximize processing and reflection. This most commonly takes the form of revisiting and re-experiencing dance/

movement therapy and music therapy practices that have been meaningful or helpful to them in maintaining holistic wellness throughout the treatment process. For example, a cohort might decide to close with a mindful walking meditation followed by a drum circle, and then conclude with a brief writing exercise to capture their experiences.

Unique IOP group: Incorporating Families

During the fourth and final week of the IOP, patients' family members (e.g., spouses, partners, children, siblings, parents) are invited to participate in informational and experiential sessions. This provides family members with the opportunity to learn more about the treatment their loved ones have received at the NICoE and gain a deeper understanding of the patient perspective. Music therapy family sessions typically take the shape of a couples session or a family session with multiple family members present. In couples sessions, the music therapist can shape musical experiences that support communication and celebrate connections to one another, which can be generalized outside the clinical space. Spouses and partners often express enthusiasm and support for the integration of music in the home environment. In family sessions with children, the music therapist typically introduces the family to music therapy interventions that the patient has experienced, such as music-assisted relaxation or group drumming. Roles within the family system often emerge while music-making together, allowing the music therapist to assess areas of interpersonal strength and potential growth (Chilton *et al.*, 2020). Songs written by the patient in individual or group sessions can be performed for the family members, which often leads to in-depth conversations about the songwriting process and the subjective meanings of the lyrics. Additionally, family members can engage in structured or improvised music-making as well as songwriting as a family.

Unique longitudinal group: Six-Week Music Therapy Group series

The Six-Week Music Therapy Group meets once a week for six consecutive weeks. It is designed to expose new patients to a variety of musical instruments (e.g., ukulele, guitar, bass guitar, piano drums), to identify and select preferred instruments, build group cohesion, and inspire creative decision making. The main goals of the Six-Week Music Therapy Group series are to achieve positive socialization, increase complex cognitive functioning, improve memory, and strengthen frustration tolerance. These combined goals support reintegration, which is a secondary gain of this group. Active music-making in a group format provides opportunities for positive socialization and cognitive training. Learning new musical skills (e.g., chords, notes, strum patterns) is a complex cognitive task, therefore it is not uncommon for patients to get confused or frustrated. Music therapists can address this by acknowledging it and encouraging patients to work through the confusion, breathe through the frustration, and engage in positive affirmations. Utilizing these strategies to learn frustration tolerance skills can transfer to a myriad of life experiences. Sometimes patients have difficulty attending each session due to work schedules, military training exercises, family emergencies, and Alaskan weather conditions. Because this group is progressive, if a patient misses a session it can be difficult for them to catch up, so if a patient has to miss a session, they are scheduled for an individual session to keep them up to speed on the group's progress. Overall, patients have reported enjoying the progressive nature of the group and have requested that it extends longer than six weeks.

Unique longitudinal group: Music and Wellness

Music and Wellness Groups are co-treated with the pain psychologist and/or occupational therapist once a week for 60 minutes. This group is designed for patients with TBI and PTSD who experience related symptoms such as physical pain, headaches, sleep disturbance, anxiety, frustration, and irritability. Interventions are based on the iso-principle (meeting patients in the moment) and use the NMT technique of patterned sensory enhancement to entrain hyperactive internal stimuli with soothing external auditory stimuli using intentionally sequenced music (Thaut & Hoemberg, 2014). A combination of traditional instruments (e.g., guitar, mini harp, steel tongue drums, buffalo drum) and digital music-based relaxation apps (e.g., *Relax Melodies*) are used. The session teaches strategies for patients to independently engage in deep-breathing techniques, grounding skills, and mindfulness exercises, coupled with learning how to intentionally select appropriate music to accompany these practices.

Music therapy and military band collaborations

In 2016, the Creative Forces music therapy program at NICoE began collaborating with military bands, specifically the U.S. Air Force Band in the National Capital Region (Kramer, 2016). These initial collaborations set the foundation for continued opportunities for music therapy programs and military bands to work collectively at sites across the Creative Forces network, as each military branch has an associated band, and therefore, bands are present on most bases. For example, at JBER, the 9th Army Band has approximately 40 members. Clinically based collaborations entail smaller ensembles that provide live music for intentional listening and music-assisted relaxation sessions in the partial hospitalization program and on inpatient units. Community-based collaborations include the 9th Army Band rock ensemble providing musical support for members of the Jam Group by joining them for performances. More formalized collaborations between music therapy programs and military bands include the Music Mentorship Program, which pairs band members (mentors) with music therapy patients (mentees) with the aim to advance learning and musical proficiency on selected instruments. Inclusion criteria of music therapy patients to engage in the Music Mentorship Program include: 1) cognitive and physical capacity; 2) ability to manage scheduling; 3) achievement of music therapy goals; and 4) preparedness for transition from the clinic to community. Additional collaborations include using the band's high-quality production equipment, which can be used to record patient songs.

Music therapy telehealth with active-duty service members

The use of telehealth has been pioneered by the VA for decades and is growing in the DoD (Vaudreuil *et al.*, 2020b). The rationale for telehealth services includes increased access to care, reduced need for temporary duty leave for treatment, mitigation of treatment costs such as medical-related travel, and enhanced access to specialty care (e.g., creative arts therapies) for service members stationed in remote locations or veterans residing in rural areas (Levy *et al.*, 2017). During the writing of this chapter, telehealth became more frequently utilized across healthcare settings in response to the COVID-19 pandemic and the restrictions placed on in-person clinical services. Telehealth services are typically provided between designated clinics or from clinic to homes via video-teleconferencing platforms transmitted through a government-secured network. Facilitation of telehealth music therapy sessions requires heightened situational awareness, increased use of verbal communication, video framing to properly display musical tasks, the ability to adjust facilitation depending on audio and video latency, and troubleshooting technical issues (Spooner *et al.*, 2019). Furthermore, due to the COVID-19 pandemic, Creative Forces music therapists have adapted group sessions to virtual environments, both clinically and as community engagement. Jam Group, Six-Week Progressive, and Music and Wellness Groups have successfully transitioned to a virtual platform. Additional information about music therapy and telehealth integration is included in Chapter 8.

Summary

Group music therapy treatment is a powerful tool for addressing the needs of military service members and veterans with TBI and PTSD. Assessment of relevant symptoms leads to the formation of both rehabilitative and behavioral goals. Both intensive and longitudinal programs can be designed to incorporate such goals through group music therapy sessions that address physical, psychological, and social domains of functioning. Providing a structured group context within which each domain is supported through interpersonal musical experiences bolsters group interactions and facilitates individual growth and change. This is exemplified through the wide variety of group formats, interdisciplinary co-treatments, and unique groups designed for specialized care, as presented in this chapter. Development and dissemination of group protocols and music therapy approaches for military populations provides knowledge of available resources shared among clinicians, thus strengthening the network of care available for service members and veterans. It is imperative to engage one's own clinical knowledge while adapting standardized protocols into practice. The importance and impact of this process has been demonstrated throughout this chapter by the feedback of two music therapists currently utilizing these protocols within their respective programs. Further research studies are needed to directly measure the impact of music therapy group treatment for military populations. The work presented in this chapter represents multiple ways that music therapy groups are currently being applied in the treatment of military and veteran populations with the hope to inspire ideas for new and continued programming and future research.

Chapter 7

Caring for the Caregiver: Supporting Military Families Through Music

CLAUDIA AVILA AND LISA FAGAN
INTRODUCTION BY REBECCA VAUDREUIL

> *Service members are the foundation of our nation, military families are the backbone for service members, and caregivers are the core of military readiness.*
>
> Claudia Avila, military spouse

Introduction

It is an honor and privilege to introduce this chapter. These two authors exemplify dedication, strength, resiliency, and service to their country, communities, families, and the warriors for whom they love and care. As someone who aspires to integrate selfless service and employ altruism across the multifaceted aspects of my professional and personal landscapes, knowing these two women over the past decade and witnessing how they manage multiple roles as parents, spouses, caregivers, professionals, public speakers, advocates, and authors has been nothing short of transformative. Their strength, resilience, and spirit are exceptional and unparalleled. Every encounter I have with them, whether it be it a quick conversation or an in-depth interaction, fuels my passion for service, ignites my inspiration for music, and encourages me to be more empathetic, understanding, holistic, and human.

Military families are known for their strength and resiliency, despite the unique demands of military life, which includes high occupational stress, elevated operational tempo, and deployments. However, these factors can gradually generate a familial environment wherein the frequent and prolonged absence of one parent can impair parent–child attachment and destabilize spousal/partner relationships (Chilton *et al.*, 2020). This instability can create vicarious traumatization, diminish communication, and reduce the sense of safety of family dynamics (Creech *et al.*, 2014). Additionally, frequent orders to move can be a regular part of military service that impacts families. Mandatory relocations typically leave military families without a say in where they will be transferred, leading to a sense of lack of control. These elements of military life may exacerbate already existing stressors through the inclusion of social, occupational, and educational disruptions, which can lead to isolation (Lowe *et al.*, 2012).

Furthermore, the invisible wounds of war that so many service men and women have endured from combat operations, namely traumatic brain injury (TBI) and post-traumatic stress disorder (PTSD), can complicate interpersonal functioning and familial relationships. Family members may experience grief, depression, and anxiety as they process the experiences of their loved one's enduring symptomatology associated with TBI and/or PTSD (Butera-Prinzi & Perlesz, 2004) and work towards reconciling the pervasive impact of these invisible wounds on the family system as a whole. Cultivating family resiliency is essential as the aforementioned factors can stretch even highly functioning families to their limits (Cozza *et al.*, 2018). The creative art therapies have demonstrated beneficial outcomes with service members, veterans, and military families by fostering socialization, improving communication, and generating empathy and creativity through meaningful familial interactions (Vaudreuil *et al.*, 2019a; Vaudreuil *et al.*, 2019b; Walker *et al.*, 2017). In this way, the creative arts therapies can leverage existing strengths and resiliency of military families to propel their individual and collective experiences of using the arts to overcome and heal together. By supporting military families, our military is stronger and more prepared. This chapter shares the perspectives of military caregivers—the spouse of an active-duty Army Captain and the mother of a retired Marine Corps Sergeant—regarding the impact of music therapy on their recovering warriors, as well as on their family systems as a whole.

PART 1: PERSPECTIVE OF A MILITARY SPOUSE

Claudia Avila

Military culture, tradition, resilience, and readiness

Since 2001, the United States (U.S.) Army and the military in general have been my home and my family. The military is unique in its history, structure, and mission, and it's been a gift to experience and participate in this way of life.

Being a military spouse is a career in and of itself, as my family has moved to many locations, each with a different environment and culture.

Culture, ceremonies, and tradition

As my husband, Captain (CPT) Luis Avila, and I raised our family, our three sons—Luis Jr., Miguel, and Jose—learned about military culture from the moment they were born. It is a lifestyle full of rich history and prominent traditions. For example, when a service member deploys there is a ceremony to send them off. During the deployment, families and military organizations work together to send packages and letters to support our warriors from afar and remind them we are awaiting their return. In preparation for homecoming ceremonies, we make welcome posters, decorate the barracks with new pillows and sheets, and create gift baskets with the comforts from home that they likely missed while they were deployed. We do this for all returning troops, not just our spouses. The Army provides a protocol for these traditions to guide us in creating these memories of military life and legacy. Each ceremony is dedicated with honor, respect, and duty. Additionally, formal balls are among the most elegant of military traditions, along with the playing of military songs at various ceremonies, and the accompanying honor of being able to stand when your service song is played.

Camaraderie, readiness, and resilience

Elements of military training that foster readiness and resilience enable warfighters to recover from a spectrum of invisible wounds, such as TBI and PTSD. This strengths-based mindset empowers them to overcome their struggles, achieve desired outcomes, adapt to changes, and learn and grow with faith, hope, love, friends, family, and service to country. The daily goal of making a difference—one service member or one military family at a time—is a testament to the resiliency and unique bond of military life, providing the capacity to manage the negative effects associated to military service such as relocation(s), deployment(s), and the impact of combat on our loved ones. As a military wife, I have found Girl Power through bonding with other spouses, and we are stronger together. Military spouses play an important role in supporting our service members and their units, as well as school systems for our children, and volunteering as needed in our communities, which provides a sense of security, fellowship, and camaraderie. The importance of most military friendships is that they withstand distance and time, and this is helpful to spouses who move around frequently. The strong bonds that we create help us pick up swiftly where we left off. For service members, this camaraderie is essential to mission readiness, resilience, and survival. When the service member is injured, this camaraderie is of equal importance to the readiness, resilience, and survival of military families, and our family experienced this first-hand. Luis was injured a few days after Christmas 2011, while on deployment to Afghanistan. The following description of his injury is an excerpt from an article that he co-authored, "Music Therapy Applied to Complex Blast Injury in Interdisciplinary Care: A Case Report," about his injury and recovery through music therapy:

> In August 2011, U.S. Army CPT Luis Avila, Sr. was deployed to Forward Operating Base Justice in Afghanistan. He was assigned to the 720 Military Police (MP) Battalion...charged with the oversight of 240 military policemen and 80 Soldiers. On 27 December 2011, while returning from a mission to recover a downed unmanned aerial vehicle, CPT Avila's convoy was hit by an IED [improvised explosive device] constructed from 600 pounds of explosive matter. During this attack, CPT Avila lost five pints of blood, sustained anoxic and traumatic brain injuries, survived two cardiac arrests, suffered two cerebral vascular ischemic events, and broke three vertebrae (C5, C6, C7). He later underwent amputation of his left leg at the high transfemoral level because of extensive lower limb injuries. (Vaudreuil *et al.*, 2019a)

I am proud of our family for continuing to persevere and overcome adversity every day, as we work alongside Luis in his recovery. Service members are the foundation of our nation, military families are the backbone for the service members, and caregivers are the core of military readiness. Additionally, military children are the hidden heroes and deserve to be acknowledged as the foundation of service members, veterans, and military families.

A caregiver's bond with music therapy

Music has been part of my life for as far back as I can remember. I find peace with, connection to, and enjoyment from the beautiful sounds of music. Part of Luis' treatment that continues to be essential to his recovery and helps strengthen us as a family is music therapy. When Luis was wounded and medivacked from Afghanistan, I met him in Germany and stayed by his side in the hospital. Music and praying helped to recharge and inspire me during this time. I was always praying and playing his favorite songs for him such as *Ode to Joy* and military marches. Artists such as Bruce Springsteen, Paul McCartney, and The Beatles helped us to heal our souls and reconnect. Music is a testament to how we embrace and see life; it creates meaning, inspires purpose, and helps us to dream as we travel in our imagination to more opportunities and possibilities. The songs that I played day and night for Luis were our prayers put to music, and our prayers came true—Luis is still here with us today.

Where words fail...

Poets and authors alike have attributed music to being a universal language as well as being a force far surpassing that which we are able to put into words. Where we can understand and recognize that there are many different types of music that traverse the world with consideration to culture, ceremony, and tradition, universally speaking, regardless of culture or theoretical understanding of music, humans are able to detect basic emotions (e.g., happiness, sadness, fear, anticipation) in music. This is the premise of the quote in the text box below, which means to me and my family that life is full of endless opportunities as music has brought us through dark times and provided light to help us shine through. Music is inclusive, promotes wellness, increases welfare, boosts morale and helps to prevent feelings of isolation. Especially during the COVID-19 pandemic, music has been the most effective mechanism for us to stay connected, have purpose, and thrive. Music therapy helps us process our emotions, grief, and traumas, and find meaning.

> "Music is the universal language of mankind." Henry Wadsworth Longfellow

The author, Hans Christian Andersen, is credited for the famous quote, "Where words fail, music speaks," and this rings true for our family, as when Luis first awoke from his coma and was in the acute stages of his rehabilitation, he couldn't speak. Actually, Luis' prognosis was extremely defeating, as we were told that he was never going to be able to speak, eat, or see again. With the dedication of Luis' medical team, he can do all of the things that we were told he wouldn't, and more; he sings every day! We don't see disabilities anymore; we only see possibilities! Singing became a primary part of music therapy to help with his speech goals, and I am in awe of the music therapists who have worked with Luis throughout his recovery. They exemplify love and compassion in conducting their sessions, with so much admiration for our service members for their service and sacrifice. An important quality that Luis and I have found in the music therapy team is that they keep positive attitudes which help motivate all of us in the therapy process—everyone in the family has a role! There is always a clear plan of care and ways to measure progress. Luis' music therapists have been open to learning as he teaches them new music and helps shape his goals using the music that he loves. It is empowering for a patient to teach something to a provider, and it takes a level of security and humility on the provider's part, which, unfortunately, isn't common.

Music as a motivator

Caregivers constantly advocate for treatment opportunities for our warriors. Through our road to recovery, the only discipline we never had to fight for to help Luis or beg not to give up on him has been music therapy. When other therapists said that Luis' progress had plateaued, the music therapists encouraged him to continue working harder, sing more challenging songs, and start playing the harmonica to activate his breath. Luis sings many of the songs I played for him while he was in a coma, and he is motivated to sing outside the therapy session. He performs on base at events like Creative Forces Creative Arts Cafés, and in the community at memorials, galas, and other events that support the military (Vaudreuil *et al.*, 2019a). Luis created a beautiful rendition of "God Bless America" in music therapy that he sang for the Memorial Day Capital Concert in 2017 (U.S. Department of Veterans Affairs, 2017) and at the Armed Forces Welcome ceremony for the Chairman General Mark Milley (C-SPAN, 2019). In addition, Luis sang "The Army Song" at the 243rd Army Birthday Celebration, accompanied by a choir of his fellow Soldiers, Army Senior Leadership, and with me by his side (U.S. Department of Defense, 2018). Luis enjoys and appreciates every opportunity to share his journey as music helps him overcome his challenges and helps us heal as a family and a community. Figure 7.1 shows Luis among family and friends after his performance at the U.S. Capitol on Memorial Day in 2017.

Figure 7.1: Captain Avila (front/center) with his wife, Claudia (behind), son, Jose (right), mother-in-law (left), and other family, friends, and his music therapist post-performance at the U.S. Capitol, Memorial Day, 2017

The road to recovery

Music therapy has played a crucial role in Luis' physical, emotional, and neurological recovery by taking a patient-centered approach to care. Music has helped Luis to retrain his brain, improve his cognition, activate his short- and long-term memory, restore and relax his body, reduce pain, increase his range of motion, decrease spasticity, enhance his articulation, and enrich our overall quality of life. Luis has a severe TBI, which is accompanied by chronic pain, making it extremely hard for him to engage in other activities. When Luis listens to music, his pain decreases, and he can concentrate on other things. In addition, it calms him down, which is helpful to our familial dynamic and social relationships. Music encourages his participation in his entire rehabilitation program (e.g., physical, occupational, speech therapies) and motivation to be active in our community. Our family's healing process has been like song lyrics—we have had moments of sadness, happiness, joy, despair, and hope—and there has been a song that we can relate to every step of the way. With music, everything is better; for example, our daily life is infused with Luis practicing his songs, reaching and holding the high notes he is aiming for, and always improving his singing, which gives him a purpose to continue serving in the military. He went from MP (Military Police) to emcee in his new role as a musician. Through singing, he can share the miraculous journey on his road to recovery, using the power of music therapy.

Luis' rehabilitation process continues to teach our family so much—most importantly, that our faith is the foundation to make the impossible possible. As we started our journey, one of the most remarkable things I learned was the impact of interdisciplinary treatment executed through multidisciplinary collaboration and partnership. Music therapy was the discipline that connected Luis' care in this way, and this coordination has helped me to stay focused on his treatment and home care plan, as well as prioritize his needs for his continued recovery and his military career.

Lessons learned

Finding the balance in navigating many systems (e.g., family, military, medicine) while simultaneously raising our family has been challenging at times; however, I have learned to take every situation in my stride, one day a time, and sometimes hour by hour and minute by minute. We follow a strict treatment regimen every day, but at the same time, have to remain flexible to accommodate the unknown. Our experiences have taught me to be the best project manager, advocate, spouse, and mother, which requires strong skills in leadership, communication, problem solving, delegation, team building, and integrity, and to show the most genuine passion and enthusiasm to shape, create, adapt, and apply myself in order to be successful. As a caregiver, it is my duty to help Luis get the best medical care that will maximize his potential for rehabilitation on our continued journey to his new normal. This includes taking him to medical appointments, procedures, and surgeries, as well as making adaptations to our home for maximal functioning. I help Luis in his activities of daily living, administer medication, and, especially during the COVID-19 pandemic, have facilitated a lot of his manual therapies that he was unable to receive in person. Another balance is to have my voice heard while advocating strongly, but with grace, and keeping the mindset that when one door closes, God will open another one. Having the determination and discipline to never give up and the courage to keep going, one step at a time, recognizing that even small progress is progress towards your goal, is essential. Music therapy has given us the power to help meet our goals and push ourselves to higher goals as we continue to progress. Luis is a full testament to the power of music therapy. Every day is made up of songs that reflect the soundtrack of our lives, and we are forever thankful for the music.

Resources for resilience

The role of the caregiver depends on the needs of the service member or veteran whom they are caring for, and each is unique and complex. Therefore, it is vitally important to identify resources to support our daily lives and share our knowledge with others to help them find the essential tools for their journeys. We have seen warriors with mild, moderate, severe, and catastrophic cases, and the severity of the injury itself can determine the level of support that the warrior needs. Education is a key to strengthen self-reliance, enhance readiness, and provide the tools to navigate these situations—and the military provides resources to help this process. One of the most amazing trainings I have received is the Army Family Team Building (AFTB) program, and I highly recommend that any new spouse or anyone new to the military culture takes this course. The AFTB has four levels: Level 1 focuses on basic skills and knowledge to understand military life; Level 2 teaches how to become community leaders; Level 3 trains how to mentor others to be leaders; and Level 4 provides information about becoming an AFTB instructor.

Closing thoughts

In closing, I want to commend other caregivers for being the voice for your warriors and families. Please know that you are never alone, and don't hesitate to reach out for help when you need it. I have learned to accept help when needed, and I am much stronger and more resilient than I ever thought possible. Stop at nothing to improve the quality of medical care and the quality of life for your loved ones, but at the same time, remember to take care of yourself and don't allow negativity to surround your new normal. Always carry a heart full of gratitude, keep the faith that things will get better, and work hard to make a difference. All of the angels that come into our lives are the answers to our daily prayers and are true miracles that keep our journeys blessed. Keep spreading love, grace, and joy everywhere you go, and find beauty in everything, even in the things that don't look beautiful yet. Always be ready to adapt to any situation and don't let your emotions control your behavior. Treat people the way you would like to be treated, always with dignity and respect. Stay focused on achieving the goals you have set to have a purpose in your daily adventures, and don't forget to have fun in the process! Our service members, veterans, military families, children, and supporting communities embody the true love, dedication, and commitment to God and country. My family is honored to belong to the best institution in the world, our Armed Forces, and we are forever grateful for and proud of our heroes!

PART 2: INSIGHTS FROM A MILITARY MOTHER

Lisa Fagan

Finding hope in heartache

I am the proud daughter and mother of Marines; my father was a pilot in the United States Marine Corps (USMC) and my son and daughter both served our country in the USMC and gave all they had to protect our nation. On March 23, 2006, my son, Sergeant Benjamin Tourtelot, USMC, Retired, who we lovingly call Ben, suffered a TBI during a routine training. Figure 7.2 shows Ben as a Corporal in 2003, three years prior to his accident. The following part of this chapter reflects a miraculous journey of recovery, resiliency, and rehabilitation. As well as being a decorated Marine, Ben is a dedicated father, brother, uncle, nephew, cousin, friend, and my one and only son. Since Ben was a toddler, he has had an adventurous spirit, frequently coming home with scraped knees that needed bandaging and broken bones that required casts. But all the bumps and bruises in the world could never prepare me, us, for the magnitude of the injuries he sustained in 2006. The journey that followed included exemplary medical intervention, music therapy, and an abundance of faith and perseverance; it was truly life changing.

Figure 7.2: Benjamin Tourtelot pictured as a Corporal in 2003

It all began...

March 23, 2006 is a day that I will never forget. I was at Irvine Valley College in California, coaching a student for an upcoming speech competition when I received a call from my daughter-in-law informing me that Ben was hurt. I don't remember the details that she recounted on that call, but what stuck in my mind was that he'd hurt his arms and his head.

Initially, I didn't understand the severity of his injuries, but as our conversation progressed, it became clear that Ben was in a critical condition. He was in the intensive care unit (ICU) at Tripler Army Medical Center in Honolulu, Hawaii, and the medical team working on him were doing everything they could to save him. I remember feeling a sense of shock and fear along with a dull calm that descended on my heart. My daughter-in-law's mother made arrangements for us and we were on the next flight to Hawaii, which departed the following morning. It was the longest flight of my life. I sat next to the window staring at Ben's picture and praying the same prayer over and over non-stop, "Dear God, heal my son. Dear God, heal my son."

As we anxiously walked through the airport, we were met by two Marines, one of whom was Ben's First Sergeant, Tony. They somehow knew who we were and quickly approached us. I could not stop myself from asking the dreaded question, "Is he alive?" Tony answered, "Yes. He is alive and I am taking you to him now." When we got to the hospital, we were met by my daughter-in-law who took my hand and led me to his room. I remember her preparing me for his appearance—his eyes were purple, and his head was swollen. He was connected to so many machines and he was in a coma, but all I remember is seeing my son's face and that he was breathing. I put my hand on his bandaged hand, kissed his forehead, and whispered, "I'm here Ben. Mom is here." From there forward, we were on a rollercoaster ride of hope and despair. Hearing the doctor say the phrase "100 percent mortality" is something you never forget. However, after many surgeries, heroic medical care, and the countless hours his wife and I spent at his bedside, Ben survived. As this chapter continues, I am grateful and humbled to share Ben's story with you; our journey of shock, fear, despair, acceptance and, yes, joy.

The fall

As the Chief Instructor at Marine Corps Base Hawaii in Kaneohe Bay, Ben's day started out like any other but ended very differently. Ben was instructing his class of Marines on how to safely rappel from a helicopter. Just as he had many times before, Ben started the class by demonstrating an Australian rappel. An Australian rappel is a bit different from traditional rappelling where people use a rope to descend feet-first, for example, down the side of a cliff or tall building and in this case from a helicopter to the ground. An Australian rappel is different because instead of descending feet first, the rappeler descends head-first. This is an essential survival technique used when troops are landing in a combat zone, actively under attack, and may need to return fire as they make their way to the ground.

On that Thursday, March 23, 2006, Ben was in a helicopter that was hovering about 110 feet above the tarmac, and just as he was exiting the aircraft to start the demonstration, something malfunctioned. We suspect Ben's wrist snapped the moment he exited the helicopter rendering him unable to grasp the rope and stop his trajectory towards the tarmac, but we will never truly know what happened to cause the events that followed. Ben fell headfirst towards the tarmac, gaining speed on the 110-foot fall. It is my understanding that one of his fellow Marines recognized what was happening and quickly took action to assist the belayer (the Marine who was supporting the rappelling rope on the ground) in bringing the rappel rope taut at the last millisecond. It was too late to stop the fall, but perhaps it was in just enough time to save his life. Ben broke both arms, shattered both wrists, obliterated part of his skull, and consequently had to have part of his right frontal lobe removed, as it was beyond repair. These injuries have had a lasting impact and resulted in the full loss of vision in his right eye and partial loss of vision in his left eye. Peripheral vision in his left eye is also very limited.

Ben's accident was classified at 100 percent mortality by the neurosurgeon, meaning that there was no expectation for survival; however, due to the incredible talent of that same neurosurgeon, a myriad of dedicated healthcare professionals, and the advancements in military medicine, Ben woke up after being in a coma (not medically induced) after almost two and a half weeks. He remained in the ICU with a team of caring, diligent, and dedicated doctors and nurses for another two months, at which time he transitioned to a different rehabilitation facility, and then another. This process continued over the next several years. We knew it was going to be a long road, and one that we would have to walk with steadfastness, flexibility, and, most of all, faith.

The long road to recovery

I have learned so much during this process. For example, did you know that motivation is literally a part of your brain? Apparently, motivation is controlled by communication between the amygdala (e.g., emotional center) and the prefrontal cortex (e.g., task planning, execution, reasoning station), and is reinforced by the neurotransmitter, dopamine—the "feel-good" hormone. Later in Ben's recovery, this is where music therapy came into play in his continued rehabilitation; it helped immensely with his motivation. Along with the chronic pain and short-term memory loss that Ben continues to experience as a result of his TBI, he has little to no motivation. Now, add lack of motivation to the fact that in order to visually see any of his surroundings, he must constantly scan left and right, up and down. I cannot tell you how many times he has walked into a wall, stepped off a curb and fallen, or tripped over something the rest of us would easily see through our peripheral vision. With these combined challenges and the amount of energy it takes to execute simple tasks, it's no wonder that even getting out of bed each day becomes a major challenge, and one that Ben was not always able to accomplish. It is a great loss to go from being a successful Marine who was running a schoolhouse to an injured Marine lying in bed praying for the pain to go away by any means necessary. Seeing your child seriously injured, in constant pain that you cannot relieve, and knowing he is changed forever is a very difficult experience for a parent. But I often remind myself that the gift of him surviving a 100 percent mortality classification is a miracle for which his entire family and I are indescribably grateful. It is an understatement to say that the road to recovery is not an easy one and watching your child's friends slowly fade away is heartbreaking. They don't mean to turn away, but the fact is that social isolation often results from TBI. Ben is no longer the person he was and only a few of the most devoted friends are able to accept the changes he has undergone. TBI is a true test of friendship. I am grateful to those who passed that test, and understand those who could not.

Ben has always been an upbeat, positive person, and still is, but the first two years post-injury were discouraging, confusing, and at times felt hopeless. To further complicate the situation, many of the closest people to Ben were unable to understand the level of pain he was enduring and couldn't fathom the hopelessness he was experiencing, which left him feeling isolated and frustrated. How do you get someone to understand that the pain you are feeling is real when they are used to you "shaking it off" or "sucking it up," as Marines do? We navigated Ben's recovery as a family, but throughout the process it became clear there were no solid answers to most of our questions. In many ways, this was uncharted territory with no maps to guide us or even point us in a specific direction. The brain is a complicated system and when this very intricate organ is severely injured, it's impossible to provide a simple answer to questions like "How long will healing take?" "Will certain senses and functions return?" "What are the long-term effects of TBI?" The one question that his medical team could answer was one that took us a long time to accept: "Will he ever be the same?" His neurosurgeon was honest with us right from the start. She said, "The person you knew is gone. Ben will never again be who he was before the accident." We refused to accept this, but over time we realized that what his doctor told us was the truth, and Ben realized it too.

By 2009, Ben had lost his career, drifted away from those close to him, and was struggling just to get out of bed each day. Daily pain was a constant companion and he had no motivation to do anything. He was living in a neurorehabilitation center in California and adjusting to life away from his wife and baby daughter. Fortunately, his rehab center was only an hour or so from our house, so we spent the weekends together. I would pick Ben up after work each Friday and take him back to the center on Sunday evenings. I was grateful to spend any time with my walking miracle. This also allowed me to see what he was physically, mentally, and emotionally enduring and gain a better understanding of the sorrow and loss he felt, as well as his constant battle with head pain. As we made progress with his pain, I could still see his loneliness and lack of direction. I tried creating outings for him but going out or attending events required too much energy and was often overstimulating. He wanted to be included but could not endure lengthy activities; he could manage maybe an hour if we were lucky. Ben continued to feel lost and alone and I didn't know how to help him. Then another miracle happened.

Miraculous music

Music walked into his life in the form of a music therapist, Rebecca Vaudreuil, and everything changed. I was picking Ben up from the neurorehabilitation center for the weekend, but I couldn't find him. He was not in his room, ready and waiting to go as he usually was on Fridays. The staff directed me to the main building where I found Ben with a young lady who was sitting on the floor playing a guitar. I couldn't believe my eyes. Ben had a beaming smile on his face! The two of them were singing together and Ben was obviously enjoying himself! Normally, any kind of unusual noise triggers Ben's head pain, but not this time. I could see that he was fully engaged in the singing.

From that moment on, a change came over Ben, and it was dramatic and immediate. Although Ben has always loved music, I never really heard him sing very much. Suddenly, Ben was singing every day! Rebecca continued to open even more horizons for him. She taught him how to play different instruments, which was a huge benefit for his healing wrists and hands, and helped him gain dexterity, strength, and coordination. They wrote songs that captured the experiences he had lived through. He wrote about his accident, injuries, and the new life he was learning to accept. He was able to process his ongoing recovery through songwriting, recording, and performing, and it gave him a sense of pride and accomplishment to present his family and friends with CDs of his songs, as shown in Figure 7.3. He even started performing in public, initially with Rebecca, and then he graduated to solo performances as a continuation of care. I was truly amazed at how much Ben was embracing creativity and music, and I was grateful he'd found something that gave him hope, comfort, and some relief from his constant pain. The impact of music was huge! Ben was able to express his feelings using music and lyrics through which he poured out his love for his daughter by writing her songs and singing them to her when they talked on the phone each day. I truly feel music brought Ben back to us on so many levels.

One of the most memorable musical moments I experienced with Ben was one weekend when his daughter was visiting. She was three or four years old at the time and we were walking around the block together. She kept asking Ben to sing her song, "Sing my song, Daddy. Sing my song!" As soon as he'd finish, she would launch into "Sing Mommy's song, Daddy!" He obliged, of course. It was an incredible experience for me to stand back and see my son not only walking but holding his little girl's hand and singing his original songs with her! I remember feeling overwhelmed with gratitude to see his smiling face reflected in his daughter's equally beautiful smile as they sang together. It wasn't a momentous event by most standards, but it was one of the greatest and most humbling moments of my life. I remember thinking "He's going to be okay. He's going to be okay." That's all any parent wants for their children and I started to feel hopeful for the first time in a long time.

Figure 7.3: Ben's first album, Sung in the Key of Love, that he created and recorded in music therapy

Walking to the beat of a different drummer

As time passes, Ben continues to heal and improve, as seen in Figure 7.4. The improvements are incremental for the most part, and we rejoice in each one. For example, Ben recently regained a very faint sense of smell after almost 13 years of having no sense of smell at all. He actually smelled the barbeque grill the other day and it was an unbelievable breakthrough! I ask you to take a moment and think of what it would feel like to smell your favorite food cooking after not experiencing that sensory input for a decade and a half. Take a moment, breathe in deeply, and give it a try.

Ben still has very limited vision. Imagine walking through life using a telescope (not binoculars), just a single lens, to navigate daily activities like going to school, work, or the grocery store. Try this, close one eye and look through a paper towel holder with the other eye and add some gauze at the end of that holder to make it nice and blurry. Give it a try. Now you see what Ben sees. Frustrating, isn't it?

Physically, Ben is on the mend. His arms and wrists were repaired, but never regained full strength and he lost some of the feeling and dexterity in his fingers. To compensate for the loss of his pituitary gland and naturally occurring hormones, he has a robust daily medication regimen required for him to remain neurochemically balanced and vital. His TBI resulted in short-term memory loss as well as the loss of reasoning ability, pertaining to certain aspects of his life, such as sense of time, basic decision making, and in some circumstances, patience. His memory plays tricks on him as well. This is distressing to him and he asks that we always be honest when he shares a false memory that is completely removed from the truth. The biggest challenge continues to be the chronic and severe head pain he struggles with every day of his life. TBIs can heal to a certain extent but finding relief from pain is a huge challenge.

We are grateful that, regardless of the pain, Ben's sense of humor is intact and his love for people and all living beings is as strong as ever. He and his dog Frank, a Saint Bernard, are neighborhood favorites as Ben walks Frank several times a day around the two-block area surrounding our home. This is about all he can handle. Ben and his former First Sergeant, the one who greeted me at the airport and visited Ben in the hospital almost every day, continue to stay in close touch, and Ben and his now ex-wife remain good friends as they raise their daughter and put her needs first. Additionally, Ben keeps in close contact with his first music therapist, Rebecca, and they still write new songs together from time to time, most of which are dedicated to his daughter, rich with lyrics that instill life lessons about honesty, integrity, kindness, and faith.

Figure 7.4: Ben in 2018, 12 years after his injury

Looking back

In the first days after Ben's accident, I began writing him a letter every day as I was confident that he would recover and would want to know what happened during that time. In hindsight, I can see that writing to Ben was also a coping strategy for me as I struggled to remain hopeful during the darkest days of my life. I have included a few excerpts from my collection of "Letters to My Son" in Appendix A, which includes time-indicated passages that correspond with the days that followed his accident. The excerpts conclude with a "Letter to My Friends" written on day 43 of Ben's recovery, providing updates on his miraculous process and progress, included in Appendix B.

Looking forward: 15 years later

As I reread some of my letters to Ben and to my friends, I see some really long paragraphs that clearly indicate how my grief and fear were presenting through my writing and word selection. It is obvious to me that this was the form my own personal therapy took, and that the blank pages were a place where I could unburden my heart—just as playing music and writing songs in music therapy provided healing for Ben.

Over the years, Ben struggled with depression, and some days still does. A few years after the accident, he and his wife separated and eventually divorced. She continues to support him and to this day they remain good friends and work together to co-parent their daughter, who is now a teenager. After discharge from the neuro-rehabilitation center, Ben was placed in a senior living center to ensure that he received his medications throughout the day and proper nutrition; however, the setting was too lonely for such a people-loving guy. Ben now lives with my husband and me, as he needs to have family and friends around him. Figure 7.5 is a photo taken at Ben's 40th birthday on January 15, 2020. We are blessed to have our family together again! There is a lot of silliness, loud laughing, and music in our home every day! Life has been interesting to say the least and it has taught us to cherish and find joy wherever we can, which is not that hard to do if you take a moment to look and appreciate what life provides you with!

The three of us have started a new and exciting chapter of our lives. We moved from California to Texas. Go Longhorns! Ben has come so far and is doing so well. He still struggles with daily pain and does not live the life I had imagined he would, but we recognize how much he has progressed and are grateful. Music continues to be a huge part of Ben's life; it's in his heart, and singing is a part of who Ben is now. He is constantly writing songs. I don't know what would have happened to Ben without music therapy and I am grateful every day for the direct and positive impact it made on Ben, his daughter, and our whole family!

Figure 7.5: Ben (pictured middle with mother, Lisa) celebrating his 40th birthday

Appendices

Appendix A: Excerpts from "Letters to My Son"

DAY 2 | SATURDAY, MARCH 25, 2006 | 8PM HST (HAWAIIAN STANDARD TIME)

Hi Ben,

You had surgery on your hands and arms today. The doctors said they didn't think you'd be okay under anesthesia for too long, so they'd do the shorter "moped" (as in "scooter") surgery. But you tolerated the anesthesia so well, they went ahead and did the "Cadillac" surgery on your arms. Shane is here. He got here first. Poor Pete. It took him so long to get here. Just couldn't get the flights to cooperate. But he finally made it yesterday at 5.50pm. Chris, Josh and Googs got here yesterday too. Then Dirk arrived today. Looks like most of your groomsmen are here!

We got to see the images of the baby today. Your little daughter was kicking and moving her hands and head all around. What a cutie patooty!

Poor Googs and Josh have colds so they can't go in and see you. It's killing them, but they understand.

As for me, my heart is heavy, Ben. I'm on a rollercoaster ride. I've been hopeful—and yet so scared. The panic feeling just sits on my chest. There's nothing to be done. Just waiting and hoping and praying. I go in and see your beautiful face. Your eyes are unfocused and it's an unreal sensation to see my boy so helpless. I love you son. No matter what happens I am so thankful that God gave me you to be my son. I love you, Benjamin. I love you. Love, Mom

DAY 5 | MONDAY, MARCH 27, 2006 | 3:22AM HST

Hi Ben,

Looks like you're having a better night tonight. Your temp is down (99°). Your oxygen is at 100 saturation (woo hoo! 90 and higher is the magical number!). They re-wrapped your arms to make them more movable, plus a doctor is here who just watches and watches you.

I recited Horton Hatches the Egg to you. I can't believe I remember so much of it. Each time I go over it in my head, a bit more of it comes back to me.

All your numbers are looking pretty good right now. We're really happy about that. The three of us (both moms and of course your sweet wife) are taking shifts. Every two hours we sit up and talk to you so that you are never alone. That way we each get a bit of sleep. I'm going to try and get some sleep now. Sweet dreams, Ben. I love you so much. I'm trying to be very strong, so don't even worry about that. You have always been my angel, Ben. You will always be my angel, Ben. I love love love you. I know you're hanging on and I'm grateful for this extra time you are giving us. Thank you, Ben. I love you so very much. Good night, son.

PS—Pete is thrilled that ya'll want him to be your baby's godfather. I'm thrilled too. What a perfect choice. (*Thank you for my granddaughter*) Love, Mom

DAY 12, EXCERPT 1 | TUESDAY, APRIL 6, 2006 | 5:23PM HST

Note: Ben had just undergone a second surgery trying to save him and get oxygen to his brain—this surgery had never been done a second time on a patient before and when the surgeon talked to me after the operation, I asked her, "It's going to take a miracle, isn't it?" She just looked at me and nodded her head.

Hi Ben,

Jobe (nurse in training) stopped by your room to tell me that he was there while you were having today's procedure done and that the doctors used very encouraging words. He is such a kind soul. He reminds me a little of you. I remember when you were 12 years old or so, and we saw something on the news (I think it was an earthquake or something like that). And you took one look at me and said "Mom, let's pray for them." This is what Jobe did. He held my hands and prayed such a beautiful prayer. What a kind soul he is. Just like you,

son. I'm sorry I lost my hope earlier today. My fear overcame my faith. Please don't judge me too harshly. I'm starting to think that you are going to have a profound effect on some people you don't even know. Your Master Sergeant was here and told me about one Marine's life you have already changed. This Marine was going to get out of the Corps and go work for that company you'd been talking about (protection for certain people in Iraq or something like that). Your accident made him re-think his decision. He's not going to go into that incredibly dangerous business after all. He wants to see his daughter grow up, so he's re-enlisting. I wonder about the other lives you will change before it's all said and done. You've certainly changed my life, son. God blessed me when he gave me you. I thank Him for the gift of you. Between you, Lisa Marie, Danielle, and Jennifer I don't believe there is a luckier mom on the face of the earth. I love you so very much, Ben. My boy. My heart.
Love, Mom

DAY 12, EXCERPT 2 | TUESDAY, APRIL 6, 2006 | 7:00PM HST

Oh, Ben. We need a miracle and you're the only one I know who can pull it off. Ben, I want what you want son. Whatever you want—I support you. I love you more than I can bear. I love you, son. Love, Mom

LATER THE SAME DAY

I stood by your bed and talked to you tonight. I told you that I know you're in conference with God right now making a big decision—and whatever decision you make I will support you. You have always made me proud and that will not change. I have always been proud of you and now I am going to make you proud of me. Whatever it is, I am going to accept your decision. I will be strong, BUT, if you haven't decided yet, if you're still on the fence about whether or not to stay with us, just remember…I need you…Dad needs you…your wife needs you…the baby needs you. I love you, Ben. My boy. Love, Mom

Note: Ten hours later, Ben awoke from his coma and squeezed my hand on command.

Appendix B: "A Letter to My Friends"

DAY 43 | FRIDAY, MAY 5, 2006

Here's the latest on Ben:

Last Friday, the speech language pathologist (SLP) came by and we asked about getting Ben some kind of trachea that would allow him to speak. She pointed out that Ben was not even mouthing any words yet, but when he did, she would look at getting him the different trachea. Naturally, his wife and I spent the entire weekend trying to get Ben to mouth the words "Yes" and "No." Some of his friends were visiting from California and spent most of the weekend watching over Ben, trying to do anything they could for him (literally trying to straighten his sheets or fluff the pillows under his arms, etc.) They are such sweethearts. But the best part is the way Ben interacts with them. Picture this poor kid, lying in bed most of the time with his eyes closed. Then there's good old Chris and Josh, reminding him of all the trouble they used to cause in high school. All of a sudden you would look at Ben and there he is, looking like he is asleep, with a little smile on his face! Priceless!

At one point, the nurse was removing the A-line (arterial line) from Ben's arm. This isn't a big ordeal, except there is tape and arm-hair involved (you get the picture). Chris was feeling sorry for Ben and said, "Ahhh Ben, would it make you feel any better if I had the nurse put some tape on my arm and rip my hair out too?" Ben actually got a grin on his face and nodded his head "Yes!" Haha! That was an amazing moment.

By the time Monday rolled around, Ben was mouthing all kinds of things like "Okay" and "Yes." Strangely enough, we couldn't get a "No" out of him. I figured since that was his first baby word, that would be the easiest, oh well.

Anyway, he passed the speaking test on Monday and the SLP showed us how to place our gloved finger over the trachea hole while Ben was exhaling, and he could talk! Very softly...not very distinctly...but he was definitely making sound! I cannot tell you what a thrill it was to hear Ben's voice after six weeks of silence! His first word was "Ben" (she asked him his name)...but his SECOND word was "Mom." YAY! Okay...to be fair, we were trying to give him simple, one syllable words, and "mom" is pretty basic! Hahaha!

He spent the rest of the day talking—off and on. It was VERY, VERY hard to understand him most of the time, and it really wore him out. That night, everyone went to dinner and I was alone with Ben doing physical therapy. We do this three or four times a day. When he was done, he was wide awake. I asked him if he wanted to talk and he nodded yes, so I just stood and talked for a while. But then he got that "Mom I want to ask you something" look on his face. So, I asked him if he wanted to ask me a question and he nodded yes. He tried to tell me with words, but I just could not make out what he was saying. So, we started playing 20 questions. This was quite a process, but the bottom line is that I finally figured out that he wanted to talk about the accident. Here's how the conversation went from there:

Me: Are you asking about the accident?

Ben: Yes. *(Ben is nodding his head "Yes" and shaking his head "No")*

Me: Do you remember the accident?

Ben: No.

Me: Do you want me to tell you what happened?

Ben: Yes.

Me: Okay. Do you remember that you are the Chief Instructor for HRST [Helicopter Rope Suspension Technique]?

Ben: Yes.

Me: Okay, you were teaching a class on how to rappel out of a helicopter and there was an accident.

At this point, Ben mouthed some words, but I couldn't understand what he was saying. He kept saying the same thing over and over and over. I would try and try to get it but couldn't. I would have to wait for him to catch his breath, and then ask him to try again. I felt so bad because he kept saying the same thing and he had a look of frustration and defeat on his face. I told him, "Please don't give up on me, I know you're trying to say something. I am going to get it. Let's try again. Say it very slowly. Say it like you're shouting. Try using only one or two words." Finally, after several frustrating minutes, I understood.

Ben: Every…one…okay…?

I looked at him.

Me: Ben, did you ask me if everyone was okay?

He nodded yes.

Me: Yes Ben, everyone is okay. Nobody was hurt. You got hurt, but everyone else is okay.

Ben: Nodded his head again, closed his eyes, and went to sleep.

I know that Ben must have thought there was a helicopter crash. As time goes on, we will clear all that up but, it touched my heart when I heard his words *"Everyone okay?"* This son of mine continues to amaze me. Since that night, Ben has made leaps and bounds. He speaks very quietly, and mostly with his teeth clenched together, as he still has to wear a c-collar (cervical collar). Since he is doing so well, they capped off his trachea and are moving towards getting rid of it altogether. They are going slowly though, just in case he needs to go in for surgery again unexpectedly before he heads to rehab. As it stands now, he is only scheduled for one more surgery, to put the plate in his head to replace the skull they took out. This will probably be two or three months from now.

Ben asked me the other day about his right eye (this was still before he could speak). He kept pointing to his eye, which was a bit indistinct because he has splints on both hands. I said, "Ben, are you asking me about your right eye?" He nodded, "Yes." I told him that his eyelid was closed because he hit it hard and the muscles were strained and that we won't know for sure if he can see out of it until he can lift that eyelid and tell us. I asked him if he could see out of his left eye, "Can you see me?" He nodded, "Yes." Then he gestured to the rest of himself, so I informed him that he hit his head pretty hard and that he is wearing a c-collar as a precaution because he flipped his head vigorously forward and backward. I demonstrated this for him. I informed him that his arms were broken and I held up each arm and showed him, assuring him that they had already been operated on and were on their way to being better than before, that he was on his way to being the Terminator, at which point he kind of smiled. I was trying to get him focused on the positive as he had already come so far! I told him that even though he had braces on his feet, there was nothing wrong with his legs or feet, in fact everything else is really doing just fine. He looked skeptical. I said, "Ben, you are going to be okay and you want to know how you can tell I am telling you the truth?" He looked at me as if to say, "How?" I asked him, "Am I the biggest cry-baby you ever knew?" He nodded "Yes." "And if you weren't going to be okay, wouldn't I be blubbering right now?" He nodded. "So, are you going to be okay?" He kind of smiled and nodded his head again. Then went to sleep.

Yesterday the physical therapist sat Ben up in bed, helped him pull his legs to the side, and propped them up on a stool. He sat up for about ten minutes, really hunched over and swaying, but without getting dizzy. Unfortunately, his nose started bleeding and a little cerebral spinal fluid came out. Thankfully, this didn't seem to alarm the neurosurgeon, and she said it was likely residuals left from before. They were unable to sit him up today because his electrolytes were out of whack and he couldn't seem to wake up enough to do anything. Because he destroyed his pituitary gland when he fell, he will have to take a bunch of meds every day to keep balanced (desmopressin, thyroid, steroids, testosterone, growth hormones, etc.) They tried to switch from administering these intravenously to orally via feeding tube, and shots and creams, but they may have moved a bit too fast because his sodium dropped and his electrolytes need adjusting. They are starting the process over again, this time, more gradually.

The big news is that Ben is no longer in critical condition! He is considered stable. Their goal is to get Ben into rehab in the next week or so. He will be an outpatient in maybe six to eight weeks! Can you believe it? As each day passes it becomes clear that Ben's mind is intact. His memory seems to be fine. For example, he knows who we all are. He knows all of his own family members' names but cannot remember our dogs' names (although he knows his own dog's name). He knows he is a Marine, but cannot remember that he lives in Hawaii, not California. The bits and pieces of his memory that are mixed up may come back with time or may just have to be learned all over again. His motor skills seem to be okay, but he is still too weak to tell in some cases. His personality seems to be intact, his sense of humor is strong, and he is very polite. He continues to thrill us every day. Today a nurse stopped by to see him and I told him that she knew a friend of his named Steve. I couldn't remember his last name, so I said, "Ben, you know Steve, that guy who wrestles or grapples or whatever you call it." Ben immediately said Steve's full name! His memory is better than mine!

As his friends from the Corps visit, he calls them by name or at least by rank. When I say he is talking, bear in mind that it is very quiet and slurred, but getting better. Okay—I am heading off to bed. Need to be up and at 'em tomorrow. All Ben's physical therapy wears me out but is making my arms rather buff. Today ended on such a nice note. Ben is very restless in bed now and after a lot of squirming, pillow placement, tucking, and so on, he finally got comfortable enough to relax. I said, "You okay now?" His eyes were closed, and he nodded his head. I walked over to my green chair. Then I heard a very quiet, "Thank you, Mom."

Wow.

Chapter 8

Music Therapy and Telehealth: Serving Remote Military Populations

DIANE G. LANGSTON AND KAREN WACKS

Disclaimer: The views expressed in this chapter are those of the editor and authors and do not necessarily reflect the official policy or position of the U.S. Department, Department of Defense, Department of Veterans Affairs, or the United States Government.

Introduction

Over the year that we wrote this chapter—2019–2020—the world was significantly impacted by the COVID-19 global pandemic. Innovations in music therapy telehealth with military populations had been well underway for many years, a process in which we, the chapter authors, played an instrumental role. In fact, when this chapter was conceived, music therapy telehealth was quite limited in its use as a supplement for in-person sessions. It was primarily used in remote areas where patient safety, physical limitations, and distance were barriers to access clinical treatment, or in specific circumstances such as where an existing therapeutic relationship was established, and the client or therapist relocated (Vaudreuil *et al.*, 2020b). The impact of COVID-19 rapidly transformed the delivery of music therapy to clients, and music therapy telehealth became the primary format for therapists to continue providing services. It remains unclear as to how long telehealth will be used at a high level, but it is anticipated that it will remain relevant in some capacity, to include hybrid models of in-person and telehealth approaches to care, for years to come.

Telehealth is a tool that many providers may not have anticipated needing to augment their practice, but many music therapists have begun facilitating group and individual sessions via telehealth to provide continuity of care for their clientele. When sudden changes in clinical processes or environment occur, music therapists must respond in a way that preserves goal-oriented treatment. Often, this transforms practices through embracing innovation, adapting to situations, and improvising to transcend obstacles. A component of music therapy education and training focuses on the ability to be creatively flexible and prepared for the unknown, which gives music therapists an advantage in adapting and expanding their practices within a short period of time. Music therapists are prepared to be flexible in the delivery of clinical services, leveraging technology to bolster adaptive approaches to care, both essential elements in successful telehealth practice.

Music therapy has traditionally been offered as an in-person service; however, as technology advances and it has become a necessity for services to be generalized to online platforms, telehealth can be used as a tool for music therapists. This allows for patients to receive music therapy services regardless of any physical, mental or emotional limitations, and extends the reach of the music therapist in reducing barriers to providing services. Telehealth offers the opportunity for music therapists to expand their practices without certain financial, physical, or geographic constraints. It is important to note that telehealth is not ideal for all populations, particularly those with deficits in reality orientation, such as psychosis, schizophrenia, Alzheimer's, or dementia.

Telehealth can be employed to sustain existing connections and build new connections. This has been demonstrated through both clinical and community models of music therapy with military populations (Spooner *et al.*, 2019). Trust is a crucial component across all environments; therefore, it is essential to establish rapport in initial sessions with military populations, creating a trusted foundation on which to build the therapeutic relationship. Dr. Brene Brown is a renowned social worker, author, and researcher who defines connection as, "the energy that exists between people when they feel seen, heard, and valued; when they can give and receive without judgment; and when they derive sustenance and strength from the relationship" (Brown, 2010, p.5). In this way, the telehealth platform extends the reach of the music therapists to establish and reinforce connection, validating patients by meeting them where they are, and maintaining quality of care on a clinic to community continuum.

PART 1: MUSIC THERAPY TELEHEALTH

Diane G. Langston

The history of telehealth in military healthcare

The profession of music therapy was initially validated and systematized in Veterans hospitals during World Wars I and II. The United States (U.S.) government—including the Departments of Defense (DoD) and Veterans Affairs (VA)—was at the forefront of telemedicine and telehealth (Sullivan, 2007) and the Veterans Healthcare Administration (VHA) is the first subsystem to regulate creative arts therapies via telehealth (Lightstone *et al.*, 2015), thus expanding the innovation of the arts in healthcare.

Telemedicine and telehealth in military medicine

The Health Resources and Services Administration of the U.S. Department of Health and Human Services defines telehealth as, "the use of electronic information and telecommunications technologies to support and promote long-distance clinical healthcare, patient and professional health-related education, public health and health administration" (Health Resources and Services Administration, 2015). Telemedicine is defined as the remote diagnosis and treatment of patients by means of telecommunications technology (World Health Organization, 2010). Spooner *et al.* (2019) defined creative arts therapies telehealth as discipline-specific care (e.g., art therapy, music therapy, dance/movement therapy) provided on a digital platform. Vaudreuil *et al.* (2020b) posited that virtual arts engagement can include psychoeducation that informs the use of creative arts techniques in home and community settings. As the field of telehealth continues to advance and creative arts practices are becoming more widely used, practitioners are uncovering various utilities of remote arts engagement on a clinic to community continuum. Table 8.1 presents various definitions pertaining to virtual healthcare and community connectivity.

Table 8.1: Telehealth terminology: definitions and examples

Terminology	Definition	Example/Description	Source
Telemedicine	The remote diagnosis and treatment of patients by means of telecommunications technology.	Consultative appointments, prescription refills, scheduling appointments, accessing medical information.	World Health Organization, 2010

cont.

Telehealth	The use of electronic information and telecommunications technologies to support and promote long-distance clinical healthcare, patient and professional health-related education, public health and health administration.	Clinical appointments, co-treatment, continuity of care.	Health Resources and Services Administration, 2015
Creative arts therapies telehealth	The use of digital platforms to provide clinical creative arts therapies service (i.e., art therapy, dance/movement therapy, music therapy, psychodrama, poetry therapy).	Individual and group creative arts therapies sessions, arts integration that support the clinic to community continuum (e.g., virtual performances, art exhibits).	Spooner *et al.*, 2019; Vaudreuil *et al.*, 2020b
Virtual arts engagement	The use of digital technology to support reintegration and community engagement.	Remote performances (music, dance, theater), arts exchanges, virtual exhibits, art and music installations.	Vaudreuil *et al.*, 2020b

As technology is increasingly accessible and continues to advance globally, it is innovating a form of universal communication that requires a level of literacy and proficiency. In addition to the impact that technology has had on social and familial connections, opportunities for occupational networking, educational engagement, training programming, meetings, summits, conferences, medical consultation, rehabilitative care, and community integration can be provided virtually through non-secure/public platforms (e.g., Skype, Facetime, GotoMeeting) and secure interactive technological interfaces (e.g., VA Video Connect, WebEx, Jabber, GoogleDUO, Zoom, Microsoft Teams). Due to the quick pivot that many healthcare systems had to make to accommodate the impact of COVID-19, telehealth regulations and restrictions were temporarily loosened, allowing healthcare workers to provide services more readily using the platforms that were most accessible to their diverse and broad client base.

A creative arts therapies telehealth program model

One model of creative arts therapies telehealth was developed through the Rural Veteran Tele-Rehabilitation Initiative (RVTRI). In 2014, art therapy and dance/movement therapy telehealth were piloted within the RVTRI, at Malcom

Randal VA Medical Center (VAMC) in Gainesville, Florida, with the intention of expanding the access of creative arts therapies to veterans living in rural areas within the North Florida/South Georgia VHA. Art therapy and dance/movement therapy were added to existing disciplines being facilitated via telehealth, including recreation therapy, physical therapy, and occupational therapy (Levy *et al.*, 2017). Music therapy was integrated into the Creative Arts Therapy Clinic at the Malcom Randall VAMC in 2017, through collaborative efforts of the National Endowment for the Arts (NEA) Creative Forces®: NEA Military Healing Arts Network, the University of Florida Center for Arts in Medicine, and the Veterans Affairs RVTRI (Vaudreuil *et al.*, 2020b). Music therapy was offered as in-person sessions that served inpatient groups and individual outpatients, and telehealth sessions that served individual outpatients.

One of the barriers to care for outpatients included travel time to and from the VAMC or other medical facility. For example, some veterans face travel times of up to three hours one way to receive music therapy and other treatments. Accessibility provided another challenge for veterans who experienced physical, emotional, cognitive, and financial limitations that inhibited them from driving or sitting for an extended period of time (Spooner *et al.*, 2019). Prior to the wider implementation of music therapy telehealth in the North Florida/South Georgia VHA, there were few other reported cases of music therapy telehealth used with military populations. These included: 1) individual treatment of a veteran in Canada (Lightstone *et al.*, 2015); 2) a service member in Southern California receiving music therapy telehealth on a clinic to community continuum to assist with retirement and life transitions (Vaudreuil *et al.*, 2020b); 3) a group of women veterans receiving music therapy telehealth for consistency of care when the music therapist relocated (Vaudreuil *et al.*, 2020b); and 4) a community partnership between the Music Therapy Department at Berklee College of Music and a therapeutic school in Lira, Uganda, for the rehabilitation and reintegration of child soldiers (Codding & Wacks, 2015).

Music therapy telehealth for military populations

Music therapy telehealth provides military-connected populations (i.e., service members, veterans, eligible dependents) with remote music therapy services. Facilitation of music therapy in-person and facilitation via telehealth have many parallels. Similarities include interventions used, musical instrument selection, cultivation of trusted relationships, support and assistance from a third party (e.g., caregiver, medical technician), to name a few. The main difference is that the provision of treatment occurs through a digital interface, but essentially a music therapy telehealth session closely resembles an in-person session. Digital platforms are intended to serve as a tool in supporting the continuity of care and the therapeutic relationship, thus supporting the concept of music therapy telehealth as accessible and accommodating.

The DoD and VA subscribe to substantial and stringent security protocols to ensure patient privacy, and these translate to the telehealth setting. For cybersecurity measures, the broadband level is high and cannot always maintain the technological needs of telehealth. This can lead to delays in both sound and image quality. While this can certainly be a hindrance to practice, it can also provide the opportunity for the veterans to practice autonomy, patience, and comprehensive verbal processing. For example, they may have to describe imagery or sound using words rather than synchronous musical demonstration. Thus, an increase of skills to employ frustration tolerance practices is aptly supported in the telehealth environment as well as in-person settings.

Continued expansion and standardization of music therapy telehealth

Partnerships supporting expansion

Due to the high level of need for remote services and the success of benchmark programs, a partnership between the VHA and Creative Forces, the RVTRI is supporting the continued expansion of creative arts therapies telehealth services to VAMCs in Ohio, Indiana, and Mississippi (National Endowment for the Arts, 2019). It is intended that there will be at least two creative arts therapists (CATs) at each site—one supported through the VA and one through Creative Forces. This expansion increases the representation of CATs who are trained in telehealth within the VHA system. The intent of this partnership is to utilize telehealth to provide clinical care for veterans living in rural and remote areas surrounding the VAMCs. These CATs are equipped to provide targeted treatment for patients who are transitioning from active duty to veteran status, assimilating to veteran status, reintegrating into their communities, and those who need health maintenance. Treatment occurs in multiple environments: in person, from clinic to clinic, and from clinic to home.

Standardization efforts

A network of music therapists working across the DoD and VA create, share, and implement standardized treatment approaches to support patients' immediate needs, long-term goals, treatment termination, and community integration and assimilation processes. This standardized clinical process is introduced as early as the assessment stage and is reinforced throughout every level of treatment, concluding with termination and transition. Figure 8.1 presents the music therapy telehealth clinical trajectory that supports patients throughout treatment on a clinic to community continuum.

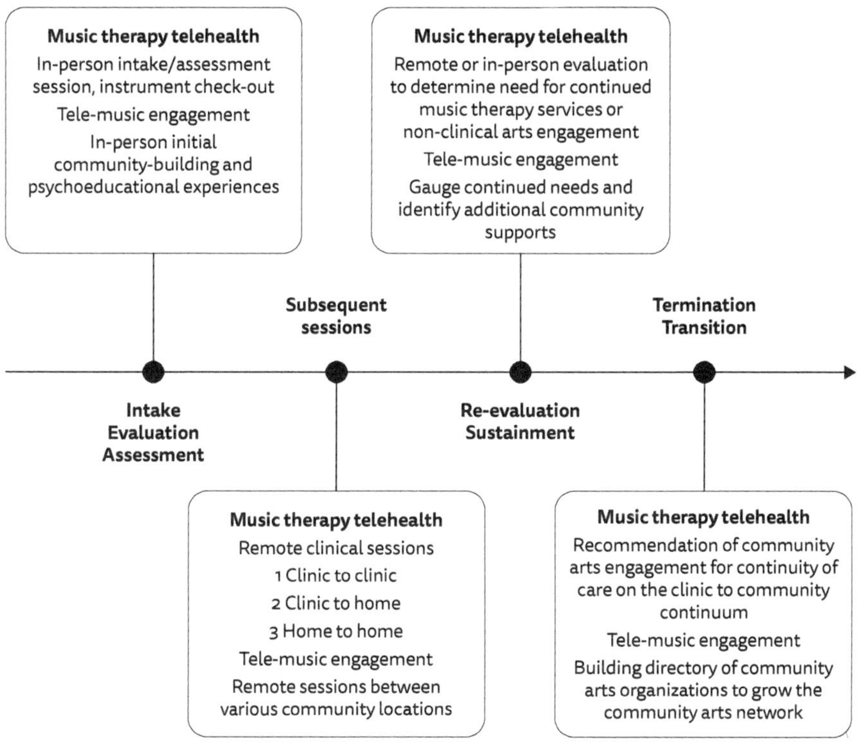

Figure 8.1: Music therapy telehealth treatment process

In addition to the efforts to standardize the clinical application of music therapy telehealth, treatment approaches are being refined across sites to assist with facilitating standardization of music therapy telehealth. The goal of standardization is to promote synchronicity across multiple sites to inform best practices that optimize patient care and, ultimately, inform future research. Three music therapy telehealth approaches are introduced: 1) individual treatment; 2) group sessions; and 3) non-clinical virtual arts engagement.

Individual music therapy telehealth

It is important that the facilitator of any clinical session is a board-certified music therapist, and this applies to telehealth as well. Individual music therapy telehealth sessions require the facilitator to have clinical training in assessment and evaluation purposes and to provide effective and ethical treatment. Specific goals and objectives are set for the individual, which are discussed and supported by the clinical treatment team. Each time the music therapist connects with the patient for clinical sessions, they must confirm the patient's current address and emergency contact information in case of an emergency or network disconnect. Another consideration for the music therapist and the patient is to develop methods of communication to compensate for the challenge of potentially missing non-verbal cues, for example determining a code word or hand signal if someone else enters the virtual clinic space.

Music therapy interventions that have been successfully employed with military-connected populations in individual telehealth sessions include active music-making to train fine and gross motor skills, auditory discrimination through active listening, and cognitive recall through remembering specific sounds and musical patterns (Spooner *et al.*, 2019). Furthermore, individual telehealth music therapy sessions have been shown to reduce depression, anxiety, and pain perception (Vaudreuil *et al.*, 2020b). Additionally, other creative arts therapies have been successfully implemented via telehealth. For example, telehealth art therapy sessions helped to promote concentration and motor skills through a patient's engagement in sculpting clay, observational drawing, and detailed pen patterns. This supported the patient's goals of developing coping strategies, promoting a more positive self-image, and improving focus, concentration, and motor skills. Dance/movement therapy facilitated via telehealth helped a patient achieve expanded movement repertoire and increased range of motion, and supported socialization goals (Spooner *et al.*, 2019).

Group music therapy telehealth

Similar concepts for individual music therapy telehealth sessions can be applied to group work, with the inclusion of multiple participants, including technicians and assistants. The goals and objectives are more group-oriented, such as appropriate communication, engagement, socialization, and reintegration support. Technology can be increasingly challenging with group sessions, as various participants have different levels of bandwidth and connectivity, which may generate higher audio and/or visual latency. Also, the music therapist has to track multiple participants in diverse environments to ensure their wellbeing, monitor engagement levels, and maintain session privacy.

Music therapy interventions that have demonstrated efficacy through group telehealth sessions include call-and-response singing and music-making, active/intentional music listening, lyric analysis, and songwriting. Female veterans engaged in a five-week group music therapy telehealth series indicated that "music facilitation through a digital platform was not a deterrent from engagement, and the transmission of music through a digital platform was effective" and they "expressed interest in additional telehealth music therapy groups" (Vaudreuil *et al.*, 2020b, p.6).

Virtual arts engagement

This is a non-clinical arm of the clinic to community continuum, focused on providing warm handoffs and smooth transitions to remote community arts engagement opportunities. This includes arts experiences that take the form of instructive classes or interactive workshops that present music, art, dance, and writing/poetry-based experientials to a wide audience in the comfort of their own homes. Because this is a non-clinical activity, facilitation by a board-certified CAT is not required, but creative arts therapies-informed insights can be advantageous to non-clinician facilitators. Instruction-based classes can be streamed on platforms such as Facebook or Instagram Live, where there is limited ability for experiential participation. Workshops with increased level of interaction are best suited to being presented on Zoom, Teams, and other platforms that allow for participants to engage at their desired level of interest through control of their audio and video functions.

The following vignette is an example of virtual music engagement between a Soldier in Afghanistan and a teaching artist from the Yamaha Music and Wellness Institute.

Vignette: Music has no boundaries

Yamaha Music and Wellness Institute connects to a Soldier in Afghanistan

By Lori Frazer

The Yamaha Corporation of America has a non-profit division, The Yamaha Music and Wellness Institute (YMWI), dedicated to the benefits of music-making and wellness using evidence-based educational practices. The YMWI was founded in 2004 and continues its work under Chief Executive Officer Dr. Barry Bittman. The YMWI collaborates with many organizations and initiatives, and one of the most exciting resulted in establishing a remote connection with a Soldier in Afghanistan through music engagement.

In early 2011, YMWI was contacted regarding the possibility of donating a Yamaha digital piano to Bagram Airfield in Afghanistan, the largest U.S. military base in Afghanistan. YMWI had previously donated guitars to this base, but this was the first request for a digital piano. The justification was that one of the soldiers stationed at Bagram, a Chief Warrant Officer Four (CW4), was having a difficult deployment and wanted an outlet for emotional support; a piano was his solution. This was the CW4's sixth deployment and he had always brought his Yamaha keyboard on all of his deployments, including this one; however, one evening when he was working late, his barracks took heavy incoming fire, and he lost all of his possessions, including his keyboard.

The fulfillment of this request required collaboration between three organizations: 1) Yamaha Corporation of America, which donated the digital piano; 2) Soldiers Angels, a non-profit which provided a new laptop computer and shipped the digital piano; and 3) TimeWarp Tech, which provided state-of-the-art music software for this project. Connecting technologically using the piano as the main source of communication has its share of technical difficulties. For example, when using general live video-streaming programs, the sound of the instrument is compressed, making it very difficult to hear clearly. TimeWarp Tech's program, *InternetMidi*, has changed the experience of tele-music communication. *InternetMidi* allows two digital instruments, in this case Yamaha digital pianos, to connect over the internet for distance learning and remote performing. The computer screen displays the animated keys, pedals, and velocity meters, as shown in Figure 8.2, visually depicting real-time happenings, while at the same time, hearing the instrument playing the music being created on the other piano. Using Skype allows visual imagery of each player, allowing face-to-face interactive communication.

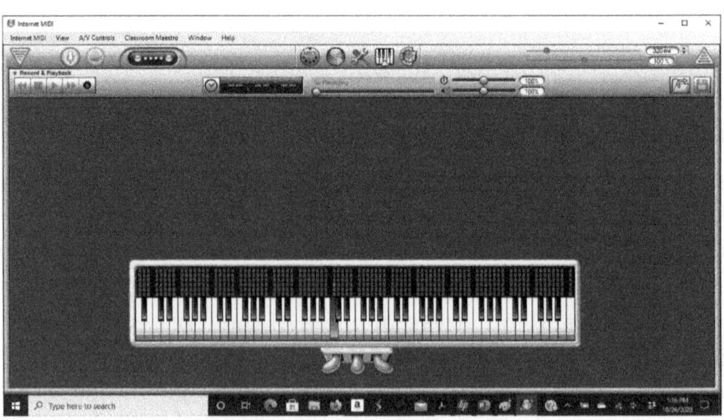

Figure 8.2: An InternetMidi screen

Due to high security and firewall systems, special permissions were needed for this project. The Yamaha digital piano was located in the CW4's barrack, where there was a strong internet connection. Scheduling was difficult due to the high operational tempo of his deployment, but we were able to meet on Thanksgiving morning of 2011. We first tested the system and made some adjustments before our pianos were able to connect and play together. Our digital pianos interfaced, and my music played on a Clavinova in Tuscon, AZ, sounded through his keyboard in Afghanistan. Most of our session was spent improvising and having musical conversations that we then talked about. We were able see each other using Skype at the same time that we played music together, as shown in Figure 8.3.

Figure 8.3: Yamaha teaching artist and a U.S. Soldier in Afghanistan connecting remotely

As the CW4 was very busy during the remainder of his deployment, our meetings were sporadic, but we always looked forward to them. Sessions typically took place after midnight in Afghanistan, after the CW4 had worked a 14-hour shift. He expressed that music was the best way to end his day and that he was grateful to achieve his mission of being able to use music as an outlet for emotional release. The CW4 has now retired from the military and continues to enjoy music with his family. We keep in touch with each other through technology and will hopefully meet in person one day. Music has no boundaries!

PART 2: EDUCATION AND TRAINING OF MUSIC THERAPY TELEHEALTH AND VIRTUAL COMMUNITY MUSIC MODELS

Karen Wacks

Training and education of telehealth in music therapy curriculum

The rapid growth of music therapy telehealth has created the need to train students in understanding new delivery methods of music therapy. This encompasses a holistic continuum of care comprised of in-person and online sessions that expand our understanding of using technology for collaborative music-making. This shift requires that students adapt their clinical practice, adjust delivery of treatment, and gain awareness of innovative technologies that they are trained and competent in using. With respect to the groundwork of music therapy telehealth and the quick shift that music therapists, interns, and students across the globe have made due to COVID-19, this practice innovation is shaping the future of music therapy. Therefore, competencies for music therapy telehealth have been created to inform training needs for continued adaptation and integration into music therapy academic curricula which will best prepare students to succeed across professional situations. This mirrors ongoing shifts in healthcare through respecting patients' unique needs.

The American Music Therapy Association (AMTA) has continued to review and establish competency-based standards for ensuring the quality of education and clinical training in the field of music therapy. As music therapy evolves in both clinical and research realms, new information is provided (e.g., telehealth), and the competency requirements must be re-evaluated regularly to ensure consistency with current trends and needs of the profession and to reflect the growth of the knowledge base of the profession (American Music Therapy Association, 2013). Table 8.2 presents adapted music therapy telehealth competencies for students and interns that were developed by Berklee College of Music in 2013 as part of a practicum class that was utilizing telehealth and remote community music models to interface with students in Lira, Uganda. This collaboration will be elaborated on throughout this chapter.

Table 8.2: Adapted music therapy telehealth competencies for students and interns (by Karen Wacks at Berklee College of Music in 2013)

1. Define the appropriate applications of music therapy telehealth for the individuals, families, communities, the healthcare team, healthcare organizations, and the broader population.
2. Define the limitations presented by the use of music therapy telehealth for the constituents.
3. Cite the differences between music therapy telehealth and standard healthcare delivery.
4. Describe common applications of both outpatient and inpatient music therapy telehealth.
5. Identify and demonstrate basic working knowledge of available telehealth platforms.
6. Perform basic troubleshooting of common network, telecommunications, connection, audio, picture, and call quality issues.
7. Examine regulatory standards and ethical principles of virtual healthcare.
8. Describe the role of the music therapy telehealth facilitator on the interprofessional team and understand the roles and responsibilities of each team member.
9. Summarize strategies for using appropriate client service skills, cultural awareness, and electronic and ethical protocols in coordinating telehealth services.

Ethical considerations of music therapy telehealth

Because our AMTA academic institutions follow the Standards for Education and Clinical Training, the Association's standards are based on a vision of the future for music therapy education and clinical training. In establishing and maintaining these standards, music therapists have a responsibility related to education and clinical training in relationship to the outside world that includes patients, professionals of other disciplines, and treatment settings. The AMTA Code of Ethics does not explicitly address telehealth practice regulations; however, some of the items pertaining to patient safety can be adapted to support and inform telehealth facilitation, as indicated by Vaudreuil *et al.* (2020b):

> **2.1** act with the best interest of clients in mind at all times. **3.12** exercise caution and professional judgment in all electronic, written, verbal, and inferred communications being especially aware of electronic messages and potential public access. **4.2** use resources available to them to enhance and better their practice. **5.3** use caution, critical thinking, and strong consideration of the best available evidence when incorporating new and evolving interventions and technologies into their practice, education, or supervision.
>
> In addition, music therapists engaging in telehealth can use the ethical decision-making models in Appendix II of the American Music Therapy Association Code of Ethics to help inform decisions regarding telehealth practice. (AMTA as cited in Vaudreuil *et al.*, 2020b, p.7)

Community-building through telehealth: connecting liberated child soldiers in Uganda with college students in Boston

In February 2013, I was invited by Samite Mulondo, Executive Director of the non-profit Musicians for World Harmony (2015), to travel to Northern Uganda and explore the use of blending performance and music therapy as part of a feasibility study on psychosocial development of liberated child soldiers. Staff and care providers at an aid-based training center in Lira were exploring different approaches to promote assimilation and reintegration both inter- and intra-personally as well as mindfulness, spiritual development, and relaxation. To address these and other life transitions and issues with societal reintegration, Samite and I used music therapy strategies integrated into dance and music experientials that were performed by the ex-child soldiers.

As in most music therapy programs, the initiative started with an assessment. Counselors were involved to discuss the needs of the children. Using both music therapy and performance techniques, the arts were used to explore therapeutic strategies and determine physical and emotional strengths and limitations. Cultural exchange through performance was key to the development of trust across cultures, and active music-making and dance were presented interactively. A major consideration was how to maintain the relationships and provide opportunities for ongoing partnerships; therefore, an effort to sustain this initiative was the integration of undergraduate music therapy students enrolled in a community music therapy practicum course, under the direction of myself and Dr. Peggy Codding.

Using the technological platforms of Skype and Google Hangout, a model of sustainability for continuation of treatment was created. When doing any collaborative global work, staying connected is often the most challenging yet vital component in achieving success. Technology provided an opportunity for both the students in Uganda and at Berklee to exchange information and develop goal-based interventions to continue fostering authentic relationships. Through these virtual platforms, music activities were shared and evaluated, and treatment plans were designed. Participants on both sides engaged in learning and growth, which expanded their worldviews, and understanding of themselves and others. Berklee students listened to and worked with a very sensitive group of clients who had experienced diverse and complex levels of trauma, and participants in Uganda expanded relationships of trust and connection. The virtual classroom brought new insight of real-life experiences and integrated a thematic concept into academic areas while incorporating a wide variety of engaging and hands-on learning experiences.

Summary

Technology has enabled multiple possibilities and potential for remote delivery of music therapy and music engagement. These opportunities have positioned the field of music therapy to be a relevant discipline on a level playing field with traditional and complementary healthcare services. Music therapy telehealth provides a compelling alternative to conventional acute, chronic, and preventive care, and has yielded preliminary data indicating improvement in clinical outcomes. In the industrialized world, it is likely that telehealth and telemedicine will continue to move healthcare delivery from the hospital or clinic into the home and community, as supported and mandated by current policy and programming in military, veteran, and civilian healthcare systems. Telehealth integration also brings awareness and access to global issues and opportunities to patients where music therapy may have been previously excluded in the treatment plan. Music therapy telehealth exemplifies the importance of music used within the clinical treatment model and compels providers to incorporate music therapy as an essential component of both in-person and remote care.

SECTION III

Expansion Efforts and Military Music Therapy Research

Chapter 9

From Clinic to Community: The Social Impact of Music

MACK BAILEY, DEMI BULLOCK, JASON DANLEY, AND BARBARA REUER

PART 1: RESOUNDING JOY SEMPER SOUND MILITARY MUSIC THERAPY PROGRAM

Demi Bullock, Jason Danley, and Barbara Reuer

Introduction

Demi Bullock

As a composer, musician, neuroscience enthusiast, health and wellness consultant, social sciences aficionado, and United States (U.S.) Marine Corps Veteran, I am a supporter of interdisciplinary health models and an advocate of creative arts therapies. My educational endeavors encompass everything from psychology to music technology to behavioral neuroscience to the intersection of music therapy, acute and chronic traumatic stress, and traumatic brain injury (TBI). My professional experiences include working alongside board-certified music therapists to develop, implement, and facilitate military music therapy and recreational music programming across the U.S. Additionally, my musical knowledge includes proficiency on numerous instruments, music theory, composition, orchestration, and music for wellness practices. Overall, I am a firm believer in personal growth and learning across the lifespan.

I picked up the guitar at the age of 15 and since then have had an interesting relationship with music that has followed me across the world. I joined the Marine Corps in December of 2007. I deployed to Afghanistan as an individual augmentee from October 2008 to May 2009 and deployed a second time from October 2010 until March 2011. I had a guitar with me for the majority of my time in the service. For me, playing the guitar provided a healthy, creative outlet in an environment where emotional expressivity and creativity were stifled.

At times, it also provided a unifying force for social bonding. For example, service members would stop by to listen when I played in the barracks lounge and I would participate in jam sessions with fellow Marines or corpsmen. I even taught guitar basics on occasion, when requested.

I was fortunate, both during and after my time in the military, to learn from many service members whose experiences took them on unique tours to combat zones and back. I personally know the effects that general military life, exposure to traumatic circumstances, and serving in a combat zone can have on an individual. Because of my own experiences and interactions with others, I became adept at identifying various symptoms of acute stress reactions and post-traumatic stress disorder (PTSD), depression, substance abuse, and sleep disturbances. By the outset of 2013, I had also become increasingly invested in my own musical abilities and the community outreach that assisted veterans in recovery through music. I attended a creative arts therapies event that highlighted the Semper Sound Band, a program of Resounding Joy, Inc., a music-based non-profit organization. I was invited to join the band as a peer music mentor. Through this experience, I learned more about how community music is facilitated using a clinically informed approach. After six months of participation, I became an intern with a national veteran service organization, which placed me with Resounding Joy. As an intern, I engaged in community events and gigs with the band, observed and assisted with music therapy groups, and learned the art and science of music therapist-facilitated recreational music groups, as compared with non-music therapy activities. After completing my internship, I moved to Massachusetts to further my collegiate education. It was there that I had the opportunity to work alongside a music therapist, and together we developed and implemented military music therapy programming throughout the Greater Boston Area.

While working as a director of a recreational band comprised of veterans, I quickly learned that facilitating groups was a substantially different experience than working in a peer support capacity with individual service members. Working with vulnerable populations who experience varying mental, physical, and emotional conditions in a recreational music capacity was challenging at times. There were specific skills and areas of additional knowledge that I had to acquire to successfully facilitate music groups and individual lessons. These included: making informed musical selections; identifying when to use different musical exercises; adapting teaching methods; knowing when to consult a clinician; and understanding and implementing the iso-principle. The iso-principle is specific to music therapy and was coined by a music therapist pioneer in the 1950s. It refers to a technique by which music is matched with the mood of a client, then gradually altered to affect desired mood states (Heiderscheit &

Madson, 2015). I realized that more formal education was required to continue this work successfully. My educational pursuits have yielded a Bachelor of Arts in interdisciplinary studies with a focus on trauma, music, and mental health from the University of Massachusetts Amherst. I also completed an advanced professional certificate in general music studies from Berklee College of Music Online, and I am currently in pursuit of a Master of Music in music technology from Southern Utah University. My past and present educational and work experiences have helped me to grow personally, professionally, and musically. I have gained unique musical perspectives, including how music therapy can inform recreational music programming, the benefits of performance-based military music therapy, and how music supports the clinic to community continuum.

Resounding Joy, Inc.: enhancing the human experience through music

Demi Bullock and Barbara Reuer

Resounding Joy, Inc. (RJoy) is a non-profit organization based in San Diego, California. RJoy enhances the human experience through therapeutic applications of music, uplifting individuals and families with challenging conditions, helping people achieve their goals, and supporting health and wellness throughout the community. Since its inception in 2004, RJoy has created many programs that provide specialized services to diverse populations. For example, the Ariana Miller Healing Notes program offers sliding scale or free music therapy to medically fragile children and their families. Music therapists provide bedside visits to hospitalized children, group music therapy sessions at partner non-profits, and in-home sessions for eligible clientele. RJoy's Community Connections initiative provides music programs for first responders, homeless populations, at-risk teens, and older adult populations. These community-based programs provide invaluable social experiences as well as improved quality of life by fostering physical wellbeing, healthy attitudes, and enrichment for the mind, body, and spirit.

The Semper Sound Military Music Therapy program was established in 2010 with the goal of empowering service members, veterans, and their families through music. The Semper Sound program enriches and fosters musical and non-musical successes aimed at symptom management, physiological and emotional regulation, and strengthening social, occupational, and familial engagement and relationships. Music therapists integrate into rehabilitation and health and wellness programming at military installations and veteran facilities, providing effective non-invasive, music-based treatment to those struggling with mental health issues.

Semper Sound Band member testimonial

"Before beginning music therapy, I got to the point where it was hard to function as a person. I wouldn't leave the house, I had a lot of anger, and I didn't have an outlet for that anger or the frustration of waking up in the middle of the night, and not having anywhere to put that. Now I have this tool of music and music has given me a way to process a lot of things. Music allows us to have words to some things that maybe we don't even know what they are yet." Semper Sound Band member

The Semper Sound program began by providing a weekly music therapy group at one base in San Diego, and this was soon followed by the addition of individual sessions in 2011. By 2013, Semper Sound programming expanded across San Diego County to include individual and group music therapy services on three military installations and a Department of Veterans Affairs (VA) residential program. In 2014, RJoy launched an extension of Semper Sound in Boston, MA, called RJoy East, which included music therapy and recreational individual and group sessions for veterans in both long-term and transitional residential programs, and provided specific groups for female veterans. RJoy East engaged the community by providing music therapy workshops for veteran retreats in partnership with a non-profit organization serving military populations in Massachusetts and the music therapy department at Berklee College of Music. Figure 9.1 shows a timeline of the growth, development, and expansion of the Semper Sound program.

The integration of performance and music therapy was a natural occurrence in the Semper Sound program. Therefore, the Semper Sound Band was established for service members, veterans, community musicians, and industry professionals with the aim of community engagement via music performance. In San Diego, the Semper Sound Band included active-duty service members from multiple bases and veterans from the community. On the East Coast, the GI Jams Band consisted of veterans who resided at the VA facility served by RJoy East. Both bands included weekly rehearsals facilitated by board-certified music therapists and recreational music facilitators who supported performances on-site and in the community. Performance was often a feasible next step after completing music therapy programming, as it supported service members and veterans (re)integrating into their communities in an informed way that also promoted reciprocal awareness building of military and arts cultures. Informed by music therapy facilitation, band rehearsals and jam groups utilized a recreational music approach that integrated principles of music theory, performance techniques, skill building, and adaptive and customized music to meet the needs of participants.

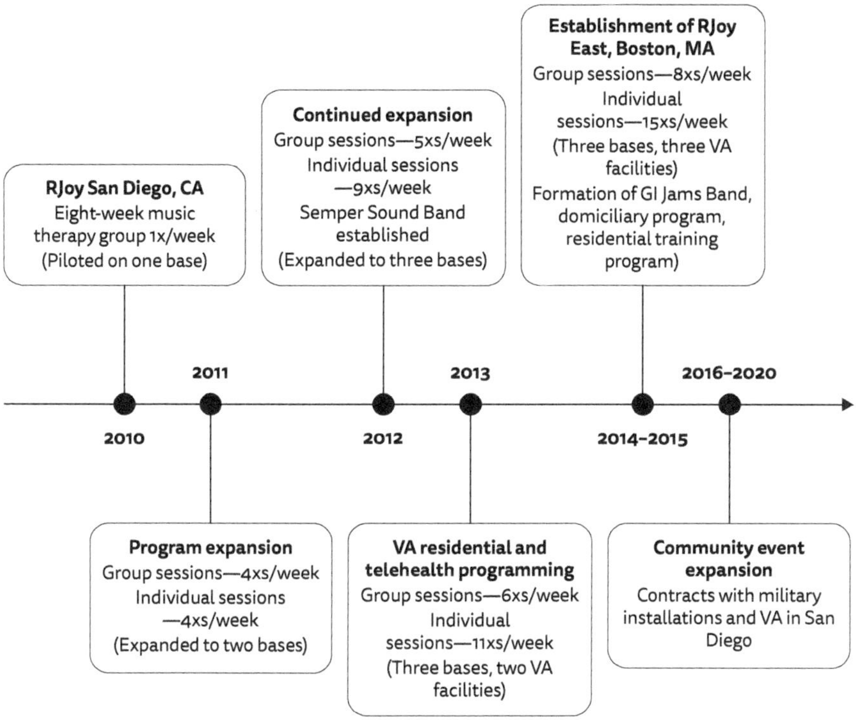

Figure 9.1: Semper Sound program timeline

Performance integration into music therapy programming with military populations enables "service members to increase awareness of self-perceptions, challenge belief systems, and view treatment as an evolving mechanism of change" (Vaudreuil *et al.*, 2019b, p.2). It supports community engagement and promotes opportunities for collaboration within and outside of military and veteran treatment facilities, thus serving as a catalyst for social transformation. Rehearsals can take the form of individual lessons, small performance groups, and whole band "prep groups." Performances occur at military installations, local community establishments, and regional venues. Audiences include families, clinicians, peers, community members, industry professionals, and military band members. Military band members often perform alongside Semper Sound program participants in support of goals such as reintegration and social engagement. Performances enable a reframing of experiences for audience members and performers. Participants are able to develop an awareness of their internal and external experiences, feel validated, and cultivate resilience. According to Vaudreuil *et al.* (2019b), audience members are able to view the results of music therapy, develop a strengths-based perspective of service members, and "understand how to construct supportive communities that better accommodate service member reintegration" (p.3). The culmination of individual and communal experiences creates a platform for further communication and development that otherwise may not have transpired.

Semper Sound Band member testimonial

"Playing music allows me to focus on something that is positive and fun. Preparing for and performing with the group allows me to set goals that are attainable and rewarding. More importantly for me, music evokes emotions that have been suppressed throughout my military career. My involvement with the Semper Sound Band has helped me to better understand an unseen injury that I (and many combat veterans) carry."
A.J.F. Bautista, USN Retired

From active duty to veteran and clinic to community: a service member's journey

Demi Bullock and Jason Danley

In the context of clinical treatment, music therapy often serves as a foundation for the transition to community music engagement via recreational music and performance. This occurs through the generalization of clinical goals (e.g., emotional regulation, improved motor coordination) to non-clinical settings. Retired U.S. Navy Corpsman, Jason Danley, experienced the clinic to community process. During an interview for this chapter, Jason shared his history, which includes his military service experiences and musical journey. His story captures a spectrum of transformation—both personally and professionally—across micro, mezzo, and macro levels.

Early military career and deployment experiences

I joined the Navy in 2006 when I was 19 years old. I was inspired to serve my country because I admired a friend serving in the military and because of the events that took place in the U.S. on September 11, 2001. After basic training, I was assigned the military occupational specialty (MOS) of Navy Hospital Corpsman, which is an MOS that aligns with my personal and professional interests and desire to help others. In 2008, I was attached to the 3rd Battalion 4th Marine Division and deployed with them to Iraq. This was my first deployment and my assignment on a daily basis included foot patrols. I would treat the medical conditions of the Marines I was deployed with as well as civilians in the local community. Less than a year later, I was deployed again, at which time I spent seven months in Afghanistan. After returning from my second deployment, I started to struggle with readjusting and found myself to be irritable and angry, which was not reflective of my usual mood or disposition. Thoughts of deployment became more prevalent and I experienced difficulty sleeping. With so many things going on, I found myself getting overwhelmed, was referred to psychotherapy, and diagnosed with PTSD.

After meeting with the therapist for a few months and being prescribed different medications to help with anxiety, depression, and sleep, I was not improving. In fact, it seemed to be making things worse. As time passed, I felt less like myself, and one day I ended up having two grand mal seizures back-to-back. I was rushed to the emergency room, and after diagnostic testing, the doctors determined that the seizures were a result of having a low tolerance for the cocktail of medications I was taking as prescribed. After my seizures, and in addition to struggling with PTSD, I began having vision problems. At first, the vision problems were not hindering my daily functioning and the doctors attributed them to stress and anxiety; however, they progressively worsened to the point where I experienced double and blurred vision daily.

Rediscovering music as therapy

Due to my low tolerance for psychopharmacology intervention, doctors were limited as to the medication that they could prescribe me, and we reached a standstill regarding treatment options. I was referred to recreational therapy at a local military treatment facility. I started hiking, cycling, surfing, and overall feeling rejuvenated by getting back to doing the activities that I always enjoyed. One day, I saw a music therapy group listed as an option. Prior to military service, I played the bass, but I hadn't played for a long time, and so, as I had reclaimed my outdoor activities, I thought this would be an excellent opportunity to re-engage with my lost love of music. I really didn't know what to expect of music therapy, but I imagined it would be like other therapies—sitting in a chair, listening to soft music, and talking about my "problems."

It was nothing like I imagined or expected. The music therapist had drums, guitars, and a stereo, and we ended up doing a lyric analysis of Bob Marley's "Redemption Song" in the first group I attended. We dived into the music, relating to the lyrics, and feeling the interplay between the melody and rhythm. It provided the opportunity for the music to speak to me and for me to speak to others about how music impacted me. I was able to express how I was feeling, process what I was going through, and explore the emotions I was experiencing—all of which many combat veterans lose touch with. The more I learned and got involved with music therapy, the more I realized how much it was helping me. The music therapist would assign homework and that's how my family was able to get involved; they even attended some music therapy sessions with me. I can honestly say that the shared love of music helped strengthen our family. The more involved I became with music therapy, the better I was feeling about many aspects of my life. I started playing bass guitar again and was inspired to explore performance. To further this goal, I joined the Semper Sound Band in 2011, through which I met other service members and veterans who played music and performed as a team, playing gigs in the community.

The continued impact of music post-service

I medically retired from the Navy in October 2012 and continued to play with the Semper Sound Band, which became a band of brothers and sisters who shared similar life experiences and were bonded through music. Often when veterans leave the military, they lose the feeling of camaraderie and it's tough to get it back. The Semper Sound Band allowed that camaraderie to continue. Along this journey of music therapy and the Semper Sound Band, I was inspired to write my own music. I started creating hip-hop beats with a fellow band member, Ben. I would write the beats and music, and he would write the lyrics. "The Cycle" was the first song we collaborated on. After listening to the beat, Ben asked me what I wanted the lyrics to be about. I wanted the song to reflect our shared experiences since we were working on it together. At the time, we were both struggling with depression and anxiety, and we talked about our experiences. These are the lyrics of the chorus that Ben wrote:

> People say this life's a blessing—
> Then why are so many people stressin'?
> Pumped up on meds to fix their heads that are messed with
> Only to perpetuate the cycle of depression.

The lyrics of the chorus really stood out for me, because that's the cycle that I was in before I had my seizures. They spoke volumes between both Ben and me because we had had different paths in the military and different experiences and injuries, but we came together through collaborating on this song and were able to collectively express what we were going through. This song is also significant because it was the first song that I performed live with the Semper Sound Band. Ben wasn't feeling well the day of the show, so I performed it alone, which sparked my interest and pursuit of writing and performing hip-hop music, lyrics, and beats as my main form of therapy. I've always loved hip-hop and rap music since childhood but had never thought of writing or performing it. The Semper Sound Band concert inspired me to pursue performance and, since then, it's been an effective way of coping for me.

Reflecting back

Another original song, "Reflections," was the first song that I wrote both the music and lyrics for, with the guidance of the music therapist. She helped me musically portray a journey through the process of joining the military, experiences from both deployments, and how the second deployment was a turning point in my life. We specifically focused on events related to my deployment to Afghanistan and returning to my new wife and son. Here's an excerpt from "Reflections":

> Now that I'm back/Reflections run deep/My mind races/Can't get any sleep/
>
> The days get better with family/In their presence/I feel peace/
>
> Still have—good and bad days/Take them in stride—finding positive ways/To maintain the pride, not in vain/I pass down to my son/Caleb's his name.

Even today, as a veteran, I reflect on my deployments from time to time, as many veterans do. Yes, the reflections still run deep, at times my mind still races, but the most important thing is that the days continue to get better. I feel most at peace when I am around my beautiful and supportive wife and three sons. Involving my family with the camaraderie of the band and music therapy sessions motivated us to use music together and bring it into our home. My oldest son, Caleb, and I co-compose music and make hip-hop beats, and all three of my children have adopted music into their lives. We all play instruments and record music together, and Caleb now writes his own songs as well.

Moving forward with music

From 2013 to 2018, I focused on writing my own music. Then, in December of 2018, I reconnected with RJoy and started working as the Semper Sound Band coordinator. I assisted the Semper Sound Band director in rebuilding the band, managing equipment, booking gigs, networking, and also playing bass with the band. Through that process, I built camaraderie with a new group of service members, veterans, and civilians, which was something that I had missed. We played at various community establishments, such as veterans' retirement homes, and events including the Creative Forces Pop-up Community Creative Arts Cafés. I met more veterans with shared interests of the arts and got more veterans connected with the Semper Sound Band. The combined power of this work reinforced the passion to continue writing my own music and inspired self-reflection on my new place in the band, my community in general, and on music. I realized that I was serving as a mentor helping active-duty military and veterans who were new to music therapy. Because of my experiences in music therapy, I understood where they were at in their recovery and helped them realize how to use music in processing their military experiences, rehabilitation, and transitions.

Seeing how music therapists work with the military—from both sides of the process—and gaining the understanding of the power of music therapy, I knew how much of an impact I was making working for RJoy and realized that I could make an even greater impact in the military community by pursuing music as an academic venture. I am now a full-time student and musician, with plans to pursue a degree in music.

Tying it all together

Back in 2011, I never thought that music therapy would be so influential in my life and help guide me on the path that I am on. Starting out, I never expected to be working for a music therapy company or pursuing a music degree. These experiences have taught me how important music is to me, personally, and how music therapy can have a lasting impact on the military community. A service member once told me that this program saved their life and got them out of the darkest places. I resonate with this, as it helped me in these ways as well. I will continue my journey and educational pursuits, doing my part to make sure that access to music therapy and recreational music programs continues and expands for military populations.

Summary

Engagement in the Semper Sound Military Music Therapy program and the Semper Sound Band provided benefits that were unique, versatile, effective, and long lasting. Participation provided positive coping mechanisms and support that far surpassed scheduled clinical sessions and band rehearsals. It extended into numerous aspects of the lives of service members and veterans—personal, familial, social, and occupational. Jason's story exemplifies this extension of support and how powerful music therapy can be as he described the results of his participation that began at the individual level and expanded to collaboration with his peers, family, and ultimately the community at large.

If we reflect on these experiences, it is apparent how important the process is for each individual, and that the product—a result of what can be an attempt to process—truly reflects growth, hard work, perseverance, and dedication. The culmination of establishing and developing musical abilities, working with others, socializing even when one may not initially want to, improving self-awareness, self-esteem, cognitive and emotional wellness, and having the courage to express oneself in a public venue is an incredible demonstration of one's personal evolution.

Semper Sound Military Music Therapy participant testimonial

"I am a 13-year-retired disabled veteran of the best navy in the world. I have been a part of the music therapy program provided by Resounding Joy for over a year. I had almost given up on life. With the help of the Resounding Joy music therapist, I now have a purpose in life again. There is no telling how many lives have already been saved by this music program, and certainly our band has helped brighten the lives of many. Veterans helping veterans saving lives through music." William Z, USN Veteran

PART 2: MUSIC THERAPY OF THE ROCKIES VETERAN RETREATS

Mack Bailey

Introduction: music as a divine inspiration

Music has been an integral part of my life since I can remember. I grew up listening to my father's folk albums and learned to sing and perform by listening to Glenn Yarbrough and the Limeliters, The Smothers Brothers, John Denver, to name a few. When I was 15, I played the courier in a community production of *1776*, which led me to attend the North Carolina School of the Arts as a junior in high school. This experience gave me the opportunity and education to understand what music meant to me, how I resonated with it, and how it completed me. In 1987 I joined a band, The Hard Travelers, which used music to help others through organizing benefit concerts. Over the course of 19 years, we raised over $11 million for cystic fibrosis research and other charitable organizations. In 1999, I was in a marriage that was falling apart. As things continued to unravel, I experienced depression and started engaging in negative behaviors that affected my wellbeing. I never sought help nor shared my feelings and at the time did not see divorce as an option. Much like the image and persona of the warfighter, I felt that above all, I was supposed to be the strong father and husband, and just "get over it." As my thoughts grew darker, I realized that if this was what life was going to be like indefinitely, I did not know how much longer I wanted to keep going.

One day I found myself standing in my daughter's room pondering a final message to leave with her to remember me. The first thought that came to my mind was "just because you can't see me doesn't mean I'm not there." I became intrigued, one could say inspired, by this thought, and I started singing the phrase. A phrase became two phrases, then a verse, and before I knew it, I had written a song. It was emotional and raw. I found myself immersed in the process of songwriting, as it seemingly structured my thoughts and helped me process them in a creative and cathartic way. They were no longer free-form bursts of darkness whirling in my head like a tornado.

After I completed the song, I realized I had deciphered the dire helplessness I was feeling for so long; writing the song saved my life, but I still did not own up to the story. I played the song for others, who openly shared what it meant to them, but I still didn't share my own story. After the song was out there, I still struggled with my purpose in life; however, through a stream of fortunate events, I started working for a company that provided music services to nursing homes in the Washington/Baltimore area. Seeing and experiencing the power of music on a one-to-one level gave me a purpose I had never known existed. It was not about writing hit songs and getting record deals. It was music and healing—a perfect pairing, and one that ignited a passion within me to dedicate my life to making a difference in other people's lives.

In 2011, I chose to end my career as a touring musician to pursue my true passion of using music for healing. I enrolled at Colorado State University in Fort Collins and earned my master's in music therapy. I was grateful that the curriculum was founded on the principles of neurologic music therapy. During my degree program, I learned more about how the brain responds to trauma and music. The foundation from the music therapy program at Colorado State informed and inspired the creation, development, and implementation of Music Therapy of the Rockies (MTR), a non-profit organization that I founded. MTR provides evidenced-based music therapy retreats for veterans diagnosed with PTSD and includes a continuing education course for music therapists called Music and the PTSD Brain in Military Veterans. The remainder of this chapter provides a description of services offered at MTR retreats and shares feedback from veteran participants about the impact of their experiences.

Background of MTR

The foundational philosophy of MTR is based on the concept that "it's not what you get out of the music, but what the music gets out of you!" Goals of the MTR retreats are aligned with this notion and aim to assist veterans in re-framing their stories through songwriting by pairing them with professional songwriters to shape their experiences through music and lyrics. We engage veterans in interactive music designed to improve cognition, promote healthy communication, and assist in the development of coping skills. MTR retreats use a structured yet flexible approach to music-making and songwriting in which veterans gain autonomy, while being supported throughout the process. This tactic yields itself to encouraging reminiscence and sharing of experiences with safeguards in place that scaffold the musical process to manage risk of various potential triggers. Veterans at our retreats often express that in their day-to-day lives they do not feel that their voices are heard, and that they are not empowered to take an active role in their rehabilitation. Songwriting gives people a voice, music-making is empowering, and combining lyrics and music into performance of songs allows for voices to be heard.

Hirschi has conceptualized the categorization of social bonds for decades and identifies four elements of social bonds: 1) attachment; 2) commitment; 3) involvement; and 4) belief (2017). These components are addressed during the retreats through social interaction, dedication to improve one's situation, engagement, and trust in the people supporting these processes. These factors play an integral role in normalizing the veterans' perceptions regarding life after military service. We adapted MTR practices in response to COVID-19, which has increased experiences of isolation and disconnect. Socialization is maintained through virtual gatherings of veterans from all retreat locations. One veteran shared, "These virtual sessions help me connect with other people during this time of social distancing" (Charles, verbal communication, May 18, 2020).

Studies have shown that songwriting demonstrates a reduction of PTSD symptoms in numbing and hyperarousal scales as well as depressive symptoms and stress reactivity (Hirschberg *et al.*, 2020). Furthermore, collective music-making has the power to transform (Vaudreuil *et al.*, 2019b). At MTR, we have often found that the most effective catalyst for change is to provide veterans with a safe and supported space in which they openly explore and access new experiences that may help them in their recovery. In some cases, we have worked with veterans who are resistant to or weary of traditional therapies. The systems they rely on for medical care are oversaturated and often understaffed, which impacts access to care. There can be long wait times for appointments and the time in between is critical in preventing isolation by using healthy coping strategies and engaging in positive activities (Campbell, 2016).

Theoretical frameworks of MTR retreats

The design of the MTR retreats is developed from a neurologic perspective. We design music experiences to focus on two areas of the brain, including the prefrontal cortex and the amygdala (the limbic system). The prefrontal cortex is where executive functioning takes place regarding attention, focus, and decision making. The limbic system is where memories and emotions are stored and processed. In the brain of someone with PTSD, neuroimaging reveals a hypoactive prefrontal cortex and a hyperactive amygdala and limbic system (Shin *et al.*, 2006). This can translate to actions that drive decisions based on memories and emotions rather than looking at situations from rational perspectives. This helps explain why some veterans socially isolate, physically position themselves with a wall or barrier at their backs, and may experience prolonged hypervigilance. Picture a seesaw where the prefrontal cortex is low on the ground and the amygdala is in the air. Each of the techniques we incorporate throughout the three-day retreats is designed to counteract this situation by using the properties of music to address these imbalances.

A neurologic and mindfulness approach to stress responses

Brain scans of neural activation and responses to music show increased activity in the prefrontal cortex, especially during creative activities. The basic concept of structure in music is valuable in organizing the thoughts of the PTSD brain (Beaty, 2015). Mindfulness techniques such as deep breathing, active listening to music, and goal setting provide the veterans with coping skills to address symptoms of PTSD through slowing the physiological responses of PTSD. MTR retreats incorporate music into mindfulness exercises. For example, the veterans are encouraged to identify the first physiological reaction to a situation (e.g., increased heart rate, sweating, physical tension such as a clenched fist or jaw). These responses are initial indicators that stress is building, and if attention can be brought to the forefront at the first noticeable sign of stress, then coping skills can be applied and the effects of the episode may greatly diminish. By identifying physical reactions and gaining control over somatic responses, the veteran is better positioned to address the situation causing distress. It is very difficult to address symptoms as they are happening in the moment. Many veterans we work with report difficulty focusing due to memories that are seemingly "swirling around in their heads like a tornado" and other stress responses; these can be debilitating if not addressed. Techniques such as active listening and deep breathing to music provide opportunities to acknowledge and manage these symptoms.

Sensory integration

Active listening allows the brain to pinpoint location and qualities of sounds and therefore shapes how we respond to them. I remember when I was at an Alison Krauss concert at Red Rocks Amphitheatre in Morrison, CO, and her acoustic band stood around one microphone as they all played a song. I concentrated on the mandolin player and what he was playing, and I could hear him above the other instruments; he appeared to move closer to me while the others remained stationary. He became the visual and auditory focus while the other band members seemed to blend into the background. This is not because the mandolin player physically moved forward or because his amplification was turned up, it is because I focused on him above the other instruments. At our retreats, one of the exercises is to sit and listen to the sounds around us. MTR retreats are held in an outdoor area, such as a farm, surrounded by sounds ranging from birds singing to the wind rustling in the trees. This environment is well-suited for mindfulness exercises, as it allows participants to be present and in the moment. We acknowledge that mind wandering occurs, and that is okay. The goal is to realize when mind wandering starts happening, acknowledge it, and then find a new or familiar sound to focus on. Over the course of the exercise, distractions may present themselves numerous times, but eventually participants are able to start learning and implementing skills in the moment, which helps them to gain control of mind wandering and create techniques to help address distractibility.

Biochemical considerations

It is also notable that daydreams or wanderings of thought are fed by the brain. We start with an initial thought and then the mind takes off, creating scenarios, interactions, or conversations that we play out in our mind. Dopamine is a chemical neurotransmitter responsible for signaling between the nerve cells of the brain. We usually think of dopamine as a reward chemical or the "feel-good" happiness chemical, but when your thoughts turn dark, your brain still feeds off dopamine. Dopamine is not capable of distinguishing between our perception of happiness and what we want in our thoughts. Without an effort to control our thoughts, our minds can go to very dark places and still be rewarded by the dopamine. One of the most frequent comments we hear from veterans suffering from PTSD is that they want their lives "normalized." MTR retreats provide experiences that allow participants to feel comfortable and supported while engaging in treatment approaches different than traditional rehabilitation disciplines. The more we can normalize how we promote recovery, the more veterans can feel normalized.

Applied positive reframing

In addition to neurobiological and mindfulness practices, we use positive reframing exercises to contextually shape music experiences that build positive strategies and formulate healthy mindsets. For example, during military service, veterans had a weapon (usually a rifle), which was an essential instrument for survival. At MTR retreats, each veteran receives a new acoustic guitar and we present it as a new instrument to assist with survival outside the military. Our goal is not to just teach songs and chords, but rather to create a bond with a safe coping mechanism to access when symptoms arise. For example, the first guitar-based activity we do is to place the index finger of the right hand under the high E string and pull it up towards the B string without letting go—feeling the tension and then lowering the finger while still holding the string. Repeating this exercise a few times has led to more than one veteran comparing that sensation to their trigger finger, which connects to the military experience. These shared music-making opportunities often lead to conversations about lived experiences. Veterans have shared testimonies such as, "I don't remember my life before I joined the military" or "It took me three years after I discharged to get used to hearing my first name again." Another veteran added, "You don't realize the intimacy of your first name until you don't have it." There are so many unique situations and each one furthers our goal to help veterans reintegrate in life outside the military.

Songwriting

As the veterans become familiar with their new instrument, we introduce songwriting to assist in reshaping their narratives, based on their lived experiences. The therapeutic songwriting part of the retreat gives the veterans a chance to reframe their stories and take control of them, rather than the stories controlling them. The process of songwriting helps structure and clarify thoughts, and as the songwriter and veteran explore what stories to base song topics on, the sharing is part of the structure as the songwriter seeks clarity and continuity. Our goal is for everyone to be in the best position for success; therefore, the pairing of veterans and songwriters is crucial. Music therapists assess veterans at the beginning of the retreat (e.g., welcoming dinner), which enables the music therapist to determine preferred styles of music, personalities, and level of PTSD symptoms. In addition, knowing the professional songwriters' styles and personalities is essential in creating an appropriate veteran–songwriter pairing. There is also a level of consideration that we take in creating veteran–songwriter pairings regarding gender, race, and personalities. We aim to create a supportive and structured environment in which veterans and their families can engage outside their comfort levels, as appropriate for each participant.

Program logistics and retreat schedule: veteran and family participation

MTR retreats last two and a half days, starting on a Friday night with a welcome barbeque and ending on a Sunday with a closing concert. The welcoming event serves multiple purposes. For veteran and family member participants, it informs them what they will be doing throughout the retreat and establishes familiarity in a new and unfamiliar environment. For MTR staff and music therapists, it provides the opportunity to assess participants and pair them with a songwriter who best fits their musical abilities, preferences, and goals. This is crucial in the relationship-building aspect of the therapeutic songwriting process and can shape the entire retreat experience.

The retreat experiences run for approximately eight hours each day, 20 hours total. Table 9.1 details the full retreat schedule. Participants do not stay overnight unless the location is remote and does not accommodate daily travel. We find it helpful for participants to return home after each day and start putting the therapeutic skills they learn into practice after the first day. For example, we have witnessed numerous examples of participants experiencing changes between Saturday and Sunday. Their appearances and verbal communications reflect a decrease in emotional stress. On two different occasions, a veteran brought their service dog with them on Friday and Saturday, but not on Sunday. When asked why they did not bring their dog on Sunday, they responded that they felt safe, and did not feel they needed the additional support. When asked about other times that they leave their service animal at home, one reported "Never" and the other stated, "I think I went to the store once without him."

Table 9.1: MTR retreat schedule for veterans

Day 1	Time	Event
	5:00–7:00pm	Opening dinner for participants and families
Day 2	**Time**	**Event**
	8:30– 9:00am	Breakfast
	9:00–10:00am	Mindfulness circle
	10:00am–12:00pm	Half the group participates in guitar workshops, half the group works with songwriters
	12:00–1:00pm	Lunch
	1:00–3:00pm	The groups switch between guitar and songwriting workshops
	3:00–4:00pm	End of day discussion and processing

cont.

Day 3	Time	Event
	8:30–9:00am	Breakfast
	9:00–10:00am	Mindfulness circle
	10:00am–12:00pm	Half the group participates in guitar workshops, half the group works with songwriters
	12:00–1:00pm	Lunch
	1:00–3:00pm	The groups switch between guitar and songwriting workshops
	3:00–4:00pm	Wrap up of the retreat with final goal setting, concert preparation, post-retreat surveys, and retreat processing
	4:30–6:00pm	Closing concert featuring veterans' songs for participants, families, support teams, and guests

Setting the stage for post-retreat success

Appropriate termination is crucial in ensuring optimal potential for ongoing and long-term success. On the final day of the retreat, the veterans engage in experiences that support retreat closure. These include: 1) a final goal-setting exercise for post-retreat skill implementation planning; 2) preparations for the closing concert; and 3) completion of a post-retreat survey. MTR retreats directly serve the veterans and their families through music experiences, while also recognizing the importance of their external support systems such as social networks, occupational environments, educational systems, religion and spirituality, communities, and society in general. If we can improve the situation for veterans and their families, then we are on the path to improving our community and society as a whole. The detailed elements of retreat termination that MTR employs are provided below.

Final goal-setting exercise

Goal setting is critical in helping the veteran establish objectives following the retreat. They are asked to write goals with clear objectives and action steps. Action steps are essential in guiding the veterans towards commitment to achieving their goals. For example, during this exercise, one veteran posed a goal of becoming a songwriter. Since he had written a song during the retreat, it was validated that he had already achieved becoming a songwriter. This helped him shape his goal to come back to a future retreat as one of the songwriters. His action step was to continue writing songs between the end of this retreat and when he came back to a future retreat as a songwriter.

Preparing for and participation in the closing concert

The concert provides an opportunity to showcase songs written during the retreat. Participation in the concert is completely voluntary; however, we have found that the veterans gain increased confidence during the retreat through learning a different method to tell their story. Therefore, veterans commonly opt to perform their songs, or at least introduce them and delegate someone else to play them. Each concert is digitally recorded and the recordings are given to the veterans as a take-away from the weekend, along with the guitar they have trained on throughout the retreat. We find that song recordings are an effective tool for veterans to use for constructive learning and self-improvement purposes as well as providing them with the opportunity to relive their and other veterans' performance experiences. An aspect of our retreat program is that a unique song is written with each veteran, so each retreat produces up to 12 songs. To help protect the ownership of the song, MTR Healing Music and MTR Retreat Music were established as publishing companies to represent and protect the veterans' publisher's share of the song. The songwriters retain their writer's and publisher's share and the veterans retain their writer's share, while MTR retains the publisher's share of the song.

Retreat evaluation

We administer a pre-survey that is implemented as part of retreat registration and provides a baseline for each participant. This survey is based on the PCLM PTSD scale for military and veteran populations. The questions focus on PTSD-related symptoms such as upsetting memories, physiological reactions, avoidance, isolation, distorted cognitions, and other PTSD symptoms. Each veteran participates in post-retreat surveys that help MTR collect data to learn what worked well and how to improve subsequent retreats. The post-survey also contains questions regarding changes in PTSD symptoms. As previously mentioned, MTR staff observe changes within the two days, and this is often reflected in the responses to post-retreat surveys. We realize that this data may be biased due to the power of the retreat and the participants completing the survey on-site; therefore, we also administer a follow-up survey six months after the retreat to glean information pertaining to skill generalization and continuation of music engagement, and to identify any trends in reporting. Results to date show marked improvement in the most extreme responses to PTSD.

Continuing education for music therapists

As an addition to the program that runs the veteran retreats, MTR is an approved provider of Continuing Music Therapy Education courses by the Certification Board for Music Therapists. This additional curriculum was developed to share the research that is the basis of the program and to provide a hands-on learning opportunity to equip music therapists to work with veterans, aimed at expanding music therapy programming with veterans on a national scale. We can also identify music therapists with similar passions and abilities for this work who can be trained to run MTR retreats. Increasing the number of retreats will benefit more veterans nationwide. Music therapists learn the targeted approaches to MTR retreats (neuroscience, mindfulness, etc.), foundational information about creating a retreat, and experience partnered songwriting with other music therapists to learn the art of collaboration and co-writing. During the MTR retreats with veterans and families, music therapists engage in songwriting with the veteran–songwriter pairs to help guide more difficult aspects of the story exploration and document observations of the veterans' behaviors. Music therapists are also tasked to lead some aspects of the retreat, such as the mindfulness circles and the guitar workshops, assisting those that require added attention. Table 9.2 displays the Continuing Music Therapy Education schedule, which includes two days of training prior to the veteran retreat.

Table 9.2: MTR retreat schedule for music therapists

Day 1	Time	Workshops and training
	8:30–9:00am	Breakfast
	9:00–10:45am	Working with veterans and in-the-moment assessment
	10:45am–12:00pm	Effects of PTSD and music on the brain
	12:00–1:00pm	Lunch
	1:00–1:45pm	Addressing needs of clients with PTSD and TBI
	1:45–2:30pm	Mindfulness techniques
	2:30–4:00pm	Using the guitar (and other instruments) to address symptoms of PTSD and TBI
Day 2	**Time**	**Event**
	8:30–9:00am	Breakfast
	9:00–12:00am	Addressing symptoms of PTSD and TBI using songwriting experiential workshop (includes breaks)
	12:00–1:00pm	Lunch
	1:00–2:30pm	Program management and toolkit

	2:30–3:00pm	Evaluation and documentation
	3:00–4:00pm	Closing discussion, organization, observation, and documentation training
	5:00–7:00pm	Opening dinner for participants and families (start of MTR veteran retreat)
Days 3 and 4		Music therapists participate in the MTR veteran retreat (indicated in Table 9.1) to apply their new-found skills through engagement in experiential learning.

Summary

I can honestly attest that I am still here today because of the foundations of this program and I want to give every veteran I work with the same opportunity for revival and survival that I found through music. Our aim is to empower veterans who struggle to cope with normal daily routines, and ultimately lower the suicide rates of veterans. In closing, I would like to share a quote from one of the veterans who participated in an MTR retreat and whose PTSD symptoms were so severe that for many years he was unable to work towards his educational goals. He stated, "I never had the opportunity to go to school with the GI Bill. It's taken almost 15 years, but I finally am able to go to school, which was all I ever wanted to do. And I am alive and enjoying it because of this experience" (Jeff, US Army, Ret, verbal communication, October 21, 2017).

Chapter 10

Music Integration with the National Guard, Military Reserve Force, and First Responders

SSG BRITTANY COSTA

Introduction to the author

I initially joined the Army National Guard in 2006 because I needed money for college. I have re-enlisted several times for the benefits the military provides, security, camaraderie, and passion for the job. I served most of my 15 years in the Massachusetts National Guard and transferred to the Colorado National Guard in 2019. To date, I have earned the rank of Staff Sergeant (SSG). I have served as a military musician in both the 215th Army Band and the 101st Army Band. I also served on full-time orders for the Massachusetts National Guard for five years as a recruiting and marketing assistant and case coordinator for Guardsmen with mental health and physical disorders. In addition to my military career, I earned a Bachelor of Music in clarinet performance from the University of Massachusetts at Lowell, a Master of Science in arts administration from Boston University, and a Master of Music Therapy from Augsburg University. My goal is to use my diverse knowledge base and skill set to work as a full-time music therapist with military service members and veterans. My approach to music therapy is to integrate theories to help meet the client's needs in the moment. I use a combination of psychodynamic, behavioral, cognitive-behavioral, music-centered, humanistic, and resource-oriented theories to provide my clients with the best possible care.

Background of the National Guard and Reserve Force

This chapter focuses on two military components, the National Guard and Reserve, as well as their roles as first responders. National Guard and Reserve units are similar in that they are part-time military service organizations requiring service members to typically work a minimum of 39 days a year or one weekend each month and two weeks a year. Reserve units are federally controlled by the President of the United States (U.S.), whereas National Guard units are controlled by state governors. Additionally, National Guard units may be mandated to orders by the President; however, Reserve units cannot be controlled by state governors. Both National Guard and Reserve units serve their country and the communities in which they reside. Since both of these military components require their service members to work only part time, Guardsmen and Reservists can work civilian jobs and attend college. Their civilian work is often disrupted by additional responsibilities such as supplemental and leadership training, team-building and morale days, and activations in support of state and federal homeland missions, as well as overseas deployments. In the fiscal year (FY) 2019, states called up National Guard forces 235 times and 2.1 million man-days were logged in support of state and federal homeland missions (U.S. Department of Defense National Guard Bureau, 2021, p.21).

The National Guard serves under two branches of the military, the U.S. Army and the U.S. Air Force. The Reserves serve under all military branches: the U.S. Army, the U.S. Air Force, the U.S. Navy, the U.S. Coast Guard, and the U.S. Marine Corps. Some individuals join the National Guard or Reserves after completing high school or college, while others join after transitioning from active-duty military service or after working in the civilian sector. Initial training for both National Guard and Reserves is similar to that of active duty; however, continuation of training throughout one's military career is typically condensed due to the abbreviated commitment. Condensed training can be difficult for some Guardsmen and Reservists because generally it is the same amount of information, input, and output required by active-duty service members, but in much less time and without breaks during training for physical and/or mental recovery.

Historical context and purpose of National Guard, Reserves, and first responders

The National Guard was founded in 1636 in Massachusetts in order to protect the Massachusetts Bay Colonies from threats to the Commonwealth. The National Guard was composed of the North, South, and East Regiments. These units still exist in the Massachusetts National Guard (The First Muster, 2015). Although the U.S. Army was officially formed in 1775, the Army Reserves was not founded until 1908. Despite their formal establishments being centuries apart, both the National Guard and Reserves act as the reserve components for the U.S. Army, working missions both in their local communities and on domestic and international deployments. Guard and Reserve assets include search and rescue units, medical units, communications support, aviation assets, and route clearance engineers (Luckey, 2020). Guardsmen and Reservists may be activated for natural disaster support, working as first responders during community events, providing homeland security, and assisting with states of emergency. The 2020 activation of the National Guard in response to the COVID-19 global pandemic, civil unrest across America, and wildfires in California and Colorado highlight their diverse utilization. In 2020, the deployment of Guardsmen under state authorities peaked at 86,367 in June (Sonne, 2020).

As highlighted above, in the many missions that they fulfill, National Guard and Reserve members serve as first responders. First responders are individuals trained to respond and react to emergencies such as accidents, natural disasters, and terrorism. For example, in FY 2019, the National Guard responded to 63 natural disasters (U.S. Department of Defense National Guard Bureau, n.d.). Many occupations are considered first responders, including: police officers, firefighters, emergency services personnel (e.g., emergency medical technicians), healthcare workers, and trained military service members. Due to the intense and urgent nature of the work of first responders, Guardsmen, and Reservists, their lives are often at risk. This creates a stressful occupational environment, and if this stress is unaddressed, it can impact other areas of life, health, and wellbeing. Therefore, provision of health and wellness resources for all of these individuals is a high priority, but unfortunately these resources are lacking.

Healthcare considerations

The Military Healthcare System (MHS) and Veterans Health Administration (VHA) focus on treating active-duty service members and veterans; however, Guardsmen and Reservists' eligibility to the programs and services provided by these entities is varied and dependent on factors such as the status of a member on active duty and if they were activated under a state or federal mission. Guardsmen and Reservists on orders for fewer than 30 consecutive days are responsible for obtaining their own healthcare and health insurance (Kizer & Le Menestrel, 2019). Additionally, when members have both military and civilian healthcare, determining which providers they should seek care from is not always clear (Myers, 2019). While some Guardsmen and Reservists hold status as veterans that qualifies them for healthcare through the Department of Veterans Affairs (VA), not all Guardsmen and Reservists meet the service qualifications and eligibility criteria for this benefit.

Guardsmen and Reservists are expected to adhere to the same physical fitness requirements of active-duty service members, who have free access to fitness centers on military installations. Guardsmen and Reservists only have this access if they live or work near a base. Furthermore, Guardsmen and Reservists may not feel comfortable using facilities for active duty because they are not considered traditional service members (Vaudreuil, 2020). Otherwise, they are required to fund their own fitness routines as required by their military obligations. The health insurance plan offered to Guardsmen and Reservists provides access to many healthcare needs; however, unlike many civilian health insurance plans that offer a stipend for individuals paying for a fitness plan, the health insurance plan offered to Guardsmen and Reservists does not.

Mental health considerations

Healthcare does not solely pertain to physical health; it includes mental health as well. Mental health is a growing concern among military populations. According to a study by the VA (U.S. Department of Veterans Affairs 2019b), there are approximately 20 veteran suicides per day in the U.S. The study showed the suicide rate from 2005 to 2017 of veterans who were clinically diagnosed with various mental health disorders such as depression, post-traumatic stress disorder (PTSD), bipolar disorder, substance use disorder (SUD), or general mental health conditions. Although there were several spikes and dips in that 12-year gap, the suicide rate generally increased over time across all listed variables. These statistics do not include suicides of veterans not diagnosed with a mental health disorder. Looking specifically at the Guard and Reserve components, the 2018 Department of Defense (DoD) Annual Suicide Report found that the suicide rate for the National Guard and Reserve units has remained steady from 2013 to 2018 with a rate of 22.9 suicides per 100,000 Reservists and 30.6 suicides per 100,000 Guardsmen. The same study also noted while "Suicide rates for military families, the Active Component, and Reserve are comparable to U.S. population rates after accounting for age and sex; National Guard rates are higher than U.S. population after similar adjustment" (U.S. Department of Defense, 2019, p.5). However, the 2019 DoD Annual Suicide Report indicated a drop in the suicide rate for the National Guard with a rate comparable to the U.S. population and statistically down from 2017 (Cronk, 2020).

This demonstrates a severe need for resources accessible to all veterans, with and without diagnosed mental health conditions. Needed resources may include financial support, medical care, job assistance, and family support. A 2020 National Guard Bureau report identified the most widely used resources by Guardsmen:

> The Army National Guard Family Assistance Centers addressed more than 1.6

million resource and referral inquiries and outreach calls in FY18 at 400 geographically dispersed National Guard armories and Reserve centers. The services most used were finance, ID Cards/DEERS and community outreach. (U.S. Department of Defense National Guard Bureau, 2020, p.27)

National guard and reserve contributions to combat operations

Some of the causes of mental health conditions experienced by veterans are occupational or related to deployment. National Guard and Reserve contributions to combat operations are significantly impactful to the readiness and health of the fighting force of the U.S. Armed Services. In FY 2020, nearly 18,000 National Guard Soldiers were deployed in support of missions in Afghanistan, Kuwait, Bahrain, Jordan, Qatar, Ukraine, Poland, Kosovo, Eastern Europe, the Horn of Africa, Central and South America, and Sinai Peninsula. That number does not include Reservists or active-duty military. Since 9/11, the National Guard has been continuously engaged in countering violent extremist organizations and supported more than 1.1 million overseas deployments to Iraq, Afghanistan, Kuwait, the Balkans, Guantanamo Bay, Sinai, and other locations since 9/11 (U.S. Department of Defense National Guard Bureau, 2020). In addition, it has been reported that "the military has relied more heavily on Reservists than at any time since the Korean War" (Kapp & Salazar Torreon, 2018, p.2). Because of frequent deployments and other types of full-time activation, Guardsmen and Reservists experience difficulty with attaining and retaining civilian employment. The Uniformed Services Employment and Reemployment Rights Act (USERA) prohibits civilian employers from discriminating against military service members in the hiring, retention, promotion, and other processes; however, a study found that 11 percent of resumes indicating current employment by the National Guard were rejected compared with resumes indicating former National Guard employment (Figinski, 2017). Civilian employers may be hesitant to hire Guardsmen and Reservists due to the nature of unplanned and often long-term periods of time away from the civilian job. Additionally, Guardsmen and Reservists with civilian employment must balance their civilian and military duties. At times, this can result in one job taking precedence over the other, which may lead to missed opportunities or slower advancement at the subordinate job.

Not only do Guardsmen and Reservists experience difficulty with managing schedules of civilian jobs with their military duties, but they also struggle to find time for personal and professional development such as civilian sector education or training, quality time with family, and other responsibilities. The strenuous requirements of military obligations that service members face can cause homelessness, SUD, loss of employment, family strains, and other hardships (Vaudreuil, 2020). These considerations are especially heightened on return from deployment and transitioning back to home life. While active-duty service members often return to a military community where their peers have had similar experiences, during demobilization, "National Guard and Reserve members usually return to their hometowns and civilian jobs, which may not be close to any fellow unit members or military resources that can assist them with their transition or post-deployment issues" (Military OneSource, n.d.-d; Kizer & Le Menestrel, 2019, p.39). This indicates another area of need for these populations to have access to programs that foster resilience, promote health and wellness, and emphasize the importance of training coping skills and techniques to improve quality of life, therefore filling the need gap.

Military music therapy: roots to contemporary practice

According to the American Music Therapy Association (AMTA) (2014), music therapy has been rooted in the treatment of military service members since the end of World War II when service members convalescing in Army hospitals responded to live music played by community musicians (U.S. War Department, 1945). Since then, the profession of music therapy has been further developed and regulated in the facilitation of music interventions to achieve clinical goals through the therapeutic relationship of board-certified music therapists and clients. As a growing discipline, music therapy has established a scientific evidence base that spans qualitative and quantitative research studies (American Music Therapy Association, 2015). Unfortunately, only a small percentage of those studies have focused on military populations. This research gap may be due to many considerations including: music therapists' lack of formal education and training regarding military populations and culture; limitations in music therapy service provision at military treatment facilities; and the stigma of mental health treatment in military culture, which often creates a barrier for military populations to seek help. Fortunately, there are actions in place to fill these gaps. A review of music therapy and the military population was published in 2019, stating that there are about 8000 music therapists in the U.S., some of whom work directly within DoD and VA facilities and others who work in communities with active-duty military personnel, veterans, and their families (Gooding & Langston, 2019).

Publications demonstrating the use of music therapy and creative arts therapies as a part of interdisciplinary treatment in both intensive outpatient and longitudinal programs and in co-treatment with traditional disciplines with military populations show promise for wider application (Bronson *et al.*, 2018; Vaudreuil *et al.*, 2019a). These models are now being replicated at several military treatment facilities and VHA clinics across the country. Bronson and colleagues described diagnoses (e.g., PTSD, TBI) and symptoms (e.g., hyper-vigilance, sleep disturbance, memory loss) that military populations commonly experience as well as general information about the population. These publications are valuable for music therapists interested in working in military and veteran healthcare systems to learn essential information about the unique experiences and needs of military-connected populations. Furthermore, in the past five years, the number of music therapists working with service members and veterans has grown and innovative research is on the horizon.

Resources for National Guard and Reserve populations

Although Guardsmen and Reservists do not have access to all the same resources available to active-duty service members, there are multiple systems in place and resources available to ensure the health and wellbeing of these populations. Federal resources (i.e., provided through the DoD or VA) include Vet Centers, Military OneSource, and the Yellow Ribbon Reintegration Program (YRRP). Additionally, within each National Guard unit there are entities such as Family Readiness and Assistance Centers, and Directors of Psychological Health that provide service and support around resilience and mental health. Furthermore, the National Guard Bureau has implemented several initiatives in response to the findings of the 2018 DoD Suicide Report. These initiatives include the Warrior Resilience & Fitness Innovation Incubator, Suicide Prevention and Readiness Initiative for the National Guard, the VA Center Outreach Initiative, and Star Behavioral Health Providers Program Expansion (U.S. Department of Defense National Guard Bureau, n.d.). Brief descriptions of some of these programs are provided below.

Directors of Psychological Health

Directors of Psychological Health (DPH) exist at multiple levels throughout the Guard. Every state has a DPH. Additionally, within the Air National Guard each wing has their own Wing Director of Psychological Health (WDPH). At the state level, "The DPH ensures, maintains, and enhances mission readiness by promoting individual, family and community resilience through readily accessible and exceptional psychological health services" (Bacalzo, 2020).

National Guard Family Program

The sole purpose of the National Guard Family Program is "supporting and educating families along the path of their National Guard life" (Military OneSource, n.d.-a). Components of the National Guard Family Program include the national office, and a State Family Program Director and one to four Wing Family Program Coordinators within each state. State family program offices provide "strategic planning, inter-service coordination and liaison with higher headquarters, other military services, state and federal government, and non-government (profit and non-profit) agencies and organizations" (Military OneSource, 2020). Other entities within the National Guard Family Program include Family Readiness Groups/Key Volunteer Groups, Family Readiness Assistants, and Family Assistance Staff (Military OneSource, n.d.-a). Family Programs provide assistance, guidance, and support aimed at enhancing quality of life for service members during peacetime, wartime, and on mobilization. Services and resources provided by the entities and organizations that make up the Family Programs include "family readiness, resource management, mobilization and deployment coordination, crisis intervention, outreach, volunteer recruitment, training, management, information, referral and follow-up, life skills education, review and analysis of program effectiveness, and youth development" (Military OneSource, n.d.-a).

Yellow Ribbon Reintegration Program (YRRP)

The Yellow Ribbon Reintegration Program is a DoD-wide effort that connects Guardsmen, Reservists, and their families and communities to resources through the deployment cycle to promote their wellbeing. Yellow Ribbon events connect service members and loved ones with local resources before, during, and after deployment (Yellow Ribbon Reintegration Program, n.d.).

Warrior Resilience & Fitness Innovation Incubator programs

These include state-level pilot programs designed to enhance the readiness, wellness, and resilience of all geographically dispersed National Guard members (U.S. Department of Defense National Guard Bureau, n.d.). In 2019, there were 12 distinct projects piloted. Topics covered by these pilots include substance abuse issues, physical fitness, access to behavioral health services, sexual assault prevention, and employment assistance (Myers, 2019).

Vet Centers

Operated through the VA, "Vet Centers are community-based counseling centers that provide a wide range of social and psychological services, including professional readjustment counseling to eligible Veterans, active-duty service members, including National Guard and Reserve components, and their families" (U.S. Department of Veterans Affairs, n.d.-i). In addition to the brick-and-mortar Vet Centers, there are also mobile and remote Vet Centers and a 24/7 call center. Psychosocial services provided at Vet Centers include individual, group, and family counseling for military-related issues, community events for education and outreach, employment assessment, and medical screening and referrals (U.S. Department of Veteran Affairs, n.d.-i). Through the Vet Center Outreach Initiative, mobile centers will be utilized to provide counseling services to full- and part-time Guardsmen living in remote locations during drill weekends (U.S. Department of Defense National Guard Bureau, n.d.).

Military OneSource

Military OneSource is a DoD-funded program that "offers a wide range of individualized consultations, coaching and non-medical counseling for many aspects of military life" (Military OneSource, n.d.-b). Military OneSource provides information about resourcing and programming available to Guardsmen, Reservists, and their immediate family members at the state and unit level. In addition, training on how to navigate and maximize federal benefits and resources is provided for all service members (Military OneSource, n.d.-c)

In addition to resources available through the DoD or VA, there are several other organizations and programs that provide resilience and mental health resources to Reserve and National Guard Service members. Examples of these program types include Give an Hour, the Star Behavioral Health Providers Program, and Cohen Clinics. Many of these programs have formal partnerships or working relationships with the DoD and VA. Give an Hour has a Reserve-specific program component that "works with existing Guard and Reserve programming to encourage help-seeking behavior, promote available mental health services, recruit additional service providers, and raise awareness of the Five Signs of Emotional Suffering" (Give an Hour, n.d.). It also holds a Memorandum of Understanding with the National Guard Bureau and the Army Reserve with the intention of increasing access to services provided in support of mental healthcare for Guardsmen, Reservists, and their families (Give an Hour, n.d.) Additionally, the National Guard partners with universities and other academic institutions in support of Star Behavioral Health Providers, which educates community-based behavioral health providers about military culture and competencies (e.g., deployment cycles) and trains to the standards of evidence-based treatments for PTSD, depression, insomnia, and suicidal behaviors (Smith, 2020). While services provided through these organizations are available to National Guard and Reserve members based on their service history and current status, availability may be limited based on a service member's location.

Treatment intervention and innovation: answering a call

All military populations can incur both visible and invisible injuries during their service. According to the U.S. Department of Veterans Affairs, 11–20 percent of service members who served in Operation Iraqi Freedom and Operation Enduring Freedom meet the criteria for PTSD in a given year. Service members exhibit PTSD at 12 percent and 30 percent for Desert Storm and the Vietnam War respectively (Gradus, 2017). The DoD released a report prepared by the Defense and Veterans Brain Injury Center showing that from 2000 to 2017 there were 370,688 cases of traumatic brain injury for the US Army, Navy, Air Force, and Marines (U.S. Department of Defense Traumatic Brain Injury Center of Excellence, 2020). Other service members may experience military sexual trauma, depression, anxiety, adjustment disorders, SUD, amputations, hearing loss, and mobility issues (Bronson *et al.*, 2018). These physical and psychological impairments create barriers to achieving optimal quality of life, social connectedness, and reintegration.

In addition to understanding wounds of war within military populations, music therapists must also be informed as to how injuries were sustained, which often depends on the type of combat tactics employed. "Every war has its own weapons. Every war has its own strategies, and every war has its own injuries. In Vietnam you were being shot. In Afghanistan you're being blown up" (Glasser, 2011, p.3). Modern warfare has changed the wounds of service members returning from combat. Improvised explosive devices are commonly used in current conflicts and have caused numerous fatalities and injuries including TBI, PTSD, hearing loss, post-concussive syndrome, and a plethora of physical injuries (U.S. Department of Veterans Affairs National Center for PTSD, 2015).

Music therapy interventions

Many music therapy methods can be applied to support treatment goals, as shown in Table 10.1. These include improvement in the areas of speech and language, cognition, motor coordination, social integration, emotional expression, family dynamics, auditory perception and tolerance, and emotional regulation. Additionally, music therapy promotes relaxation, informs mind–body connections, enhances problem-solving skills, assists with interpersonal communication and exploring self-preferences of music, and processes treatment outcomes and experiences (Bronson *et al.*, 2018).

Table 10.1: Music therapy methods and interventions

Music therapy methods	Music therapy interventions
Receptive/Passive	• Active music listening • Music-assisted relaxation • Lyric analysis and song discussion
Expressive/Active	• Instrument playing (re-creative or improvisational) • Singing • Music performance • Movement to music
Compositional	• Songwriting • Music production and recording
Collaboration and resourcing	• Music therapy co-treatment with other creative arts therapies and rehabilitation disciplines (e.g., physical, occupational, speech and language therapies) • Psychoeducation through music

An area of research that could be particularly helpful to National Guard and Reserve populations, as well as first responders, is using music to train coping skills. Coping skills are imperative for all humans, but especially during times of significant stress such as deployments and other first responder activations and/or missions. Many service members and first responders endure various types of trauma, often compounded throughout their careers; therefore, music therapists working with these groups must have an understanding of these specific considerations. It is recommended that music therapists working with military-connected populations and first responders have experience in trauma-informed care and adhere to work within in their scope of practice.

Considerations for program planning and development

Since Guardsmen and Reservists have abbreviated military service schedules, which entail a minimum of 24 inactive-duty days per year and 15 days of active duty each year, there is limited access during their condensed service hours and training time. Therefore, it may be most effective to work with these service members during off-duty hours. Examples of interventions that may be suitable for providing an introduction to music therapy include instrumental improvisation, intentional music listening, and music-based relaxation. After establishing a baseline understanding of music therapy and a therapeutic relationship, more in-depth work can be explored, such as lyric analysis and songwriting, which deepen the verbal processing of introductory exercises. For example, Bradt and colleagues (2019) found that songwriting can be a very powerful intervention with military populations through a thematic analysis of songs written by service members, which uncovered themes of personal struggles and barriers to recovery, relational challenges, positive relationships and support, and moving forward. It is important to note that accessing memories and associated thoughts, feelings, and experiences through songwriting with traumatized individuals can be triggering. Therefore, this work should only be done by board-certified music therapists who are trained to handle the depth of this work.

Clinical providers are often resistant to recommend that their patients participate in programs they are not familiar with, and directors of programs providing community arts engagement opportunities for military-connected populations have noted the importance and efficacy of word-of-mouth program promotion. Therefore, it is helpful to make connections with entities already providing services. For example, networking with existing resources that provide services for military-connected populations (e.g., Military OneSource) can assist with initiating processes to support program implementation for the National Guard and Reserve populations. Additionally, providing information and resources regarding community outreach and connecting service members and their families with local, regional, and national programs is essential for access to and consistency of services. Many of the organizations and entities detailed earlier in the chapter have digital resources (e.g., websites, social networking, virtual assets) that contain information for providers who want to serve National Guard and Reserve populations. Working with established entities increases access and outreach to service members and their families and streamlines processes for providers to offer complementary and innovative rather than duplicative services.

Another avenue of programming to consider with National Guard, Reserve, and first responders is a train-the-trainer approach. These models can provide creative arts therapy-informed psychoeducational resources for community artists to guide implementation processes for clinically informed, community-implemented programming. There are multiple programs within the military that provide specialized training to service members who in turn train other individuals or groups within their unit, thus increasing opportunities for information dissemination and access to services. Examples of programs utilizing this approach include the DoD's Sexual Assault Prevention and

Response Victim Advocates program and the Army's Master Resiliency Training Program. Advantages of this approach within the National Guard and Reserve populations include the ability of service members to facilitate arts engagement in collaboration with trained community artists, either within or outside a drill weekend, which leverages local community-based resources in proximity to the units, to include remote and rural areas.

Summary

This chapter highlighted several topics pertaining to the National Guard, Reserve Force, and military first responders. These include roles, similarities, and differences, some of their indicated needs, and ways in which music therapists working with these military subgroups can provide services. My personal experiences, knowledge, passion, and skills encourage my desire to work with these communities. My hopes are to expand the number of music therapists serving National Guard and Reserve populations through promoting awareness of music therapy and the value and simultaneous vulnerability that exists across military populations. The music therapy interventions, considerations for program development, and resources outlined in this chapter provided readers with foundational information to collaborate, create additional resources, develop programming, and advocate for continued research with specific focus on the National Guard and Reserves.

Chapter 11

Historical Overview and Research Trends and Gaps in Military Music Therapy

LORI F. GOODING, DONNA BETTS, AND JOHN D. HOGUE

Disclaimer: The opinions contained in this chapter represent the private views of the authors and are not to be construed as official or as reflecting the views, opinions, or policies of the Henry M. Jackson Foundation for the Advancement of Military Medicine, Inc., the Department of Defense, the National Endowment for the Arts, or the U.S. Government. Mention of trade names, commercial products, or organizations does not imply endorsement by the US Government. This document was created free of branding or market affiliations. The authors are operating solely as contributors.

Introduction

The United States (U.S.) Department of Defense (DoD) and Veterans Health Administration (VHA) support the use of complementary and integrated treatment approaches for active-duty service members, veterans, and their families. In fact, complementary approaches, which include the creative arts therapies disciplines (i.e., art therapy, dance/movement therapy, drama therapy, music therapy, poetry therapy), as well as techniques such as mindfulness and meditation, have been made a priority in treating military-connected populations (Madsen *et al.*, 2017; U.S. Department of Veterans Affairs, 2018). The growing interest in complementary and integrated approaches to care is driven by several factors, including 1) evidence-based practice such as the integration of current research, clinical expertise, and patient values and preferences into clinical practice; 2) the integrative medicine model, a whole-person approach to health (Madsen *et al.*, 2017); 3) patient demand; and 4) the desire to reduce healthcare costs (Taylor *et al.*, 2019). Therefore, complementary and integrated approaches supported by research evidence are most likely to be used in the treatment of military populations.

A survey of veterans was conducted in July of 2017 to better understand the use of complementary and integrated health (CIH) approaches by military personnel (Taylor *et al.*, 2019). Researchers found that over 50 percent of veterans served through the VHA had used a CIH approach, and 84 percent were interested in trying or learning more about CIH approaches. However, creative arts therapies, including music therapy, were among the least used CIH approaches, with only 8.2 percent of participants reporting that they had received treatment from a creative arts therapist (CAT). Yet, despite being among the least used, creative arts therapies had some of the highest satisfaction rates, ranking seventh out of 24, with 75.6 percent of those who had used a creative arts therapy-based CIH approach reporting satisfaction with treatment. Creative arts therapies were also ranked second out of 24 in terms of military personnel's interest in learning more about or trying them. Given the interest in creative arts therapies and the focus on evidence-based practice, there is a need for comprehensive research on the use of creative arts therapies with military personnel. This need is especially important because increased research has the potential to elevate access to CIH approaches, such as music therapy (Gooding & Langston, 2019).

This chapter focuses specifically on military music therapy research by providing an overview of research related to military-connected populations, including historical research, synthesizing the current state of music therapy research, and presenting gaps in knowledge to inform future studies regarding music therapy with these populations. We discuss how music therapy is used, who uses it, and documented outcomes, through the description of an exemplar initiative of the National Endowment for the Arts (NEA), Creative Forces®: NEA Military Healing Arts Network. The development and application of conceptual frameworks to guide research with military-connected populations is also illustrated through discussion about the Creative Forces program.

Music with military populations: early research trends (1899–1950)

Music has long been associated with health and wellbeing, and both music and medicine were integral to physician training for hundreds of years (Taylor, 1981). During the 18th and 19th centuries, however, the fields diverged, and it was not until the 19th century that interest was renewed in the use of music to treat medical and mental health conditions (McCaffrey, 2015; Taylor, 1981). By the late 19th century, music had been systematically introduced in German psychiatry (McCaffrey, 2015), and was being used as a day-time diversion and sleep aid in hospital treatment (Taylor, 1981). Physicians also began conducting systematic experiments using music to treat behavioral-emotional and sleep disorders (McCaffrey, 2015) and exploring the physiological effects of music on both humans and animals (Taylor, 1981). Results from these studies indicated that music led to changes in cardiac output, respiratory rate and volume, pulse rate, and blood pressure. These positive outcomes led to an increased interest in music as therapy, and the term "music therapy" emerged (McCaffrey, 2015).

During and after World War I (WWI), interest in music as therapy increased and music began to be prescribed for "war neurosis, aphasia, temporary insanity, and paralyzed muscles" (Goetz Gilliland, 1944, p.18). Scholars have suggested that some of the greatest strides in music therapy were made during this time period (Goetz Gilliland, 1944), and early music therapy pioneers stressed the need for well-trained and qualified musicians to provide music programs in hospitals (Spencer, 2013). This led to the development of training programs, including the first university training course in music as therapy developed by Margaret Anderton, who was directly influenced by her work with Canadian Soldiers wounded in WWI (Taylor, 1981). Additional trainings, offered by organizations like the National Foundation for Music Therapy, also emerged. These trainings regularly included courses that explored the use of music in the treatment of war casualties (Solomon, 1984).

Early in World War II (WWII), the use of music in the military was discouraged (Rorke, 1996), despite the growth in research and training. This was likely due to skepticism among physicians and hospital administrators regarding the use of music to aid healing (Spencer, 2013). However, in 1942 a Music Advisory Council was formed to examine the value of the use of music with wounded and disabled veterans (Spencer, 2013), and by 1943, the Army had authorized the use of music as a morale builder and the military began to examine the usefulness of music in the treatment of wounded and disabled veterans (Rorke, 1996; Sullivan, 2007). In 1944, the National Federation of Music Clubs partnered with the American Red Cross to send musicians to hospitals (Goetz Gilliland, 1944), and the Music Research Foundation began conducting music research authorized by the Surgeon General of the Army at Walter Reed General Hospital, the Army's medical center (Taylor & Paparte, 1958). By 1945, music had been integrated into the Reconditioning Program, a program designed to help military personnel transition back to civilian life (Rorke, 1996). As a part of this program, music was used for physical rehabilitation, education, socialization, and in neuropsychiatric treatment. Ultimately, instructions on the use of music in education, occupational therapy, physical reconditioning, and recreation were published in the Technical Bulletin 187: *Music in Reconditioning in ASF Convalescent and General Hospitals* (US. War Department, 1945). Yet even though the military was interested in examining the medical applications of music, there continued to be little scientific evidence on the therapeutic functions of music (Goetz Gilliland, 1945). As a result, a group of military medical personnel that included the Army Surgeon General, the Chief of the Navy's Bureau of Medicine and Surgery, and the Veterans Administration Chief of Medical Services, disallowed the use of the title of "music therapist" until research validated music therapy (Lewis *et al.*, 1947; Taylor, 1981).

Music with military populations: research trends post World War II (1951–2014)

After WWII, scholars continued to promote music therapy (Wilson, 1989). However, the need for a scientific approach to music therapy remained (Schullian & Schoen, 1948), as did calls for training programs and research (Edwards, 2008). Early leaders in the field of music therapy strongly believed that the dissemination of research-based knowledge was key to the development of the profession and worked diligently to create a foundation of knowledge on which to build clinical treatment theories (Solomon, 1993). This led to the establishment of publications like the *Journal of Music Therapy*, with the first volume/issue published in 1964. This journal was developed to review and disseminate "original investigations and theoretical papers pertaining to Music Therapy..." (Sears, 1964, p.30). This helped to propel music and health research, with studies investigating topics ranging from the use of music in dental procedures to the use of music to reduce sedation during surgery (Taylor, 1981).

Research specifically targeting music therapy with military populations between 1950 and 2014 was inconsistent and episodic (American Music Therapy Association, 2014). Most of the works about music therapy and military populations were published between 1993 and 1999, and 2007 and 2014. The most common type of publication was historical reviews, with six publications providing profiles of early music therapists and their work with military populations. Though these publications were not clinical research, they provided important context and information regarding music therapy with military populations which can be used to help identify directions for future research (University of Southern California, 2020).

Case studies and anecdotal reports were the second most common type of publication during the second half of the 20th century and early 21st century. Case studies generally provide "single-participant qualitative descriptions of successful music therapy interventions" (Silverman, 2006, p.4), and this type of research has historically played an important role in music therapy. When looking at the case studies and anecdotal reports about music therapy interventions with military personnel, we find descriptions of the use of interventions like the Bonny Method of Guided Imagery, directed imagery (Blake, 1994), and drumming interventions (Burt, 1995). Moreover, most of the case studies focused on Vietnam veterans (Blake, 1994; Burt, 1995) and explored both individual (Blake, 1994) and group music therapy (Burt, 1995).

According to Yun-Springer and Silverman (2014), case studies were categorized as Level VI evidence on a commonly used and widely accepted evidence classification system constructed by Melnyk and Fineout-Overholt (2005). This system has a total of seven levels, with higher levels providing greater support for the interventions under investigation. Therefore, even though case studies provide rich descriptions and are useful because of their flexibility (Silverman, 2006), they do not provide the high level of evidence needed to support the use of music therapy interventions in evidence-based practice. As a result, access to music therapy services during the later 20th and early 21st centuries remained limited (Gooding & Langston, 2019).

Additional types of music therapy research focused on military-connected populations conducted between 1950 and 2014 included white papers/reports, mixed-methods research, and narrative inquiry (Gooding & Langston, 2019). White papers are authoritative reports or publications that provide information and argue a specific position (Purdue Online Writing Lab, n.d.), but like descriptive case studies, white papers represent a low level of evidence (Yun-Springer & Silverman, 2014). Mixed-methods studies include both qualitative and quantitative data, integrating multiple ways of knowing. This type of research can promote the highest quality of care by helping music therapists integrate the most current research into their clinical decision making (Bradt *et al.*, 2013). Two publications used mixed-methods designs, and both addressed inpatient services for active-duty Israeli military personnel with PTSD between the ages of 20 and 23 (Bensimon *et al.*, 2008; 2012). One explored the use of group drumming (Bensimon *et al.*, 2008) while the other explored the therapeutic process of group music therapy (Bensimon *et al.*, 2012). However, these publications may have limited application for work with military personnel in the U.S. Finally, Spencer (2013) conducted a historical review/narrative inquiry that explored the development of music therapy with veteran populations, specifically focusing on the VHA system.

Music with military populations: contemporary research trends (2015–2020)

In 2013, Dunphy *et al.* reported that music therapy had the largest body of research—broadly speaking—of all the creative arts therapies. Despite the abundance of research, however, studies focusing specifically on music therapy with military populations are still emerging. In a 2019 scoping review of music therapy with military populations, Gooding and Langston (2019) found that 10 of the 14 clinical publications included had been published since 2015. This suggests a growing interest in research on music therapy with military-connected populations. However, the level of evidence for much of the research remained low, and the authors stressed the continued need for higher-level studies to improve access to music therapy for military-connected populations.

Though research on music therapy with military-connected populations is still emerging, research since 2015 has broadened in scope. Study designs have included:

- retrospective studies (Bradt *et al.*, 2019)
- case studies, case reports, and case vignettes (Lightstone *et al.*, 2015; Stewart, 2018; Vaudreuil *et al.*, 2019a; Vaudreuil *et al.*, 2019b; Wellman & Pinkerton, 2015)
- single group, pre-test/post-test designs (Garrison, 2016; Vaudreuil *et al.*, 2020a)
- double-blind, randomized, pre-/post-intervention trials (Gantt *et al.*, 2017)
- feasibility studies (Story & Beck, 2017)
- descriptive studies (Shing, 2016).

Research topics have expanded and include the impact of music therapy:

- as a co-treatment (Lightstone *et al.*, 2015)
- during rehabilitation (Vaudreuil *et al.*, 2019a)
- on mood and emotional balance (Wellman & Pinkerton, 2015).

Populations included have also broadened, with recent research focused on veterans (Garrison, 2016), active-duty military personnel (Bradt *et al.*, 2019; Bronson *et al.*, 2018; Vaudreuil *et al.*, 2019a; Vaudreuil *et al.*, 2019b), student veterans (Shing, 2016), and female veterans (Story & Beck, 2017; Wellman & Pinkerton, 2015; Vaudreuil *et al.*, 2020b). Likewise, the conditions found among those served has also expanded, to include conditions like military sexual trauma (Story & Beck, 2017) in addition to commonly studied conditions like PTSD and TBI (Gooding & Langston, 2019). Furthermore, the research protocols appear to integrate a broader range of music therapy interventions and strategies, including:

- music-assisted relaxation (Garrison, 2016; Vaudreuil *et al.*, 2020a)
- embedded theta brainwave frequency in music using binaural beat technology (Gantt *et al.*, 2017)
- music-making and songwriting (Bradt *et al.*, 2019)
- guided imagery (Story & Beck, 2017)
- individualized listening programs (Wellman & Pinkerton, 2015)
- performance (Vaudreuil *et al.*, 2019b)
- neurologic music therapy (NMT) techniques (Vaudreuil *et al.*, 2019a)
- active and receptive interventions (Stewart, 2018).

Equally important, scholars have begun including family members (Chilton *et al.*, 2020) in their work, and their findings have suggested that family members value music therapy and believe that participation in sessions promotes continued improvement outside sessions (Vaudreuil *et al.*, 2019a).

Another addition to the research literature on music therapy with military-connected populations has been the inclusion of telehealth services. In 2015, a retrospective case study of music therapy and clinical psychology co-intervention delivered via remote technology (Lightstone *et al.*, 2015) was published, and in 2017 teleservices were added in response to the VA's attempt to expand programs and services to ensure improved access and care (Davis & Else, 2019). Subsequently, a clinical program description was released about delivering creative arts therapies for veterans via telehealth (Levy *et al.*, 2017), which was followed by case studies in art, dance/movement, and music therapy (Spooner *et al.*, 2019). Most recently, a paper by Vaudreuil *et al.* (2020b) presented three case examples illustrating participants' positive experiences with music therapy and community music engagement through telehealth. Overall, patients reported a decrease in depression, pain, and anxiety; they found that telehealth did not prevent them from continued engagement with music, and they requested continued telehealth sessions and recommended music therapy to their peers. Distance delivery of music through online platforms was found to support participants on a clinic to community continuum.

The body of literature regarding music therapy with military-connected populations benefits the field of music therapy as a whole. However, while research on music therapy with military-connected populations continues to expand, gaps remain, thereby perpetuating the need for increased research and higher levels of evidence.

Research needs

The American Music Therapy Association's (2014) status report on music therapy for military populations reiterates the need for diverse, integrated research methodologies and higher levels of evidence. Recommendations issued in the status report are included in the text box below.

1. Test and adapt established interventions.
2. Replicate studies conducted on civilian populations for military-connected populations.
3. Conduct experimental studies that have adequate power and sample sizes.
4. Use mixed methods and feasibility studies.
5. Engage in interdisciplinary research.
6. Translate research findings to clinical practice.
7. Evaluate how music therapy works with technology.

In 2020, several of the contributors to this book conducted a survey to inform the present chapter as well as Chapter 12 (Gooding *et al.*, 2020). The survey included questions about clinical practice with military-connected populations, along with questions about research with military populations. Eighteen practitioners working with active-duty service members and veterans across the U.S. (six music therapists, one art therapist, one physician, one healthcare administrator, and nine other professionals) responded. Results indicated that research is an area that needs improvement and most respondents (n=11) identified research support as needed to address existing and emerging demands of music therapists in military and veteran healthcare environments. Practitioner comments suggested securing more partnership programs, pursuing more robust research, creating an agenda for stakeholder involvement, establishing quantitative and standardized treatments, and seeking more support from local research infrastructure/resources. This last point parallels the AMTA's recommendation of "including qualified music therapy scholars/researchers in military and VA study sections and human subjects/IRB committees" (American Music Therapy Association, 2014, p.35), underscoring the relevance of this identified gap.

Survey participants largely agreed that music therapy research in the military is a priority (with 86 percent marking "agree" or "strongly agree"), that they can easily digest the literature on this topic (80%), and that they have interest in conducting research (80%). Despite these results, the respondents indicated ambivalence about 1) applying research findings to their practice (with only 47% choosing "agree" or "strongly agree"); 2) feeling adequately trained to do research in the military (53%); and 3) having a support system to help with research (73%). Moreover, few respondents agreed or strongly agreed that they had the resources to conduct a research study (13%).

AMTA's 2014 research recommendations and the 2020 survey results are consistent, providing support for the premise that music therapy with military-connected populations would benefit from further research that provides high levels of evidence. The 2020 survey, however, suggests that more training and resources are needed to support music therapy research with military-connected populations, which aligns with research constraints and barriers identified in the profession as a whole (Waldon, 2015). Two salient examples of these needs are seen in AMTA's recommendations: 1) use of mixed methods and feasibility studies; and 2) engage in interdisciplinary research.

Mixed methods and feasibility studies

Mixed-methods design, which integrates qualitative and quantitative data collection procedures, addresses research questions in more depth (Betts & Deaver, 2019). The rationale for employing mixed methods should be based on theory and appropriate for research purposes (Bradt *et al.*, 2013). If deemed appropriate, this type of research could be advantageous on a practical level; the quantitative data could provide visuals to convey the treatment's impact, and the qualitative data could provide the service members' treatment experience in their own words (Bradt *et al.*, 2013).

Because service members tend to trust their own peer group more than they trust civilians, as indicated by Garcia (2017), their words are likely to better connect to other service members, breaking through the trust barrier. The combination of the service members' narrative experiences and data visuals (e.g., figures and tables) would provide a more solid foundation to enable a richer understanding of the research. Despite the obvious benefits, the mixed-methods design requires training in both quantitative and qualitative data analysis, as well as data integration methods (Bradt *et al.*, 2013). Therefore, this type of research is often utilized by integrated teams with relevant training in data collection, management, and analysis to integrate and generate clinically meaningful data (Robb & Meadows, 2015).

Interdisciplinary research

Music therapists working with military-connected populations often work within an interdisciplinary model of care, so using this natural advantage (Robb, 2014) to investigate practical problems and life experiences may provide rich evidence of effectiveness (Robb, 2014). Exploring the effect of music therapy only, other discipline(s) only, and a combination of disciplines while comparing against a control group, as ethically indicated, would provide a higher level of evidence and generate meaningful findings to guide clinical practice. These multi-arm designs could also help music therapists disseminate findings to consumers, advocates, and policy makers, supporting the addition of music therapists to integrated care teams as employed entities and licensed independent practitioners in military and veteran healthcare systems. One challenge in conducting these types of studies, however, includes the need for extensive resources like research personnel, site support, expertise in other disciplines, and budgeting capabilities.

Future considerations

As the demand for diverse research methodologies increases, in addition to diverse methodologies (e.g., mixed methods) and interdisciplinary research, it will be important to also consider process frameworks, development of theory-based approaches, and meaningful integration of collective findings (Robb & Meadows, 2015). This process will improve the translation of research to practice and will further support communication with a variety of stakeholders. In the next section, we discuss how an exemplar clinical program addresses challenges inherent in military music therapy research and serves as a model for integrating existing knowledge, developing new knowledge, and translating knowledge into clinical practice.

Creative Forces as a model program for research and clinical work

Creative Forces®: NEA Military Healing Arts Network, an initiative of the National Endowment for the Arts in partnership with the U.S. Departments of Defense and Veterans Affairs and the state and local arts agencies, seeks to improve the health, wellness, and quality of life for military-connected populations exposed to trauma, as well as their families and caregivers (National Endowment for the Arts, n.d.). Administrative support for the initiative is provided by Americans for the Arts and the Henry M. Jackson Foundation for the Advancement of Military Medicine, Inc. Established in 2011, the program places creative arts therapists—art therapists, music therapists, and dance/movement therapists—at the core of patient-centered care at clinical sites across the U.S., including telehealth services, and increases access to community arts activities.

Compelling preliminary evidence supports use of the creative arts therapies in promoting rehabilitation and recovery for military and veteran populations exposed to trauma (Betts, 2020). Studies published by Creative Forces network-affiliated researchers justify continued growth of the program, supported by the Creative Forces research strategic framework and agenda (National Endowment for the Arts, 2018). This agenda formalizes a commitment to strategic objectives that guide the program to develop infrastructure, leadership, and capacity, and that inform the research and guide clinical care protocols (Betts, 2020).

Network clinicians and collaborators have published seven music therapy research papers to date (Betts, 2020). These include innovative music therapy protocols, small case series, analyses of secondary data (e.g., clinical documentation, program evaluation), a preliminary multi-site study replicating clinical programming, and a scoping review (Gooding & Langston, 2019). The interventions attributable to the work of Creative Forces music therapists, cross-disciplinary colleagues, patients, and their families promote rehabilitation and recovery across four domains (Betts, 2020):

1. Psychological/behavioral
2. Neurological/cognitive
3. Rehabilitative (physiological, physical, functional, and/or occupational)
4. Social/relational.

Examples of this research portfolio are summarized below.

Psychological/behavioral

As described by Bronson *et al.* (2018), music therapy across the Creative Forces network is provided both as integrated care and as a stand-alone treatment for PTSD, addressing such goals as emotional regulation, coping, sleep hygiene, and promoting quality of life/wellbeing. A music therapy group protocol in an interdisciplinary intensive outpatient treatment setting was shown to be beneficial in allowing active-duty service members to optimize feelings of safety, acclimate to music therapy, access and express their emotions, and reduce perceptions of threat during emotional risk taking (Vaudreuil *et al.*, 2020a).

Neurological/cognitive

Music therapy interventions address outcomes such as problem-solving, cognition and memory, focus and task attention, motor control and response, speech and language, auditory processing (auditory perception and tolerance of auditory stimuli), and headache alleviation (Bronson *et al.*, 2018). A case report by Vaudreuil *et al.* (2019a) demonstrated that NMT interventions, in collaboration with other treatment disciplines, contribute to improvements in task-attention, articulation, and compensatory strategies.

Rehabilitative

Music therapists can help ease difficulty associated with rehabilitation activities, thereby enhancing patient participation in interdisciplinary care (Vaudreuil *et al.*, 2019a). In collaboration with other disciplines across Creative Forces sites, music therapy co-treatments contribute to improvements in 1) functional use of bilateral upper extremities; 2) range of motion; 3) respiratory support; and 4) strength endurance. In addition, three case examples reflect a decrease in patients' depression, pain, and anxiety levels (Vaudreuil *et al.*, 2020b).

Social/relational

According to Vaudreuil *et al.* (2019a), music therapy interventions contribute to improvements in quality of life, social integration, and overall motivation in the recovery process. Music therapy reduces isolation, enables exploration of music preferences, fosters self-efficacy and identity, enhances interpersonal communication, and supports familial bonding/social engagement (Bronson *et al.*, 2018). Furthermore, the use of musical performance with this population can contribute to individual development and rehabilitation as a vehicle for social transformation and reintegration (Vaudreuil *et al.*, 2019b). Music therapy can raise awareness of social issues within patients' communities, give a voice to their experiences, and transform perceptions of illness or injury in audience members. Music therapy may also spur greater support and validation from patients' communities. Bradt and colleagues (2019) found that songwriting plays an important role in service members' personal growth and recovery processes as it enables them to share their thoughts, fears, emotions, and hopes with others, often for the first time. Songwriting can help service members returning from deployments by offering a window into their lived experiences of military service, injury, recovery, homecoming, and transition from active duty.

In addition to the preliminary evidence and research objectives, the Creative Forces program bolstered support for its research initiative by developing conceptual frameworks. To drive a rigorous research program for music therapy, theory-driven studies guided by compelling research questions and hypotheses to investigate further are needed (Betts, 2020). As such, conceptual frameworks have been created. This process includes developing a protocol of underlying mechanisms, priority research questions/hypotheses, rigorous study designs, associated measures, and outcomes that can support prospective multi-site trials in collaboration with professionals from related behavioral and rehabilitative health disciplines. Among the priorities addressed in this effort are the need to investigate mechanisms of change, economic efficiency, occupational benefits (e.g., return to duty), and social/emotional benefits.

The Creative Forces clinical program addresses challenges inherent in research through personnel who collect programmatic data and manage informatics, and provide training, support, and resources to the network's CAT clinicians. A Director of Clinical Research, alongside other subject matter experts, regularly provides training and guidance on research activities. Clinicians are also given time to engage in research, and resources that support clinical research efforts such as standardized documentation protocols, including templated notes, research support personnel, access to data with proper approvals, and funding are also provided.

Seven practitioners in the 2020 survey for this book chapter noted a gap area in program evaluation/effectiveness, but more respondents noted research as a more relevant gap area. Creative Forces conducts internal research for program evaluation purposes using a combination of workload reports, templated notes, and assessments. This combination demonstrates the impact of the creative arts therapies from the clinicians' and patients' perspectives.

In terms of programmatic data, one of the main collection procedures Creative Forces employs is bimonthly performance measurement reports. These track the number of sessions and patient encounters, and categorize daily hours (e.g., direct patient care, non-direct patient care, community engagement, research, administrative tasks, and program development). In the Creative Forces network, three collective years of reporting from 34 unique CATs, approximately 24 reporting each year, indicate a significant, positive correlation between the number of sessions scheduled and the total time spent on non-direct patient care ($r = .59$, $p < .01$), suggesting that the more scheduled sessions the therapists had, the more non-direct patient care hours the therapists logged. This correlation exposes a gap in both the music therapy military-specific research and the music therapy research at large: understanding the value and necessity of non-direct patient care. This gap raises questions, as displayed in the text box below.

1. How does non-direct patient care impact patient non-musical outcomes?
2. What parts of non-direct patient care are critical to patient care and what can be reduced for efficiency?
3. Does non-direct patient care contribute to therapist burnout?

The performance measurement reports also allow Creative Forces to capture activity in non-clinical work (e.g., community engagement, research/scholarly activity, media interviews). For example, within a year-and-a-half, 34 percent of the CATs' time and efforts in non-clinical work was in community engagement (e.g., facilitating Creative Arts Cafés, arts workshops, outreach), and 16 percent of their activity was in conducting professional presentations. These reports are funneled into digital dashboards (i.e., Tableau) to generate visuals that readily convey the data demonstrating the CATs' productivity and distribution of work.

Additionally, Creative Forces CATs use templated notes modeled in SOAP (subjective, objective, assessment, plan) note format and can choose from drop-down options to complete clinical documentation via templated notes with efficiency. The music therapy notes were originally developed through information gleaned from conceptual frameworks, which outline the therapeutic process for music therapy services across Creative Forces sites. They were framed within the NMT Transformational Design Model process (e.g., goals, music interventions, outcomes, evidence) and designed based on the unique needs of the clinicians and the sites, with consideration to maximizing efficiency in data analytics across the network. They were further refined to enable sharing of information with other clinicians on the site treatment teams and with consideration of the unique scopes of practice for each discipline in Creative Forces (i.e., art therapy, music therapy, dance/movement therapy). CATs have reported that the templated notes are easy to use and enable consolidation of information within the site's electronic medical record system to streamline the treatment planning.

Music therapy practice across the Creative Forces network includes standardized protocols and assessments that enable accuracy in collecting program evaluation and research data, and consistency in the treatment process (Bronson *et al.*, 2018; Vaudreuil *et al.*, 2020a). For example, the Introduction to Music Therapy group protocol includes an assessment for patients to complete at the end of session to determine the perceived helpfulness of interventions on a *not helpful* to *very helpful* four-point scale (Vaudreuil *et al.*, 2020a). Program evaluation and research endeavors provide valuable information on the impact of music therapy for individual patients, their families and caregivers, and the military health system at large. They help Creative Forces tell its story, improve programming, inform research, and optimize overall effectiveness.

Summary

Music with military-connected populations progressed from being relegated as morale-boosting in the 1940s to being part of an interdisciplinary treatment team today. However, the lack of empirical research on and evidence of music therapy's effectiveness with military-connected populations continues to be a concern. The use of music therapy with this population needs more high-level research that uses longitudinal, neuroscience, and mixed-methods designs and evaluates music therapy as part of an interdisciplinary treatment team. Even though music therapy practitioners want to do research, they need additional training and more resources, and initiatives that encourage the development of music therapy's evidence-based practice within military-connected populations.

Chapter 12

Looking Ahead: Continued Advancement of the Military Music Therapy Continuum

HANNAH BRONSON, MOIRA G. MCGUIRE, AND REBECCA VAUDREUIL

Introduction

The chapters throughout this book indicate a rich history of music in the military, the use of music as medicine, and music therapy integration into military and veteran healthcare systems. Each of these components of growth has contributed to the development of music therapy as a profession, and its advancement and current positioning as an integrated healthcare service within the Departments of Defense (DoD) and Veterans Affairs (VA). This evolutionary timeline, depicted in Figure 12.1, can be traced from the early uses of music as medicine, to the historical use of military battlefield music, to the evolution of music therapy in the VA, and finally to the establishment of national initiatives that champion creative arts therapies in the DoD and VA, supporting a spectrum of arts engagement for military-connected populations.

Considering the decades-long development in military and veteran healthcare systems indicated throughout the chapters of this book, it is rational to deduce that music therapy can and will continue to grow and expand the breadth and depth of evidence-based practices with military-connected populations (Gooding & Langston, 2019). In light of all the valuable information about military music therapy in the preceding chapters—the growth and expansion in the VA and DoD (Chapters 1–4); specific facilitation of individual (Chapter 5) and group (Chapter 6) music therapy sessions; family and caregiver support (Chapter 7); innovations in telehealth programming (Chapter 8); community music models (Chapter 9); access for the National Guard, Military Reserve Force, and first responders (Chapter 10); and an overview of historical and current research (Chapter 11)—it is rational to postulate that music therapy, among other creative arts therapies, has built a structurally sound foundation on which to continue integrating into modern medicine across military and veteran healthcare systems as well as in the civilian sector.

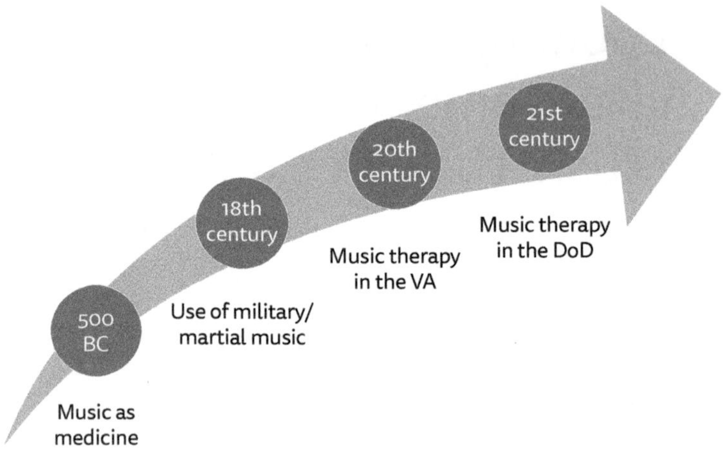

Figure 12.1: Evolution of music in medicine and military

Through current literature review and results from a survey designed specifically to inform this book's content, this chapter provides:

- an overview of current music therapy practice and positioning in military and veteran healthcare systems
- strengths, needs, and opportunities for growth of music therapy with military-connected populations
- a future-oriented focus of music therapy models of care, including community and research opportunities
- the impact of music used as an integrative tool in arts and health programming
- recommendations for the future of military music therapy.

Methods

Data collection for this chapter consists of literature review findings and qualitative research methods, including observations from the decades of the authors' clinical experiences and survey research. "Music Therapy with Military Populations: A Survey" (Gooding *et al.*, 2020) was developed to glean a deeper understanding, specific perceptions, and recommendations from professionals (e.g., creative arts therapists (CATs), military and civilian clinicians, researchers, service members, veterans, family members) regarding a variety of topics about music therapy with military and veteran populations. Needs, gaps, and growth potential of music therapy in military and veteran healthcare systems are identified, and recommendations for future foci are informed by professionals working in both arts- and non-arts-based capacities. The survey was distributed online via Qualtrics. Question types included multiple choice, Likert-type scale, and open-ended inquiries. To protect respondents' privacy, no individual responses were identifiable and questions that respondents did not want to answer were left blank. Participation was able to be stopped at any point. A total of 18 respondents completed the survey, including six music therapists, one art therapist, one physician, one healthcare administrator, and nine other professionals. Forty percent of the respondents reported past or current military service, including Army, Air Force, Marines, Navy, National Guard, and Public Health Service. Survey results are shared throughout this chapter to provide context for the recommendations regarding current and future states of music therapy with military populations.

The current states of military and veteran healthcare systems

To comprehensively understand integration of music therapy into military and veteran healthcare systems and the beneficiaries that they serve, it is necessary to understand their systemic magnitude, including availability and scarcity of resources, capacity and competence of service provision, recognition of patients' needs, and ability to identify and address gaps in care. Approximately 55 percent of veterans are diagnosed with a mental health disorder by the VA, indicating an increasing need for mental health service offerings and psychological rehabilitation for military-connected populations; however, there is a disparity in access to mental health services in the VA and DoD (Donahue, 2016). The responsibility to care for our country's warfighters is clearly defined in the VA's mission, which is aimed at serving and honoring the men and women who are America's veterans by fulfilling President Lincoln's promise, "To care for him whom shall have borne the battle, and for his widow and his orphan" (U.S. Department of Veterans Affairs, n.d.-g, para.1). The DoD's healthcare system supports a dual mission of 1) maintaining readiness of the medical branches of the U.S. Armed Forces (e.g., Army, Navy, Air Force) to care for the fighting forces and treat wartime casualties; and 2) providing for the healthcare needs of active-duty service members, veterans, and their families during peacetime (U.S. Department of Defense, n.d.-a).

The prevalence of post-traumatic stress disorder (PTSD) among service members and veterans remains high, as incidence rates consistently range from 11 to 20 percent in those who have served in support of the Global War on Terrorism (GWOT), 12 percent in the Gulf War, and 15 percent in Vietnam (Gradus, 2017). The lifetime incidence of PTSD among GWOT veterans is estimated to be 30.9 percent for men and 26.9 percent for women. In addition, it was reported that from 2000 to 2019, 413,858 military personnel sustained traumatic brain injury (TBI), 82.8 percent of which are classified as mild cases, 9.8 percent are moderate; severe and penetrating TBIs are 1–2 percent each, and 5.2 percent are unclassifiable (U.S. Department of Defense Traumatic Brain Injury Center of Excellence, 2020). Symptoms of TBI manifest with cognitive, emotional, and behavioral health symptoms (ibid.), and often are compounded by trauma comorbidities; therefore, rehabilitation professionals are often challenged with caring for service members who carry these complex diagnoses (Bronson *et al.*, 2018).

The Military Health System

The Military Health System (MHS) is the global healthcare system of the DoD, headquartered in Northern Virginia. Since the passing of the Dependent's Medical Care Act in 1956, which conceived the MHS, it has experienced significant congressionally determined evolution regarding eligibility, covered services, benefit costs, provider reimbursement, and integration of civilian sector services (Dolfini-Reed & Jebo, 2000). As of 2020, the MHS has an approximated annual budget and estimated beneficiaries served of $50 billion and $9.6 million, respectively, making it one of the largest health systems in the U.S. with mandatory and discretionary funding approved and appropriated by congress (Mendez, 2019). Currently, the MHS delivers care in over 50 military hospitals and 600 military clinics and supports a network of civilian sector providers through Tricare (U.S. Department of Defense, n.d.-a).

The Defense Health Agency

The Defense Health Agency (DHA) was established on October 1, 2013 and holds the position as America's military medical Combat Support Agency; a "joint, integrated organization that enables the Army, Navy, and Air Force medical services to provide a medically ready force and ready medical force to Combatant Commands in both peacetime and wartime" (U.S. Department of Defense, n.d.-a, para.1). As a leading integrated system of readiness and health, the DHA is making transformative changes and far-reaching strides to achieve its goal to "provide the best clinical outcomes for the 9.6 million beneficiaries within the MHS" (Military Health System, 2020, para.1). A major component of this organizational change is unifying efforts with the MHS by acquiring governance and oversight of administration and management of military medical treatment facilities (MTFs) under the MHS.

The VA healthcare system

The VA has a proposed $243.3 billion budget for the fiscal year 2021, increasing the 2020 budget by 10.2 percent. This allows for the VA to progress its continued commitment of providing high-quality healthcare and timely access to benefits and services to eligible veterans (U.S. Department of Veterans Affairs, 2020b). Additionally, the budget will support improvements in technological modernization aimed at innovative treatment approaches and advancements, which include implementation of the Whole Health initiative, as reported in Chapter 2 and 3, and expansion of the creative arts therapies delivered in person as well as remotely though telehealth (Vaudreuil *et al.*, 2020b), as reported in Chapter 8. In fact, much like the profession of music therapy was initiated in the DoD, music therapy facilitated via telehealth was conceived in the VA (Levy *et al.*, 2017). Distance delivery of music therapy is essential for consistency of services for patients who are homebound, live in rural areas, or during a crisis, such as the COVID-19 pandemic.

Systemic integration of music therapy

As exemplified through literature and clinical examples in the chapters throughout this book, music therapists are embedded in military and veteran healthcare systems and engaged in provision of interdisciplinary care through stand-alone and co-treatment sessions. Data gathered from survey responses indicates areas of success and identifies areas for improvement regarding clinical practice, community outreach, and research support.

Music therapy clinical practice in the DoD and VA

Music therapy has a solid imprint in the VA, as the VA has employed music therapists for decades; however, it was not until recently that they have been appropriately utilized for their knowledge, training, and skill sets. It has been a slower process for music therapy to gain traction in the DoD; however, over the past decade the DoD has started creating general schedule (GS) positions for music therapists, as there has been an increase in leadership support and emerging research validating the impact of music therapy treatment for military and veteran populations. To date, music therapists are embedded into military and veteran treatment clinics as part of multidisciplinary and interdisciplinary care teams that work together to provide comprehensive treatment in the areas of behavioral health and functional rehabilitation.

Reported areas of clinical success

Survey respondents indicated that music therapy has improved functioning of their patients in cognition (94%), motor (89%), and social (83%) domains. In addition, 94 percent of respondents reported that music therapy improved emotional functioning, self-regulation, and self-identity in patients. Increased self-awareness of patients receiving music therapy was reported by 89 percent of survey respondents. Improvement of self-management leisure skills was reported by 83 percent of survey respondents, and self-esteem and "other" improvements were rated less than 25 percent. Open-ended responses indicated that music therapy assisted relational development with self and others through building "improved relationships, not just social, but deeper relationships" (Gooding *et al.*, 2020). Additionally, respondents indicated that music therapy interventions supported neurologic and rehabilitative functioning through "increased vital lung capacity and breath support, improved functional communication skills, regulated dyspnea and breathing, bolstered coping skills and mood modulation, and facilitated development of neural pathways to redirect the brain and decrease negative ruminations" (Gooding *et al.*, 2020).

Reported gap/need areas and recommendations for improvements

Regarding existing need and gap areas that remain unfulfilled by music therapy services in the military and veteran facilities where survey respondents work or receive services, the top two areas indicated for improvement were caregiver services and research support (56%). These findings are supported by content related to these topics in Chapters 7 and 11 of this book and will be discussed further in this chapter as well. Family services and acute crisis services were indicated as areas of need by 50 percent of the survey respondents. Community-based services and program evaluation/effectiveness were reported needs by 39 percent of the respondents, followed by inpatient and long-term/transitional services, reported by 33 percent of respondents. Outpatient and other services were reported gaps by 28 percent of respondents, and lastly, services for individuals with specific conditions/diagnoses were reported as needs by 11 percent of the respondents.

In addition to identifying perceptions of needs, the survey was designed to capture recommendations for improvements that address gap areas. Respondents rated research and advocacy as the highest area for improvement (60%), which is congruent with Chapter 11 content, and elaborated that although interest in and knowledge of creative arts therapies are improving across military and veteran healthcare systems:

> an increase in advocacy for and evidence of creative arts therapies treatment of military-connected populations integrated into interdisciplinary care models including larger scale studies that demonstrate outcomes and define dosage is absolutely needed to increase and/or establish services amongst DoD and VA healthcare systems. (Gooding *et al.*, 2020)

Additionally, respondents identified a gap in advocacy from upper-level military leadership and indicated that the small size of many creative arts therapies departments and programs makes it difficult to generate nationwide support from high-level leadership in the DoD and VA. Specific recommendations for research support and the trajectory of music therapy investigation moving forward will be indicated later in this chapter.

Other gap and need areas indicated by survey responses included education and training (50%), licensure (45%), and reimbursement (33%). Regarding education and training, respondents posited that there are very limited resources and training opportunities for individuals (e.g., music therapists, providers, community members) interested in working with this population. Development of in-person and online education offerings could address this gap. Open-ended responses also recommended that master's-level entry for music therapists could elevate music therapy in healthcare systems and teams. This aligned with comments about licensure, which indicated that although licensure provides legitimacy, state-by-state regulatory variance limits the role of music therapy in DoD, VA, and civilian medicine, thus also creating challenges with reimbursement. Furthermore, respondents indicated a need for a process that educates, trains, and provides certification for non-clinical arts facilitators to work with military populations, which could reduce risk of potential harm, as shared here:

> I believe that music therapy should be an essential service provided at all major military installations and VA healthcare centers. These programs can be supported by local military and community musicians, creating a vibrant network of music-based health for the entire military community. (Gooding *et al.*, 2020)

Positioning, integration, and applications of military music therapy

Throughout the 21st century, music therapy has increasingly been integrated as a standard of care within the VA and DoD (Bronson *et al.*, 2018; Vaudreuil *et al.*, 2020b). Over the past decade, this integration has been amplified along with research production and dissemination that supports the need for and capacity of the multitude of evolving areas within these systems (Gooding & Langston, 2019). When examining the role of the music therapists embedded within these settings, it is important to consider the unique characteristics of the population, clinician, treatment facility, and the overall healthcare systems in which they practice. Open communication, information sharing, and collaboration between music therapists working with military populations have been essential to understanding how to develop best practices, as well as honoring the challenge of painting broad strokes in practice and research that demonstrate efficacy and promote continuous refinement and growth.

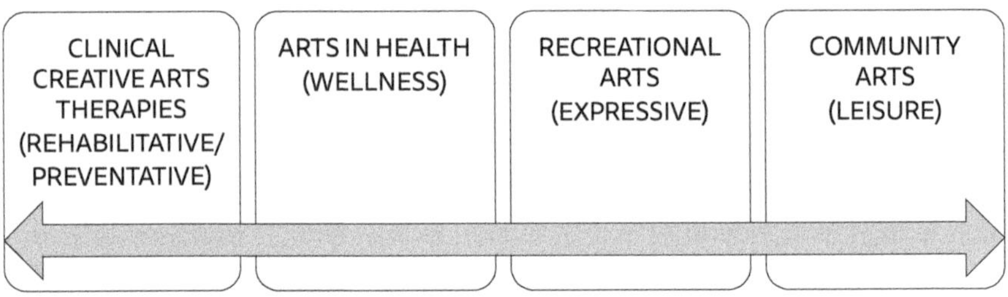

Figure 12.2: Clinic to community continuum of care

One of the unique characteristics of how music therapy can be utilized in military and veteran healthcare settings is that it has the ability to support patients across multiple levels of their military service and post-military life. Music therapists are positioned to provide care to service members recovering from injuries sustained during military service as well as during their transitions to VA care, while supporting reintegration with their families and communities throughout the entire process (Vaudreuil *et al.*, 2019b). This continuum from clinic to community, shown in Figure 12.2, can also assist in conceptualizing the role that community arts organizations and arts in health practices may play in bridging treatment gaps in treatment. By operating from a lens of acknowledgement, collaboration, and awareness, music therapists can extend the reach of their clinical operation and impact in providing lasting support for service members, veterans, and their families. CATs working within interdisciplinary treatment teams often interface with and uncover opportunities for collaborating with providers from other disciplines, as well as artists, musicians, and movement facilitators who provide recreational or wellness-based services. Clearly defining the roles of CATs and arts engagement facilitators and identifying how each contributes to the continuum of care are essential components in making informed recommendations for participant engagement and determining the most appropriate arts application.

Areas of clinical innovation

Survey results indicate that there are many areas for outreach and development where music therapy can enhance healthcare outcomes. This includes evidence-based music therapy practices such as neurologic music therapy (NMT), neonatal intensive care, pediatrics, special education, oncology, and hospice and palliative care. While much of the clinical programming and literature of music therapy with military-connected populations has focused on service members and veterans with combat-related physical and psychological injuries (Gooding & Langston, 2019), the MHS and VA healthcare system are as complex and varied as their civilian counterparts. One area of growing curiosity is integrating music therapy for resilience-building into military training. By utilizing music as an effective coping strategy, service members can be armed with additional protective factors to reduce the effects of prolonged exposure to stress, trauma, insomnia, and other psychologically harmful environmental variables associated with military service. We have seen how music can assist in providing stress inoculation training in service members who experience symptoms of trauma by regulating the nervous system (Vaudreuil *et al.*, 2020a), and research can further explore the implementation of music therapy in pre-deployment training to mitigate the effects of combat exposure.

Music therapists have experienced the unique contribution of creativity and the arts within an environment often classified by rigid structure, routine, and order that is at the forefront of military systems. Creativity as a construct, and arguably an element of intelligence, is essential to achieving adaptation in changing environments and responding flexibly to unpredictable circumstances. Anecdotally, respected and renowned military leaders are often described as having the unique capability of strategically engaging in life-saving decision making even when their training did not anticipate specific high-stress situations. Music and the arts activate shifts in perception, require the integration of complex emotional and cognitive processes, and demand increased capacity for handling ambiguous or contradictory situations. When used strategically, music therapy has the potential to increase psychological flexibility and ignite creative problem solving within essential military systems, including the individuals who work within them (McFerran & Rickson, 2014).

Research in third-wave behaviorism theory is grounded in an empirical principle-focused approach that emphasizes contextual and experiential change strategies in addition to those that are more direct and didactic (Hayes, 2004). This approach and application to psychotherapeutic processes such as acceptance and commitment therapy (ACT) supports increasing flexibility within a contextual perspective on human suffering. Furthermore, Hayes (2004) states:

> These treatments tend to seek the construction of broad, flexible and effective repertoires over an eliminative approach to narrowly defined problems, and to emphasize the relevance of the issues they examine for clinicians as well as clients. The third wave reformulates and synthesizes previous generations of behavioral and cognitive therapy and carries them forward into questions, issues, and domains previously addressed primarily by other traditions [mindfulness, Zen, Taoist practices], in hopes of improving both understanding and outcomes. (pp.5–6)

This diversion from problem solving and rule-governed responses to psychological pain (e.g., stress is bad and is something to be eradicated) results in widening of behavioral repertoire through a more open, centered, and engaged approach to living (Hayes *et al.*, 2016). This type of flexibility can also apply to treatment related to rehabilitation and healing from injury and trauma, where an individual's sense of self can experience an extreme change. Adaptability to unpredictable internal shifts such as changes in psychological or physical functioning can improve one's ability to achieve a high quality of life even when experiencing disruption and dysregulation. In fact, research indicates that engagement in music therapy has the potential to transform perceptions of injury and illness into strength and resilience, resulting in a reduction of mental health stigma (Vaudreuil *et al.*, 2019a). Further research can support emerging understanding of these concepts, and specific methods of implementing treatment to support military readiness and resilience.

As a stand-alone treatment, music therapy has unique and dynamic effects on healing complex injuries and psychological illnesses. A unique benefit to working in interdisciplinary settings that are increasingly more prevalent in military healthcare, especially in the treatment of co-occurring PTSD and TBI, is that providers can potentially increase the efficiency and impact of their disciplines by engaging in innovative co-treatment. While systemically this may seem like a financial burden and an overuse of valuable resources in a healthcare setting, pairing music therapy with other evidence-based treatments can produce potential cumulative benefits that are profound. Service members often report how rehabilitation outcomes can be improved when providers target their unique needs with combined treatment that provides overlap and offers distinctive methods of addressing clinical goals (Vaudreuil *et al.*, 2019a). For example, a physical therapy session focused on rehabilitating gait or a speech therapy intervention aimed at improving cognition can be enhanced when the patient is engaged and motivated by the addition of musical stimuli. This concept can extend to developing replicable clinical protocols created to treat specific diagnoses in military populations such as central auditory processing disorder. Additionally, integrating psychotherapeutic interventions that support people in meaning-making, such as ACT, and collaborating with other creative arts therapies to enhance the impact of self-expression is warranted. This is aligned with a 2015 report released by the American Music Therapy Association (AMTA) regarding recommendations about the future of music therapy research, *Improving Access and Quality: Music Therapy Research 2025 Executive Summary and Conclusions*. This document was a call for practice innovations, specifically compelling music therapists to design new protocols and engage in cross-discipline collaborations (American Music Therapy Association, 2015).

Furthermore, the shift from traditional models of discipline-specific treatment to a focus on interdisciplinary care can reduce provider silos and avoid disconnected and duplicative treatment experiences for patients, which can cause potential increase in fragmentation within themselves. Engaging in this type of transdisciplinary care requires providers to be comfortable with collaboration and role release, especially when boundaries between disciplines become blurred. Provider discomfort that may potentially accompany blended treatment approaches is mitigated by the unique outcomes and treatment successes of the patients. Therefore, more studies that measure this type of practice and impact are needed in order to identify and define the contributing variables that support the implementation of co-treatment methods on a systems level.

As research in evidence-based treatment for military service-related diagnoses evolves, limitations in some of the gold-standard treatment methods recommended by the DoD and the VA are revealed. For example, a literature review by Steenkamp *et al.* (2015) concluded that first-line psychotherapy treatments for PTSD such as cognitive processing therapy and prolonged exposure therapy demonstrated only marginally superior effectiveness when compared with non-trauma psychotherapy control conditions. Symptom reduction is often the primary focus of psychotherapeutic interventions and measured outcomes across westernized healthcare models; however, results from this study indicated that efficacy of treatment focused primarily on symptom reduction resulted in approximately two-thirds of service members retaining the diagnostic criteria for PTSD post-treatment (Steenkamp *et al.*, 2015). As this study suggests, further research is needed to understand the effectiveness of other therapeutic interventions and approaches to care. Creative and innovative approaches to care, such as music therapy, employed alongside scientifically validated treatments have the potential to increase their effectiveness and long-term impact. Music therapists working in military and veteran healthcare settings have often strategized approaches of integrative support to enhance service provision of psychotherapeutic interventions. Building on advancements in practice and research can further develop methods that music therapists can employ to collaborate more effectively with behavioral health providers and other traditional treatment disciplines.

Survey data collected for this chapter indicates a high percentage (>75%) of respondents reporting observed changes in patients during music therapy treatment, such as improved social functioning, improved emotional/self-regulation, and positive changes in identity (Gooding *et al.*, 2020). These areas correspond to PTSD diagnostic criteria (American Psychiatric Association, 2013) and can also assist in developing coping strategies that support continued improvement after music therapy treatment has ended. A holistic and patient-centered theoretical lens is often central to music therapists' conceptualization of their patients and informs how they develop integrative treatment plans that support individualized goal areas.

Being at the forefront of pioneering clinical treatment, creating community arts opportunities, and building the evidence base of new populations in an established profession can be both exciting and overwhelming. Potential areas of future application and integration of music therapy will continue to emerge along the journey, as a survey respondent shares below. Additionally, by focusing efforts on understanding service members, veterans, and the respective systems they are a part of, innovators can better discern the unique and evolving needs of these individuals. Ultimately, approaching clinical practice, community engagement, and research with openness, excitement, humility, and willingness to challenge and refine the existing knowledge of music therapy practice will continue to uncover areas for expansion within the field in general.

> Music therapy is a versatile treatment approach that can be used in conjunction with other forms of medical treatment. I believe that it could provide great benefit to the military population at large, especially those who have not made significant progress with traditional forms of treatment. In the next ten years, I would like to see music therapy and creative arts therapies in more VA healthcare facilities, military treatment facilities, and services in the community that are more accessible to military-connected populations. (Gooding *et al.*, 2020)

Areas for advancing music therapy research

The ever-enduring challenge of the music therapy profession to validate its own efficacy does not lie solely in academia or on researchers. Advocacy is an essential professional competency and music therapists must continually advance research to maintain a sustainable presence in healthcare systems that treat service members, veterans, and their families. Clinicians' contributions to the existing body of literature through peer-reviewed publications increase efficacy, build understanding and support from non-music therapy providers, and disseminate relevant information to potential future collaborators and decision makers who may invest resources in creating new programs. By building research-minded clinical programming, program evaluation outcomes and treatment findings have the potential to create a cascade effect on advancing further empirical studies.

Relevant research questions can be constructed from attunement to clinical processes and outcomes observed by practicing music therapists. A great deal of wisdom in identifying research priority areas comes from observing practice itself, and music therapists who have contributed to seminal literature have emphasized this point. Inductive research methods have provided a foundation for future areas of investigation, and guidance for program refinement and replication. Approximately 50 percent of survey respondents agreed that there is a need for music therapists to access methods of standardization in clinical practice. Developing a clear standard of care and clinical practice guidelines of music therapy is aligned with the missions of military and veteran healthcare systems, which emphasize treatment methods and interventions that have been rigorously tested for efficacy, as one survey respondent shared:

> I would love to see an advancement in evidence and consistency of licensure to make music therapy a covered healthcare benefit, including setting a standard for music therapy referrals built into clinical practice guidelines as indicated for specific interventions/protocols for specific populations of individuals with specific constellations of symptoms/diagnoses. (Gooding *et al.*, 2020)

In addition, clinicians can support this goal by collaborating on developing tools to support standardization such as assessment and intervention protocols, program evaluation, methods of measurement, and documentation templates (Betts, 2020). By identifying specific outcomes from clinical practice, music therapists can articulate treatment recommendations, including referral criteria, dosage, and duration required for maximum impact.

Foundational literature has focused on describing clinical practices as well as identifying areas for higher level research. Initially, it was impactful to focus on inductive methods of research design, such as case studies and retrospective analyses. These methods honor the dynamic nature of music therapy treatment, and the complex and varying clinical presentations that have made it difficult to generalize and gather normative data for the entire target population. Future research should focus on narrowing the potential mechanisms of action and variables impacting clinical outcomes. Randomized-control trials can assist in deepening this understanding and provide clinicians with methods of implementing targeted interventions. Research involving biomarkers (e.g., heartrate, respiration, endocrine activity) and neuroimaging (e.g., functional magnetic resonance imaging (fMRI), quantitative electroencephalography (q-EEG), magnetoencephalography (MEG)) can further support measured changes in behavior and self-reporting, clarifying the often complex and varying outcomes that patients experience in music therapy treatment. In addition to clinical practice standardization and protocol publication, guidelines regarding research priority areas are also outlined in AMTA's research recommendations report (American Music Therapy Association, 2015).

Over half of the survey respondents agreed that access to advocacy and educational materials can broaden the understanding of music therapy's unique value in military and veteran healthcare settings. Local and national initiatives that support these efforts by providing strategic support for clinicians and researchers are answering this call. Collaboration between clinicians and researchers can also result in better training for new music therapists entering the field with an interest in working with military populations. As academic programs grow and emerge, curricula are increasingly including developments in this area of practice. Research and program development operate hand in hand, garnering institutional support from clinics and university partnerships to create practicum and internship training opportunities for music therapy students. If we can build awareness of military populations as a viable career opportunity for music therapists, the number of competent and prepared clinicians who can fill the growing number of available positions across the DoD and VA will increase to meet high demands. The inclusion of these competencies in university settings also increases the likelihood that academicians are willing and able to support collaborative research efforts.

Approximately 50 percent of survey respondents agreed that access to resources that support clinical practice and program development is essential. Music therapy organizations such as Resounding Joy, Inc. have created useful clinical curriculums about military music therapy, which have guided much of the subsequent program development across the nation. An example of this is the toolbox and accompanying clinical training course, *An Introduction to Military Music Therapy Programming: Working with Active Service Members and Veterans* (Vaudreuil & Reuer, 2013). As national initiatives have expanded creative arts therapies programs to military treatment facilities and VA clinics across the U.S., it has been of vital importance to support these efforts with publications and resources accessible to the public (National Endowment for the Arts, 2020b). Building understanding of the cohesive theory and application of music therapy with military populations is necessary for standardization of best practices. Future research can understand the utility of existing resources and identify gap areas that can assist music therapists in efficacious practices. It is important also to consider how developing technologies can further enhance cohesion and collaborations between music therapists across the U.S. and internationally. Utilizing existing internal platforms within DoD and VA networks and those being developed by other national organizations can streamline collaboration and allow for more clinicians to participate in research efforts. As music therapists gain intimate understanding of the unique and expansive healthcare ecosystem in which they practice, this knowledge can be used to continue forward momentum in this ever-evolving area of clinical practice. In addition to research in the creative arts therapies, research across the spectrum of arts in health, recreational arts, and community arts engagement is warranted to capture the breadth and depth of impact that the arts have on health, wellness, and quality of life. These recommendations were clear, as indicated by one survey respondent:

> Consistent provision of music therapy services can assist in the transition from military to civilian life. Increased collaboration and acceptance of community artists are needed to extend access of arts programming to service members, veterans, and their families. (Gooding *et al.*, 2020)

The evolution of arts in health

The use of music and music therapy within the field of arts in health (AIH) has exciting potential and a myriad of opportunities for evaluation and research. According to the National Organization for Arts in Health (NOAH), the field of AIH, and its many subfields and affiliated fields (e.g., arts in medicine, arts in healthcare), is dedicated to "using the power of the arts to enhance health and wellbeing in diverse institutional and community settings" (National Organization for Arts in Health, 2017). Consistent with the World Health Organization's definition of health as "a state of complete physical, mental and social wellbeing and not merely the absence of disease or infirmity," AIH began to emerge as a discipline in the 1970s, with trainings focused on giving professional artists the knowledge and tools necessary to facilitate arts engagement in the promotion of health in healthcare and community settings (University of Florida, Center for Arts in Medicine, 2020). Decades later, it has become a multidisciplinary tool in an ever-expanding health and wellbeing toolkit amidst an ever-growing demand for its unique impact on the experience of those in healthcare settings and the overall health and wellbeing of individuals and communities.

AIH provides opportunities for expanding collaborations and diverse partners in the shared pursuit of health and wellbeing. Americans for the Arts (AFTA), a national arts advocacy organization, has worked for many years on developing and extending the reach of the National Initiative for Arts & Health Across the Military (NIAHM). The NIAHM aims to raise visibility and awareness of the potential impact of arts and creativity as instruments for health by advancing efforts to ensure the availability and accessibility of the arts to active-duty service members, veterans, their families, and all military-connected communities. Since its inception in 2012, the NIAHM has convened meetings, roundtable discussions, and national summits working towards strengthening networks and addressing practice, policy, and research to ensure sustainability of efforts. AFTA's *Arts and the Military* policy paper published for Arts Advocacy Day in 2020 states that arts and the military include creative arts therapy disciplines, such as music therapy, as well as artist-directed application of visual, literary and performing arts, and design. Within the AIH model, CATs, expressive arts therapists, and community artists work together to provide quality, cost-effective healthcare and wellness services for military, veterans, and their families (Americans for the Arts, 2020).

Integration of arts in health and the military health system

In 2019, the Walter Reed National Military Medical Center (WRNMMC) became the first military treatment facility (MTF) in the Military Health System to establish an AIH program. Staffed with an active-duty AIH Program Chief, and two CATs who serve as the clinical arts in health coordinator and community arts in health specialist, the new AIH program is an official acknowledgement of the importance and impact of arts engagements on health outcomes. Music was the driving force behind the historical application of arts engagement at WRNMMC, as well as the ultimate force for crossing the finish line in establishing the AIH program. The hospital's long-standing performing arts series, Stages of Healing, had long been bringing artists and performers into the hospital setting in both public spaces and inpatient units; however, its lack of sustainability, dedicated staff, and funding started to reveal itself through decreased performances. A desire from senior leadership to ensure the continuation of live music was the impetus for exploring the hospital's current offerings, identifying gaps and vulnerabilities, and embarking on a plan to generate sustainability. The resulting decision was to create and staff an official AIH program, which would continue the performing arts series as well as provide extended opportunities for creativity and expression in the pursuit of health and wellbeing hospital-wide.

The WRNMMC AIH mission, vision, goal, and approach

The mission of the WRNMMC AIH program is to build an integrated, sustainable program that provides the target population of military patients, families and caregivers, staff, students and interns, visitors, and volunteers with multiple opportunities to engage with the arts in support of their health and wellbeing. Its vision is to be a leading AIH program recognized for its quality and caliber within the MHS and the national AIH community, to integrate the arts into the standard of care in the military clinical environment, and to establish best practices to be modeled throughout the AIH industry. The goal of the AIH program at WRNMMC is to build a world-class program model targeting prevention and resilience rather than symptom management. Attaining the vision and accomplishing mission and goals requires a multifaceted approach that includes: live, recorded, and virtual real-time performances; player pianos throughout the command; rotating and permanent exhibits; CATs facilitating behavioral and personal change; artists in residence working at the bedside; and artists, performers, curators, and storytellers supporting program and service development.

The WRNMMC AIH program focuses on a wellness-centered approach that promotes prevention and resilience in all people, regardless of illness, injury, position, or rank. Working in an MTF and serving a military-connected community requires awareness of this unique setting and population. Serving as the first destination stateside for wounded, ill, and injured service members, WRNMMC is unique in its delivery of care, treatment, and rehabilitation for combat-injured service members and the complex injuries they experience. Additionally, the rank structure of military settings, and challenges adjusting to military practices and culture, create a uniquely vulnerable population in junior enlisted service members as well. Therefore, in creating the concept of operations (CONOPS) for the new AIH program at WRNMMC, the guiding principles of safety, inclusion, accessibility, quality, and wellness were identified as essential program components. Due to the nature of the aforementioned vulnerabilities present in an active-duty population, related to rank structure and combat injuries, safety is a paramount principle requiring the vetting of individuals and proposed engagements and programs. CATs are uniquely qualified to ensure a climate of safety through the appropriate application of the arts in individual, group, and community settings, the vetting of individuals and proposed programs, and the provision of educational in-services to hospital staff and students on safety considerations and practitioner roles within AIH.

The importance of inclusion and accessibility in AIH programming

The principle of inclusion demostrates the value placed on diversity and the understanding that working together as an interdisciplinary team enables the achievement and delivery of the best integrative AIH experience for the target population. The embracing of and respect for different backgrounds and points of view underpins and enables connection to a population that is culturally diverse and represents the full range of human differences and abilities. Accessibility is a critical principle, particularly considering the distinctive position that WRNMMC holds in the care of combat-injured service members in the U.S.

The DoD's Military Adaptive Sports program models the importance of both accessibility and wellness by using adaptive sports as "an essential way of understanding what each wounded, ill, and injured service member is able to achieve—focusing on levels of ability rather than disability" (U.S. Department of Defense, n.d.-b, para.7). Likewise, the AIH program strives to ensure access and appropriate access accommodations for AIH activities, deploying strategies that foster efficiency, effectiveness, ease of use, and satisfaction. As the flagship of military medicine, WRNMMC is committed to ensuring timely, patient-centered access to safe, high-quality healthcare for each and every beneficiary. Its AIH program is equally committed to quality care and strives to provide exemplary AIH experiences to the target population with a goal of being a standard of excellence from which all AIH programs can draw inspiration.

Additionally, wellness is a foundational focus and lens through which all AIH activities and programs are developed, provided, applied, and implemented. The belief that AIH is a key factor in improving wellness is valued for all patients, families and caregivers, staff, students and interns, visitors, and volunteers. The AIH program's focus is to optimize health and wellness through preventative measures, as well as creating a positive impact on patient care, treatment, and healing.

Music in an AIH program in military healthcare

Music has shown itself to be a critical asset, not only as the experience which led to the formation of a command-wide AIH program at WRNMMC, but in numerous operational aspects as well. Stuckey and Nobel identify music as "the most accessible and most researched medium of art and healing" (2010, p.255) and this has clearly been evident at WRNMMC. In the time of a global pandemic and the healthcare environment that COVID-19 has created, changes in operational tempo and limitations on volunteer activities were enacted; however, active-duty musicians were the first to return to playing at the hospital. The DoD, as the largest single employer of musicians in the world, has numerous service bands, composers, conductors, instrumentalists, and vocalists, so it makes sense that this group of uniformed service members were the first to return live performances to the public areas of the hospital. Using a phased-in approach, next steps include reinvigorating provision of music to the inpatient units, critical care settings, the hospital's cancer center, and primary care.

Findings on the use and benefit of music interventions are of particular interest in the primary care setting and include decreased anxiety, restoration of emotional balance, and improved management of pain (de Witte *et al.*, 2020). The policy paper, *Music Therapy and Military Populations*, identified the importance of music and music therapy as supportive tools to align with healthcare delivery models such as patient-centered care (American Music Therapy Association, 2014). A patient-centered medical home model is used in WRNNMC's internal medicine clinic where the emphasis for patients is on prevention and lifestyle management. True to the strengths-based approach of wellness, interventions are multidisciplinary in nature and focus on providing education, developing tools and skills, and empowering patients to take control of their health and wellbeing. Since music is one of the most represented disciplines within AIH, in addition to its previously mentioned accessibility, it is well positioned as an instrument of choice in the pursuit of wellness and improved health outcomes.

Summarizing the future

This chapter underscored many points highlighted throughout this book regarding the evolution and importance of music therapy treatment for military-connected populations. Historical developments, practice evolution, current positioning, and recommendations for continued applications and research of music therapy within military and veteran health systems were elucidated. Recommendations informed by literature and insights gleaned from survey responses of service members, veterans, Guardsmen, families, and providers offered unique perspectives about the future of music therapy and priority need and gap areas in the realms of education, training, practice, and research. Integration of an innovative AIH program at a renowned medical treatment facility was detailed and included implications for an extended impact of the arts on communities and society at large.

This chapter, and book as a whole, is an important accomplishment in the advancement of music therapy in military, veteran, and civilian healthcare systems, as well as in academia. Additionally, it is a call to action for music therapists, academicians, researchers, military leaders, policy makers, and all affiliated constituents to work in their respective roles learning and understanding about and advocating for the integration and advancement of comprehensive and creative approaches to care for military-connected populations. Much like the contributing authors, editor, and publisher of this book worked together to achieve a collective goal, through strategic planning, advocacy, and teamwork, intentional collaboration and partnerships can forge forward in advancing the arts in military and veteran healthcare. As Founding Father John Dickinson wrote in the pre-Revolutionary War "The Liberty Song" (1768), "United we stand, divided we fall." This statement rings true and captures the essence of the dedication of military service, mission readiness, steadfast familial support, and the devoted commitment of military and civilian communities and society at large to provide the highest quality care for the service members, veterans, and their families who selflessly sacrifice to protect our freedoms.

In closing this chapter and book and with anticipation of what's to come, a quote by Maxine Hong Kingston from *Veterans of War, Veterans of Peace*, is an apt summation of this book's intention and overarching mission of integrated care for military-connected populations to include the creative arts therapies existing synergistically on a clinic to community continuum. Kingston states, "When you hug one American, you hug all of us...singing, hugging, dancing, we [are] a community" (2006, p.1).

References

Ainlay, G.W. (1948). The Place of Music in Military Hospitals. In D.M. Schullian and M. Schoen (eds). *Music and Medicine* (pp.322–351). New York, NY: Henry Schuman.

American Art Therapy Association (2020). *7 Facts to Know on Veterans Day*. Retrieved from: https://arttherapy.org/blog-7-facts-to-know-on-veterans-day.

American Music Therapy Association (2011). *History of Music Therapy*. Retrieved from: www.musictherapy.org/about/history.

American Music Therapy Association (2013). *American Music Therapy Professional Competencies*. Retrieved from: www.musictherapy.org/about/competencies.

American Music Therapy Association (2014). *Music Therapy and Military Populations*. Retrieved from: www.musictherapy.org/research/ music_therapy_and_military_populations.

American Music Therapy Association (2015). *Improving Access and Quality: Music Therapy Research 2025 Executive Summary and Conclusions*. Retrieved from: www.musictherapy.org/music_therapy_research_2025_summary.

American Music Therapy Association (2019). Code of ethics. Retrieved from: www.musictherapy.org/about/ethics.

American Psychiatric Association (2013). *Diagnostic and Statistical Manual of Mental Disorders* (5th ed.). Arlington, VA: American Psychiatric Association.

Americans for the Arts (2020). *Arts and the Military: Improving the Health and Wellbeing of Military and Veteran Populations through the Arts*. Retrieved from: www.americansforthearts.org/sites/default/files/pdf/2020/events/naas/16.%20Arts%20and%20the%20Military.pdf.

Arrington, G.E. (1954). Music in Medicine. In E. Podolsky (ed.). *Music Therapy* (pp.252–287). New York, NY: Philosophical Library.

Babikian, T., Zeltzer, L., Tachdjian, V., Henry, L., *et al.* (2013). Music as medicine: A review and historical perspective. *Alternative and Complementary Therapies*, 19(5), 251–254.

Bacalzo, M. (2020). Resilience is key for new psychological health director. *National Guard*. Retrieved from: www.ang.af.mil/Media/Article-Display/Article/2242240/resilience-is-key-for-new-psychological-health-director.

Barton, W.E. (1945). The reconditioning and rehabilitating program in Army Hospitals. *Army of the United States*, 608–613.

Beaty, R.E. (2015). The neuroscience of musical improvisation. *Neuroscience and Biobehavioral Reviews*, 51, 108–117.

Bensimon, M., Amir, D., & Wolf, Y. (2008). Drumming through trauma: Music therapy with post-traumatic soldiers. *The Arts in Psychotherapy*, 35, 34–48. https://doi.org/10.1016/j.aip.2007.09.002.

Bensimon, M., Amir, D., & Wolf, Y. (2012). A pendulum between trauma and life: Group music therapy with post-traumatized soldiers. *The Arts in Psychotherapy*, 39, 223–233. https://doi.org/10.1016/j.aip.2012.03.005.

Bernstein, R. (1946). A music program for blinded veterans. *Music Educators Journal*, 33, 30–31.

Betts, D.J. (2020). *Advances in Creative Forces® Clinical Research and Applications of the Creative Arts Therapies for Treating PTSD and TBI in Military-Connected Populations*. National Endowment for the Arts. Retrieved from: www.creativeforcesnrc.arts.gov.

Betts, D.J. & Deaver, S.P. (2019). *Art Therapy Research: A Practical Guide*. New York, NY: Routledge.

Blake, R.L. (1994). Vietnam Veterans with post-traumatic stress disorder: Findings from a music and imagery project. *Journal of the Association for Music and Imagery*, 3, 5–17.

Boals, A. & Banks, J.B. (2012). Effects of traumatic stress and perceived stress on everyday cognitive functioning. *Cognition & Emotion*, 26(7), 1335–1343.

Bokhour, B., Haun, J.N., Hyde, J., Charns, M., & Kligler, B. (2020a). Transforming the Veterans Affairs to a Whole Health system of care: Time for action and research. *Medical Care*, 58(6), 295–300.

Bokhour, B., Hyde, J., Zeliadt, J., & Mohr, D.C. (2020b, February 18). *Whole Health System of Care Evaluation: A Progress Report on Outcomes of the WHS Pilot at 18 Flagship Sites*. Whole Health. Retrieved from: www.va.gov/WHOLEHEALTH/professional-resources/clinician-tools/EVIDENCE-BASED-RESEARCH.asp.

Botstein, L. (1991, March 3). Classical music; Why music in a time of war? *The New York Times*. Retrieved from: www.nytimes.com/1991/03/03/arts/classical-music-why-music-in-a-time-of-war.html.

Bowles, E. (2006). The impact of Turkish military bands on European court festivals in the 17th and 18th centuries. *Early Music*, 34(4), 533–559. Retrieved from: www.jstor.org/stable/4137306.

Boxberger, R. (1962). A Historical Study of the National Association for Music Therapy. In E.H. Schneider (ed.). *Music Therapy 1962* (pp.131–197). Lawrence, KS: The Allen Press.

Bradford, J.C. (2006). *The International Encyclopedia of Military History* (Vol. 3). New York, NY: Cynthia Parzych Publishing.

Bradt, J., Biondo, J., & Vaudreuil, R. (2019). Songs created by military service members in music therapy: A retrospective analysis. *The Arts in Psychotherapy*, 62, 19–27. http://doi.org/10.1016/j.aip.2018.11.004.

Bradt, J., Burns, D. S., & Creswell, J.W. (2013). Mixed methods research in music therapy. *Journal of Music Therapy*, 50(2), 123–148. https://doi.org/10.1093/jmt/50.2.123.

Bronson, H., Vaudreuil, R., & Bradt, J. (2018). Music therapy treatment of active duty military: An overview of intensive outpatient and longitudinal care programs. *Music Therapy Perspectives*, 36(2), 195–206. doi: 10.1093/mtp/miy006.

Brown, B. (2010). *The Gifts of Imperfection*. New York, NY: Simon & Schuster.

Browne, H.E. (1954). The Use of Music as a Therapy. In E. Podolsky (ed.). *Music Therapy*. New York, NY: Philosophical Library.

Bunt, L. & Stige, B. (2014). *Music Therapy: An Art Beyond Words* (2nd ed.). New York, NY: Routledge.

Burt, J.W. (1995). Distant thunder: Drumming with Vietnam veterans. *Music Therapy Perspectives*, 13(2), 110–112. https://doi.org/10.1093/mtp/13.2.110.

Butera-Prinzi, F., & Perlesz, A. (2004). Through children's eyes: Children's experience of living with a parent with an acquired brain injury. *Brain Injury*, 18(1), 83–101. doi:10.1080/0269905031000118500.

C-SPAN (2019). Army Capt. Luis Avila sings, "God Bless America." Retrieved from: www.c-span.org/video/?c4820132/user-clip-army-capt-luis-avila-sings-god-bless-america.

Campbell, C. (2016). Reducing waits for VHA services through use of tools of governance. *Human Service Organizations: Management, Leadership & Governance*, 40(1), 74–85.

Camus, R.F. (1975). *Military Music of the American Revolution*. Westerville, OH: Integrity Press.

Capuzzi, D. & Gross, D.R. (1998). *Introduction to Group Counseling* (2nd ed.). Denver, CO: Love Publishing Company.

Carr, C., d'Ardenne, P., Sloboda, A., Scott, C., Wang, D., & Priebe, S. (2012). Group music therapy for patients with persistent post-traumatic stress disorder: An exploratory randomized controlled trial with mixed methods evaluation. *Psychology and Psychotherapy: Theory, Research and Practice*, 85(2), 179–202.

Celina, J.G. (1977, June). A History of Veterans Homes in the United States, 1811–1930. (Unpublished doctoral dissertation). Cleveland, OH: Case Western Reserve University.

Chaiklin, S. (2020). Marian Chace Biography. American Dance Therapy Association. Retrieved from: www.adta.org/marian-chace-biography.

Chilton, G., Vaudreuil, R., Freeman, E., McLaughlan, N., Herman, J., & Cozza, S. (2020). *Creative Forces® family programming: Art therapy, dance/movement therapy, and music therapy brief vignettes.* [Manuscript submitted for publication].

Clair, A.A., Bernstein, B., & Johnson, G. (1995). Rhythm playing characteristics in persons with severe dementia including those with probable Alzheimer's type. *Journal of Music Therapy*, 32(2), 113–131. https://doi.org/10.1093/jmt/32.2.113.

Cochrane, T., Fantini, B., & Scherer, K.P. (2013). *The Emotional Power of Music: Multidisciplinary Perspective on Musical Arousal, Expression, and Social Control.* Oxford: Oxford University Press.

Codding, P. & Wacks, K. (2015, May). Music therapy with Uganda's ex-child soldier survivors. *International Association for Music & Medicine*, Newsletter, 1–3.

Comprehensive Addiction and Recovery Act (2016, July 22). 114th Congress. Retrieved from: www.congress.gov/bill/114th-congress/senate-bill/524/text.

Cordobés, T.K. (1997). Group songwriting as a method for developing group cohesion for HIV-seropositive adult patients with depression. *Journal of Music Therapy*, 34(1), 46–67.

Cozza, S.J., Knobloch, L.K., Gewirtz, A.H., DeVoe, E.R., *et al.* (2018). Lessons Learned and Future Recommendations for Conducting Research with Military Children and Families. In L. Hughes-Kirchubel, S. MacDermid Wadsworth, & D.S. Riggs (eds). *A Battle Plan for Supporting Military Families* (pp.265–287). Cham, Switzerland: Springer.

Creative Forces National Resource Center (2020). www.creativeforcesnrc.arts.gov.

Creech, S. K., Hadley, W., & Borsari, B. (2014). The impact of military deployment and reintegration on children and parenting: A systematic review. *Professional Psychology, Research and Practice*, 45(6), 452–464. https://doi.org/10.1037/a0035055.

Cronk, T. (2020). DoD releases annual suicide report for 2019. U.S. Department of Defense. Retrieved from: www.defense.gov/Explore/News/Article/Article/2370197/dod-releases-annual-suicide-report-for-2019.

Davis, J.A. (2003). Regimental bands and morale in the American Civil War. *Journal of Band Research*, 38(2), 1–20.

Davis, W.B. (1993). Keeping the dream alive: Profiles of three early twentieth century music therapists. *Journal of Music Therapy*, 30(1), 34–45. https://doi.org/10.1093/jmt/30.1.34.

Davis, W.B. & Else, B. (2019). Music Therapy with Service Members and Veterans. In S.M. Kraaz (ed.). *Music and War in the United States* (pp.291–307). New York, NY: Routledge.

Davis, W.B. & Gfeller, K.E. (2008). Music Therapy: Historical Perspective. In W.B. Davis, K.E. Gfeller, & M.H. Thaut (eds). *An Introduction to Music Therapy Theory and Practice* (3rd ed.). Silver Spring, MD: American Music Therapy Association.

de l'Etoile, S. (2000). The history of the undergraduate curriculum in music therapy. *Journal of Music Therapy*, 37(1), 51–71. https://doi.org/10.1093/jmt/37.1.51.

De Schill, S. & Lebovici, S. (eds). (1999). *The Challenge for Psychoanalysis and Psychotherapy: Solutions for the Future* (Vol. 2). London: Jessica Kingsley Publishers.

de Witte, M., Spruit, A., van Hooren, S., Moonen, X., & Stams, G. (2020). Effects of music interventions on stress-related outcomes: A systematic review and two meta-analyses. *Health Psychology Review*, 14(2); 294–324. doi: 10.1080/17437199.2019.1627897.

Dobney, J K. (2008). *Military Music in American and European Tradition*. Retrieved from: www.metmuseum.org/toah/hd/ammu/hd_ammu.htm.

Dolfini-Reed, M. & Jebo, J. (2000). *The Evolution of the Military Health Care System: Changes in Public Law and DoD Regulations*. Center for Naval Analysis. Retrieved from: www.cna.org/CNA_files/PDF/D0000437.A3.pdf.

Donahue, T. (Director) (2016). *Thank You for Your Service*. [Video file]. Gathr Films. Retrieved from: www.kanopy.com/product/thank-you-your-service.

Douglas, M. (1966). *Purity and Danger*. New York, NY: Routledge Classics.

Dunphy, K., Mullane, S., & Jacobson, M. (2013). The effectiveness of expressive arts therapies: A review of the literature. *Psychotherapy and Counselling Journal of Australia*, 2(1).

Edwards, J. (2008). The use of music in healthcare contexts: A select review of writings from the 1890s to the 1940s. *Voices: A World Forum for Music Therapy*, 8(2), 1–18. http://hdl.handle.net/10536/DRO/DU:30063095.

Elliot, V.L. (2019, July 26). Department of Veterans Affairs (VA): A primer on telehealth (R45834). Congressional Research Service. Retrieved from: https://fas.org/sgp/crs/misc/R45834.pdf.

Erkkilä, J., Punkanen, M., Fachner, J., Ala-Ruona, E., *et al.* (2011). Individual music therapy for depression: Randomised controlled trial. *The British Journal of Psychiatry*, 199(2), 132–139.

Fauser, A. (2013). *Sounds of War: Music in the United States during World War II*. New York, NY: Oxford University Press.

Health Resources and Services Administration (2015). Federal Office of Rural Health Policy. *Telehealth Programs*. Retrieved from: www.hrsa.gov/ruralhealth/telehealth/index.html.

Figinski, T. (2017). Companies are less likely to hire current military reservists. *Harvard Business Review*. Retrieved from: https://hbr.org/2017/10/research-companies-are-less-likely-to-hire-current-military-reservists.

Forrest, K. (2008). Early music musing: The music of war. *Early Music America*, 31(1), 8–10.

Gantt, M.A., Dadds, S., Burns, D.S., Glaser, D., & Moore, A.D. (2017). The effect of binaural beat technology on the cardiovascular stress response in military service members with post deployment stress. *Journal of Nursing Scholarship*, 49(4), 411–420.

Garcia, H.A. (2017). If you've never been there you wouldn't understand: The evolutionary reasons for veteran mistrust. *Evolutionary Behavioral Sciences*, 11(1), 53–62. https://doi.org/10.1037/ebs0000076.

Garrison, D.E. (2016). *The Effects of Music Assisted Relaxation on Mood Perception in Vietnam Veterans: A Pilot Study*. (Master's thesis). ProQuest Dissertations & Theses Global.

Gilliland, E.G. (1945). Music for the war wounded. *Music Educators Journal*, 31, 24–25.

Gilliland, E.G. (ed.) (1952). Preface: The development of music therapy as a profession. In *Music Therapy 1951: Book of Proceedings of the National Association for Music Therapy* (Vol. 1, pp.vii–xvi). National Association for Music Therapy. Retrieved from: https://hdl.handle.net/10217/184920.

Gilman, L. (2016). *My Music, My War*. Middletown, CT: Wesleyan University Press.

Give an Hour (n.d.). *Reserve Component Program*. Retrieved from: http://giveanhour.org/initiatives-and-programs/reserve-component.

Glasser, R.J. (2011). *Broken Bodies, Shattered Minds: A Medical Odyssey from Vietnam to Afghanistan*. Palisades, NY: History Publishing.

Gleason, B.P. (2015). Military music in the United States. *Music Educators Journal*, March. doi: 10.1177/0027432114563718.

Godleski, L., Darkins, A., & Peters, J. (2012). Outcomes of 98,609 U.S. Department of Veterans Affairs patient enrolled in telemental health services, 2006–2010. *Psychiatric Services*, 63(4), 383–385. https://doi.org/10.1176/appi.ps.201100206.

Goetz Gilliland, E. (1944). The healing power of music. *Music Educators Journal*, 31(1), 18–20. Retrieved from: www.jstor.org/stable/3386692.

Goetz Gilliland, E. (1945). Music for the war wounded. *Music Educators Journal*, 31(5), 24–25, 51.

Gold, C., Mössler, K., Grocke, D., Heldal, T.O., *et al.* (2013). Individual music therapy for mental health care clients with low therapy motivation: Multicentre randomised controlled trial. *Psychotherapy and Psychosomatics*, 82(5), 319–331.

Gooding, L.F., Bronson, H., Vaudreuil, R., & Hogue, J.D. (2020). Music Therapy with Military-Connected Populations: A Survey. [Unpublished raw data].

Gooding, L.F. & Langston, D.G. (2019). Music therapy with military populations: A scoping review. *Journal of Music Therapy*, 56(4), 315–347. https://doi.org/10.1093/jmt/thz010.

Gradus, J.L. (2017, March 30). Epidemiology of PTSD. Retrieved from: www.ptsd.va.gov/professional/treat/essentials/epidemiology.asp.

Green, R. (1947). The music program in Veterans Administration Hospitals. *Notes*, 5(1), 36–41. http://dx.doi.org/10.2307/890955.

Green, R. (1948a, May). Introducing the Newsletter. In R. Green (ed.). *Hospital Music Newsletter*, 1(1). Committee on Music in Hospitals of the National Music Council. Retrieved from: https://hdl.handle.net/10217/184827.

Green, R. (1948b, May). Hospitals Employing Full-Time Music Specialists. In R. Green (ed.). *Hospital Music Newsletter*, 1(1). Committee on Music in Hospitals of the National Music Council. Retrieved from: https://hdl.handle.net/10217/184827.

Green, R. (1948c, May). Veterans Administration Hospital Music. In R. Green (ed.). *Hospital Music Newsletter*, 1(1). Committee on Music in Hospitals of the National Music Council. Retrieved from: https://hdl.handle.net/10217/184827.

Green, R. (1948d, May). Music Program Planning. In R. Green (ed.). *Hospital Music Newsletter*, 1(1). Committee on Music in Hospitals of the National Music Council. Retrieved from: https://hdl.handle.net/10217/184827.

Green, R. (1948e, September). Music with Sports. In M. Chapman & R. Green (eds). *Hospital Music Newsletter*, 1(2). Music in Hospitals Committee of the National Music Council. Retrieved from: https://hdl.handle.net/10217/184827.

Green, R. (1949a, September). Hospital Music Research. In R. Green (ed.). *Hospital Music Newsletter*, 2(1). Hospital Music Committee of the National Music Council. Retrieved from: https://hdl.handle.net/10217/201585.

Green, R. (1949b). Hospital Music Newsletter. *Music Educators Journal*, 31, 24–25.

Guétin, S., Soua, B., Voiriot, G., Picot, M.C., & Hérisson, C. (2009). The effect of music therapy on mood and anxiety-depression: An observational study in institutionalised patients with traumatic brain injury. *Annals of Physical and Rehabilitation Medicine*, 52(1), 30–40. https://doi.org/10.1016/j.annrmp.2008.08.009.

Hanson-Abromeit, D. & Davis, W.B. (2007). A look back at the origins and development of music therapy practice and education in Iowa. *Music Therapy Perspectives*, 25(2), 155–120. https://doi.org/10.1093/mtp/25.2.115.

Hawkins, H.M. (1994). *The Healing Power of Music: The Buddha Listens to the Sounds of the Universe.* Seattle, WA: Northwest Institute of Acupuncture and Oriental Medicine.

Hayden, R., Clair, A.A., Johnson, G., & Otto, D. (2009). The effect of rhythmic auditory stimulation (RAS) on physical therapy outcomes for patients in gait training following stroke: A feasibility study. *The International Journal of Neuroscience*, 119(12), 2183–2195. https://doi.org/10.3109/00207450903152609.

Hayes, S.C. (2004). Acceptance and Commitment Therapy and the New Behavior Therapies: Mindfulness, Acceptance and Relationship. In S.C. Hayes, V.M. Follette, & M. Linehan (eds). *Mindfulness and Acceptance: Expanding the Cognitive Behavioral Tradition* (pp.1–29). New York, NY: Guilford Press.

Hayes, S.D., Strosahl, K.D. & Wilson, K.G. (2016). *Acceptance and Commitment Therapy: The Process and Practice of Mindful Change* (2nd ed.). New York, NY: Guilford Press.

Heiderscheit, A. & Madson, A. (2015). Use of the iso principle as a central method in mood management: A music psychotherapy clinical case study. *Music Therapy Perspectives*, 33(1); 45–52. https://doi.org/10.1093/mtp/miu042.

Hirschberg, R., Sylvia, L., Wright, E., Gupta, C., *et al.* (2020). Collaborative songwriting intervention for veterans with post-traumatic stress disorder. *The Journal of Alternative and Complementary Medicine*, 26(3), 198–203. http://doi.org/10.1089/acm.2019.0368.

Hirschi, T. (2017). *Causes of Delinquency*. Milton Park, Oxfordshire: Taylor & Francis.

History of Military Cadences (n.d.). Retrieved from: www.army-cadence.com/history-of-miltary-cadences.

Hogue, J., McLaughlan, N., & Vaudreuil, R. (2020). *Creative Forces®: Pilot Test of Standardized Program Evaluation in Music Therapy*. The National Intrepid Center of Excellence Research Fair. Virtual Conference. Poster Presentation.

Hong Kingston, M. (2006). *Veterans of War, Veterans of Peace*. Kihei, HI: Koa Books.

Institute of Medicine (2001). *Crossing the Quality Chasm: A New Health System for the 21st Century*. The National Academies Press. https://doi.org/10.17226/10027.

Johnson, G., Otto, D., & Clair, A.A. (2001). The effect of instrumental and vocal music on adherence to a physical rehabilitation exercise program with persons who are elderly. *Journal of Music Therapy*, 38(2), 82–96. https://doi.org/10.1093/jmt/38.2.82.

Jones, J., Walker, M., Drass, J., & Kaimal, G. (2018). Art therapy interventions for active duty military service members with post-traumatic stress disorder and traumatic brain injury. *International Journal of Art Therapy*, 23(2), 70–85.

Kapp, L. & Salazar Torreon, B. (2018). *Reserve Component Personnel Issues: Questions and Answers*. Congressional Research Service. Retrieved from: https://fas.org/sgp/crs/natsec/RL30802.pdf.

Kelly, P.J. (1997). *Creating a National Home: Building the Veterans' Welfare State,1860–1900*. Cambridge, MA: Harvard University Press.

Kintzle, S., Barr, N., Corletto, G., & Castro, C.A. (2018). PTSD in U.S. veterans: The role of social connectedness, combat experience and discharge. *Healthcare*, 6(3), 102. https://doi.org/10.3390/healthcare6030102.

Kizer, K. & Le Menestrel, S. (2019). *Strengthening the Military Family Readiness System for a Changing American Society.* The National Academies of Sciences, Engineering, and Medicine. Retrieved from: www.nap.edu/catalog/25380/strengthening-the-military-family-readiness-system-for-a-changing-american-society.

Knox, R., Yokota-Adachi, H., Kershner, J., & Jutai, J. (2003). Musical attention training program and alternating attention in brain injury: An initial report. *Music Therapy Perspectives*, 21(2), 99–104. https://doi.org/10.1093/mtp/21.2.99.

Kovner, A.R. & Knickman, J.R. (eds) (2008). *Health Care Delivery in the United States* (9th ed.). New York, NY: Springer Publishing Company.

Kraaz, S. M. (ed.) (2019). *Music and War in the United States*. New York, NY: Routledge.

Kramer, R. (2016). *Music Therapy Impacts Recovering Service Members*. Joint Base Andrews Public Affairs. Retrieved from www.jba.af.mil/News/Article-Display/Article/1034321/music-therapy-impacts-recovering-service-members.

Landless, B., Walker, MS., & Kaimal, G. (2018). Using human and computer-based text analysis of clinical notes to understand military service members' experiences with therapeutic writing. *The Arts in Psychotherapy*, 62, 77–84.

Larson, C. (1953). Music therapy—A new occupational horizon. *Etude*, 19–20.

Launay, J., Tarr, B., & Dunbar, R.I.M. (2016). Synchrony as an adaptive mechanism for large-scale human social bonding. *Ethology*, 122, 779–789. doi:10.1111/eth.12528.

Levitin, D. (2006). *This Is Your Brain on Music: The Science of a Human Obsession*. New York, NY: Penguin Publishing.

Levy, C.E., Spooner, H., Lee, J., Sonke, J., Myers, K., & Snow, E. (2017). Telehealth-based creative arts therapy: Transforming mental health and rehabilitation care for rural veterans. *The Arts in Psychotherapy*, 57, 20–26.

Lewis, R.C., Burris-Meyers, H., & Cordinell, R.L. (1947). Music as an aid to healing. *The Journal of the Acoustical Society of America*, 19(4), 544–546.

Lichtenwanger, W. (1948). The military music of the Ottoman Turks. *Bulletin of the American Musicological Society*, 11, 55–57. Retrieved from: www.jstor.org/stable/829290.

Light, G.A., Love, D.M., Benson, D.W., & Morch, E.T. (1954). Music in Surgery. In *Music Therapy 1953: Third Book of Proceedings of the National Association for Music Therapy*. Lawrence, KA: National Association for Music Therapy.

Light, S. (1946). *Music in Medicine*. Boston, MA: New England Conservatory of Music.

Lightstone, A.J., Bailey, S.K., & Voros, P. (2015). Collaborative music therapy via remote video technology to reduce a veteran's symptoms of severe, chronic PTSD. *Arts & Health*, 7, 123–136. https://doi.org/10.1080/17533015.2015.1019895.

Lim, H.A., Miller, K., & Fabian, C. (2011). The effects of therapeutic instrumental music performance on endurance level, self-perceived fatigue level, and self-perceived exertion of inpatients in physical rehabilitation. *Journal of Music Therapy*, 48(2), 124–148. https://doi.org/10.1093/jmt/48.2.124.

Lorr, M. (1949). Patient Behavior Scales. In R. Green (ed.). *Hospital Music Newsletter*, 1(3). Committee on Music in Hospitals of the National Music Council. Retrieved from: https://hdl.handle.net/10217/184827.

Lowe, K., Adams. K., Browne, B., & Hinkle, K. (2012). Impact of military deployment on family relationship. *Journal of Family Studies*, 18(1):17–27. doi: 10.5172/jfs.2012.18.1.17.

Luckey, C. (2020). *On the 2020 Posture of the United States Army Reserve: America's Global Operational Reserve Force.* Subcommittee on Defense Committee on Appropriations United States House of Representatives. Retrieved from: www.usar.army.mil/About-Us/Posture-Statement.

Lynch, R.L. (2019, December 17). American for the Arts and Americans for the Arts Action Fund issue statement in response to passage of FY 2020 spending bills. Americans for the Arts. Retrieved from: www.americansforthearts.org/news-room/press-releases/americans-for-the-arts-and-americans-for-the-arts-action-fund-issue-statement-in-response-to-passage.

Madsen, C., Vaughan, M., & Pérez Koehlmoos, T. (2017). Use of integrative medicine in the United States military health system. *Evidence-Based Complementary and Alternative Medicine*. https://doi.org/10.1155/2017/9529257.

Marriner, G.V.R. (1945). Music in reconditioning in Army Service Forces Hospitals. *Second Series*, 2(3), 161–163.

Marshall, G.C. (1944). TB MED 103. *War Department Technical Bulletin, Group Psychotherapy*, 4 August 1944.

McCaffrey, T. (2015). Music therapy's development in mental healthcare: A historical consideration of early ideas and intersecting agents. *Music & Medicine*, 7(2), 28–33.

McFerran, K. & Rickson, D. (2014). Community music therapy in schools: Realigning with the needs of contemporary students, staff and systems. *International Journal of Community Music*, 7. https://doi.org/10.1386/ijcm.7.1.75_1

McKay, L.A. (1945). Music as a group therapeutic agent in the treatment of convalescents. *Sociometry*, 8, 233–237.

McWhirter, C. (2012). *Battle Hymns: The Power and Popularity of Music in the Civil War*. Chapel Hill, NC: The University of North Carolina Press.

Melnyk, B.M., & Fineout-Overholt, E. (2005). Making the Case for Evidence-Based Practice. In B.M. Melnyk & E. Fineout-Overholt (eds). *Evidence-Based Practice in Nursing and Healthcare: A Guide to Best Practice* (pp.3–24). Philadelphia, PA: Lippincott Williams & Wilkins.

Mendez, B. (2019). FY2020 budget request for the military health system. Congressional Research Service, Report. Retrieved from: https://fas.org/sgp/crs/natsec/IF11206.pdf.

Merriam, A. (1964). Uses and Functions. In *The Anthropology of Music*. Evanston, IL: Northwestern University Press.

Michel, D.E. & Pinson, J. (2005). *Music Therapy in Principle and Practice*. Springfield, IL: Charles C. Thomas Publishing.

Military Health System (2020). DHA Director outlines how MHS standardization bolsters reform. Military Health Systems Communication Office. Retrieved from: https://health.mil/News/Articles/2020/10/15/DHA-Director-outlines-how-MHS-standardization-bolsters-reform.

Military OneSource (2020). *Kansas Military Base Overview: Military Installations*. Retrieved from: https://installations.militaryonesource.mil/state/KS.

Military OneSource (n.d.-a). *About the National Guard Family Program, Overview*. Retrieved from: www.militaryonesource.mil/national-guard/national-guard-family-program/about-the-national-guard-family-program?redirect=%2Fnational-guard%2Fnational-guard-family-program.

Military OneSource (n.d.-b). *About Military OneSource: Support for Military Life*. Retrieved from: www.militaryonesource.mil/about-us.

Military OneSource (n.d.-c). *National Guard & Military Reserves, Joint Service Support*. Retrieved from: www.militaryonesource.mil/national-guard/joint-services-support-program.

Military OneSource (n.d.-d). *Returning Home from Deployment—The Essentials*. Retrieved from: www.militaryonesource.mil/military-life-cycle/deployment/returning-home-from-deployment/returning-home-from-deployment-the-essentials.

MISSION Act (2018, June 6). 115th Congress. Retrieved from www.congress.gov/bill/115th-congress/senate-bill/2372.

Morley, I. (2013). *The Pre-History of Music: Human Evolution, Archaeology, and the Origins of Musicality*. Oxford: Oxford University Press.

"Music for rehabilitation of war casualties." (1944). *Musical Digest*, 25, 10–14, 22–25.

Musicians for World Harmony, MUSIC Heals program (2015). Retrieved from: www.musiciansforworldharmony.org/musicians-for-world-harmony-abroad-music-therapy-charity.

"Music helps veterans with impaired hearing." (1946, June 2). *The New York Times*, p.36.

"Music physically considered." (1789, February). *Columbian Magazine*, 111, 90–93.

Myers, M. (2019). The National Guard's suicide rate has surpassed the other military components. *Military Times*. Retrieved from: www.militarytimes.com/news/your-military/2019/09/26/the-national-guards-suicide-rate-has-surpassed-the-other-military-components.

NAMM Foundation (2021). *What We Do*. Retrieved from: www.nammfoundation.org/WHAT-WE-DO.

National Endowment for the Arts (2018, June). *Creative Forces Clinical Research: A Strategic Framework and Five-Year Agenda (2018–2022)*. Retrieved from: www.arts.gov/sites/default/files/CREATIVE FORCES-Clinical-Research-Framework-and-Agenda-10.23.18.pdf.

National Endowment for the Arts (2019). National Endowment for the Arts announces expansion of Creative Forces Healing Arts Network: Three veteran-serving telehealth sites to join the network. Retrieved from: www.arts.gov/news/2019/national-endowment arts-announces-expansion-creative-forces-healing-arts-network.

National Endowment for the Arts (2020a). *History, Impact, and Future of Clinical Activities of Creative Forces®*. [Video file]. Creative Forces: NEA Military Healing Arts Network. Retrieved from: www.youtube.com/watch?v=2bfEyjotlBk&feature=youtu.be.

National Endowment for the Arts (2020b). *Creative Forces: Research*. Retrieved from: www.arts.gov/initiatives/creative-forces/creative-forces-research.

National Endowment for the Arts (2021). *Creative Forces Site Locations*. Retrieved from: https://www.creativeforcesnrc.arts.gov/what-we-do/locations.

National Endowment for the Arts (n.d.). *About Creative Forces*. Retrieved from: www.arts.gov/national-initiatives/creative-forces.

National Museum of Health and Medicine (c.WWI; MIS 59-12935-406). Patient engaged in music therapy to assist with physical rehabilitation. Medical Illustration Service (MIS). Library Collection. Otis Historical Archives, OHA 233.05.

National Organization for Arts in Health (2017). *Arts, Health, and Well-Being in America*. San Diego, CA: Author. Retrieved from: https://thenoah.net/wp-content/uploads/2019/01/NOAH-2017-White-Paper-Online-Edition.pdf.

Nelson, A. (1958). Mental patients can like new music! In E.H. Schneider (ed.). *Bulletin for the National Association of Music Therapy*, 7(3) (September), 7–8. Retrieved from: https://hdl.handle.net/10217/201592.

Newsweek (1944, December 18). "Piano in your lap." *Newsweek*, 24, 66, 68.

Olson, K.E. (1981). *Music and Muskets: Bands and Bandsmen of the American Civil War*. Westport, CT: Greenwood Press.

Otto, D., Cochran, V., Johnson, G., & Clair, A.A. (1999). The influence of background music on task engagement in frail, older persons in residential care. *Journal of Music Therapy*, 36(3), 182–195. https://doi.org/10.1093/jmt/36.3.182.

Otto, D. & Woodward, L. (2020a). VHA Music Therapist Information Spreadsheet. [Unpublished raw data].

Otto D. & Woodward, L. (2020b). Therapist Reported Trends in the Delivery of VA Music Therapy Services: A Survey. [Unpublished raw data].

Paperte, F. (1946). Music in military medicine. *Mental Hygiene*, 30, 56–64.

Purdue Online Writing Lab (n.d.). *White Paper: Purpose and Audience*. https://owl.purdue.edu/owl/subject_specific_writing/professional_technical_writing/white_papers/index.html.

Quinto, L. (1951). Scope of the Hospital Music Program and Professional Opportunities in Veteran Administration Hospitals. In E.G. Gilliland (ed.). *Music Therapy 1951* (pp.70–72). Chicago, IL: National Association for Music Therapy.

Reik, T. (1954). The haunting melody: Psychoanalytic experiences in life and music. *Notes*,11(2), 308–310. doi: 10.2307/892704.

Resounding Joy, Inc. (2021). Semper Sound Military Music Therapy Program. Retrieved from: https://resoundingjoyinc.org/semper-sound/

Robb, S.L. (2014). *Journal of Music Therapy*: Advancing the science and practice of music therapy. *Journal of Music Therapy*, 5(1), 1–3. doi: 10.1093/jmt/thu005.

Robb, S.L. & Meadows, A. (2015). Cultures of Inquiry in Music Therapy Research and the Changing Landscape of Knowledge Generation and Implementation. In B. Else & A. Farbman (eds). *Improving Access and Quality: Music Therapy Research 2025* (pp.19–23). Silver Spring, MD: American Music Therapy Association.

Rorke, M.A. (1996). Music and the wounded of World War II. *Journal of Music Therapy*, 33(3), 189–207. https://doi.org/10.1093/jmt/33.3.189.

Sacks, O. (ed.) (1998). *Music and the Brain: Clinical Applications of Music in Neurologic Rehabilitation*. St. Louis, MO: MMB Music.

Sacks, O. (2008). *Musicophilia: Tales of Music and the Brain*. New York, NY: Random House.

Schäfer, T., Sedlmeier, P., Städtler, C., & Huron, D. (2013). The psychological functions of music listening. *Frontiers in Psychology*, 4(511). doi: 10.3389/fpsyg.2013.00511.

Schneck, D.J. & Berger, D.S. (2006). *The Music Effect: Music Physiology and Clinical Applications*. London: Jessica Kingsley Publishing.

Schoen-Nazzaro, M.B. (1978). Plato and Aristotle on the ends of music. *Laval Theologique et Philosophique*, 34(3), 261–273.

Schullian, D.M., & Schoen, M. (eds) (1948). *Music and Medicine*. New York, NY: Henry Schuman.

Schultz, W. (2019, May 15). Military Construction, Veterans Affairs, and related agencies appropriations bill, 2020 (Report No. 116–163) [To accompany H.R. 2745]. Committee on Appropriations. Retrieved from: www.congress.gov/116/crpt/hrpt63/CRPT-116hrpt63.pdf.

Sears, W.W. (1960). Know your Officers-President Donald E. Michel. In E.H. Schneider (ed.). *Bulletin for the National Association of Music Therapy*, 9(2) (May), 3. Retrieved from: https://hdl.handle.net/10217/201594.

Sears, W.W. (ed.) (1964). Association activities. *Journal of Music Therapy*, 1(1), 30–32. https://doi.org/10.1093/jmt/1.1.30.

Sheehan, V.M. (1946). Rehabilitation of aphasics in an Army hospital. *Journal of Speech Disorders*, 11, 149–157.

Shin, L., Rauch, S., & Pitman, R. (2006). Amygdala, medial prefrontal cortex, and hippocampal function in PTSD. *Annals of the New York Academy of Sciences*, 1071: 67–79. doi: 10.1196/annals.1364.007.

Shing, K. (2016). Music and Music Therapy: Exploring the Perspectives of Local U.S. Military Veterans. [Master's thesis]. ProQuest Dissertations & Theses Global.

Silverman, M.J. (2006). Forty years of case studies: A history of clinical case studies in the *Journal of Music Therapy*, *Music Therapy*, and *Music Therapy Perspectives*. *Music Therapy Perspectives*, 24(1), 4–12. https://doi.org/10.1093/mtp/24.1.4.

Simon, W. (1945). The value of music in resocialization and rehabilitation of the mentally ill. *Military Surgeon*, 97, 498–500.

Singer, B.A. (1983). Psychosocial trauma, defense strategies and treatment considerations in cancer patients and their families. *American Journal of Family Therapy*, 11(3), 15–21.

Smith, E. (2020). Guard suicides drop but outreach programs continue, expand. Retrieved from: www.nationalguard.mil/News/Article/2368146/guard-suicides-drop-but-outreach-programs-continue-expand.

Solomon, A.L. (1984). A Historical Study of the National Association for Music Therapy, 1960–1980. [Doctoral dissertation, University of Kansas]. Mountain Scholar: Digital Collections of Colorado and Wyoming. Retrieved from: https://hdl.handle.net/10217/184826.

Solomon, A.L. (1993). A history of the *Journal of Music Therapy*: The first decade (1964–1973). *Journal of Music Therapy*, 30(1), 3–33. https://doi.org/10.1093/jmt/30.1.3.

Sonne, P. (2020). Already facing a grueling year, National Guard revs up for election and aftermath. *Washington Post*. Retrieved from: www.washingtonpost.com/national-security/election-national-guard/2020/10/19/a7c118ae-0fd3-11eb-bfcf-b1893e2c51b4_story.html.

Sound Health (2021). *Sound Health: An NIH-Kennedy Center Partnership*. Retrieved from: www.nih.gov/research-training/medical-research-initiatives/sound-health.

Sound Health Network (2021). *About Us*. Retrieved from: https://soundhealth.ucsf.edu/about-us-0.

Spencer, J. (2013). *A Historical Review of Music Therapy and the Department of Veterans Affairs*. [Master's thesis]. ProQuest Dissertations & Theses Global.

Spooner, H., Lee, J.B., Langston, D.G., Sonke, J., Myers, K.J., & Levy, C.E. (2019). Using distance technology to deliver the creative arts therapies to veterans: Case studies in art, dance/movement and music therapy. *The Arts in Psychotherapy*, 62, 12–18.

Steenkamp, M.M., Litz, B.T., Hoge, C.W., & Marmar, C.R. (2015). Psychotherapy for military-related PTSD: A review of randomized clinical trials. *Journal of the American Medical Association*, 314(5): 489–500. doi: 10.1001/jama.2015.8370.

Stewart, K. (2018). All roads lead to where I stand: A case review. *Music and Medicine: An Interdisciplinary Journal*, 10(3), 130–141.

Story, K.M. & Beck, B.F. (2017). Guided imagery and music with female military veterans: An intervention development study. *The Arts in Psychotherapy*, 55, 93–102. https://doi.org/10.1016/j.aip.2017.05.003.

Stuckey, H. & Nobel, J. (2010). The connection between art, healing, and public health: A review of current literature. *American Journal of Public Health*, 100, 254–263. doi: 10.2105/AJPH.2008.156497.

Sullivan, J.M. (2007). Music for the injured soldiers: A contribution of American women's military bands during World War II. *Journal of Music Therapy*, 44(3), 282–305.

Sullivan, J.M. (2011). *Bands of Sisters: U.S. Women's Military Bands during World War II*. Lanham, MD: Scarecrow Press.

Taylor, D. (1981). Music in the general hospital from 1900 to 1950. *Journal of Music Therapy*, 18(2), 62–73. https://doi.org/10.1093/jmt/18.2.62.

Taylor, I.A. & Paparte, F. (1958). Current theory and research in the effects of music on human behavior. *The Journal of Aesthetics and Art Criticism*, 17(2), 251–258. www.jstor.org/stable/427527.

Taylor, S.L., Hoggatt, K.J., & Kligler, B. (2019). Complementary and integrated health approaches: What do veterans use and want? *Journal of General Internal Medicine*, 34(7), 1192–1199. https://doi.org/10.1007/s11606-019-04862-6.

Thaut, M.H. (2005). *Rhythm, Music, and the Brain: Scientific Foundations and Clinical Applications*. New York, NY: Routledge Publishing.

Thaut, M.H., Gardiner, J.C., Holmberg, D., Horwitz, J., *et al.* (2009). Neurologic music therapy improves executive function and emotional adjustment in traumatic brain injury rehabilitation. *New York Academy of Sciences*, 1169, 406–416s

Thaut, M.H., & Hoemberg, V. (eds) (2014). *Handbook of Neurologic Music Therapy*. Oxford: Oxford University Press.

Thaut, M.H., Thaut, C., & Lagasse, B. (2008). Music Therapy in Neurologic Rehabilitation. In W.B. Davis, K.E. Gefeller, & M.H. Thaut (eds). *An Introduction to Music Therapy Theory and Practice* (3rd ed.) (pp.261–304). New York, NY: McGraw-Hill College Press.

The First Muster (2015). Retrieved from: www.nationalguard.mil/Resources/Image-Gallery/Historical-Paintings/Heritage-Series/The-First-Muster.

The White House (2019, September 19). Second Lady Karen Pence hosts meeting to highlight creative arts therapies for military service members and veterans. Retrieved from: www.presidency.ucsb.edu/documents/press-release-second-lady-karen-pence-hosts-meeting-highlight-creative-arts-therapies-for.

Trotter, W.R. (2005). *The Music of War. Military History*. Retrieved from: www.historynet.com/the-music-of-war.htm.

Tyson, F. (1981). *Psychiatric Music Therapy: Origins and Development*. New York, NY: Fred Weidner & Sons Printers, Inc.

University of Florida, Center for Arts in Medicine (2020). *What is arts in health?* Retrieved from: https://arts.ufl.edu/academics/center-for-arts-in-medicine/about/what-is-arts-in-medicine.

University of Southern California (2020). The literature review. Retrieved from: https://libguides.usc.edu/c.php?g=235034&p=1559822.

Unkefer, R.F. (1961). Factors contributing to the professional growth of music therapy. *Bulletin for the National Association of Music Therapy*, 10(2) (May), 5, 11–12. Retrieved from: https://hdl.handle.net/10217/201595.

U.S. Department of Defense (2016). *NEA, DoD Launch Creative Forces Sites Expansion to Increase Art Therapies*. Retrieved from: www.defense.gov/Explore/News/Article/Article/991741/nea-dod-launch-creative-forces-sites-expansion-to-increase-art-therapies.

U.S. Department of Defense (2018). *243rd Army Birthday Live Event (1:26:30–1:28:30)*. Defense Visual Information Distribution Service, U.S. Army. Retrieved from: www.dvidshub.net//video/613163/243rd-army-birthday-live-event.

U.S. Department of Defense (2019). *Annual Suicide Report*, calendar year 2018. Retrieved from: www.dspo.mil/Portals/113/2018%20DoD%20Annual%20Suicide%20Report_FINAL_25%20SEP%2019_508c.pdf.

U.S. Department of Defense (n.d.-a). Fact Sheet: Overview of the Department of Defense's Military Health System. Retrieved from: https://archive.defense.gov/home/features/2014/0614_healthreview/docs/Fact_Sheet_Overview.PDF.

U.S. Department of Defense (n.d.-b) *About the Office of Warrior Care: Military Adaptive Sports Program*. Retrieved from: https://warriorcare.dodlive.mil/about.

U.S. Department of Defense National Guard Bureau (2020). *2020 National Guard Bureau Posture Statement: Implementing the National Defense Strategy*. Retrieved from www.nationalguard.mil/portals/31/Documents/PostureStatements/2020-National-Guard-Bureau-Posture-Statement.pdf.

U.S. Department of Defense National Guard Bureau (2021). *2021 National Guard Bureau Posture Statement: Force for the Future*. Retrieved from: www.nationalguard.mil/portals/31/Documents/PostureStatements/2021%20National%20Guard%20Bureau%20Posture%20Statement.pdf.

U.S. Department of Defense National Guard Bureau (n.d.). *Warrior Resilience & Fitness Division Factsheet*. Retrieved from: www.nationalguard.mil/Portals/31/Documents/J-1/WRF/ngb-wrf-fact-sheet.pdf.

U.S. Department of Defense Traumatic Brain Injury Center of Excellence (2020). *DoD Numbers for Traumatic Brain Injury—Worldwide Totals*. Defense Medical Surveillance System, Theater Medical Data Store, Armed Forces Health Surveillance Division. Retrieved from: www.health.mil/About-MHS/OASDHA/Defense-Health-Agency/Research-and-Development/Traumatic-Brain-Injury-Center-of-Excellence/DoD-TBI-Worldwide-Numbers.

U.S. Departments of Defense and Veterans Affairs (2016). *VA/DoD Clinical Practice Guideline for the Management of Concussion-Mild Traumatic Brain Injury*. Retrieved from: www.healthquality.va.gov/guidelines/rehab/mtbi/mtbicpgfullcpg50821816.pdf.

U.S. Department of Personnel Management (1979, September & rev. 2004, November). Multiseries position classification standard for therapist series, GS-0633/0639. *Therapist Position Series, GS-0633/0639*, TS 39.

U.S. Department of Veterans Affairs (1996, January 22). Human resource management letter No. 05-96-01: Position classification guidance for recreation/creative arts therapist positions.

U.S. Department of Veterans Affairs (2005, January 1). *About VA: History—VA History*. Retrieved from www.va.gov/about_va/vahistory.asp. (Accessed: May 23, 2020).

U.S. Department of Veterans Affairs (2017). Memorial Day concert to feature an Army captain's road to recovery after an IED blast. *VAntage Point: Official Blog of the U.S. Department of Veterans Affairs*. Retrieved from: www.blogs.va.gov/VAntage/38026/memorial-day-concert-feature-army-captains-road-recovery-ied-blast.

U.S. Department of Veterans Affairs (2018). *Health services research and development: Spotlight on evidence-based practice*. www.hsrd.research.va.gov/news/feature/ebp.cfm.

U.S. Department of Veterans Affairs (2019a, May 31). *Department of Veterans Affairs FY 2018–2024 Strategic Plan*. Retrieved from www.va.gov/oei/docs/va2018-2024strategicplan.pdf.

U.S. Department of Veterans Affairs (2019b). *2019 National Veteran Suicide Prevention Annual Report*. Retrieved from www.mentalhealth.va.gov/docs/data-sheets/2019/2019_National_Veteran_Suicide_Prevention_Annual_Report_508.pdf.

U.S. Department of Veterans Affairs (2019c). Veterans Health Administration. Appendix G60: Recreation and creative arts therapist qualification standards GS-0638. In *VA Handbook 5005: Staffing* (pp.1–47). Retrieved from: www.va.gov/vapubs/Search_action.cfm?formno=&tkey=&dType=2&SortBy=pub_num&sort=desc&oid=0.

U.S. Department of Veterans Affairs (2020a, June 1). Office of Community Engagement. *The Office of Community Engagement Serves Veterans Through Partnership*. Retrieved from: www.va.gov/healthpartnerships.

U.S. Department of Veterans Affairs (2020b). VA strengthens care and benefits for Veterans with $243 billion budget request for fiscal year 2021. Office of Public and Intergovernmental Affairs. Retrieved from: www.va.gov/opa/pressrel/pressrelease.cfm?id=5393.

U.S. Department of Veterans Affairs National Center for PTSD (2015). *Traumatic Brain Injury and PTSD*. Retrieved from: www.ptsd.va.gov/public/problems/ traumatic_brain_injury_and_ptsd.asp.

U.S. Department of Veterans Affairs (n.d.-a). *VA Capitol Health Care Network: Our History*. Retrieved from: www.va.gov/VISN5/about/history.asp#:~:text=In%201930%2C%20VA%20consisted%20of,more%20than%20doubled%20to%2097.

U.S. Department of Veterans Affairs (n.d.-b). *The Department of Veterans Affairs Human Resource Strategic Plan 2005–2010*. Retrieved from: www.va.gov/ofcadmin/docs/hra_strategic_plan.pdf.

U.S. Department of Veterans Affairs (n.d.-c). *Rehabilitation and Prosthetic Services*. Retrieved from: www.prosthetics.va.gov.

U.S. Department of Veterans Affairs (n.d.-d). *Veterans Health Administration: VA Adaptive Sports & Therapeutic Arts*. Retrieved from: www.blogs.va.gov/nvspse.

U.S. Department of Veterans Affairs (n.d.-e). *National Veterans Creative Arts Festival—History*. Retrieved from: www.blogs.va.gov/nvspse/nvcaf-history.

U.S. Department of Veterans Affairs (n.d.-f). *Veterans Health Administration: About VHA*. Retrieved from: www.va.gov/health/aboutvha.asp. (Accessed: May 31, 2020).

U.S. Department of Veterans Affairs (n.d.-g). *Mission Statement*. Retrieved from: www.va.gov/landing2_about.htm.

U.S. Department of Veterans Affairs (n.d.-h). *Whole Health*. Whole Health. Retrieved from: www.va.gov/wholehealth.

U.S. Department of Veterans Affairs (n.d.-i). *Vet Centers (Readjustment Counseling) Home*. Program Homepage. Retrieved from: www.vetcenter.va.gov.

U.S. Veterans Administration (1948). *Annual report: 1947*. Retrieved from: www.va.gov/vetdata/docs/FY1947.pdf.

U.S. Veterans Administration (1949). *Annual report: 1948*. Retrieved from: www.va.gov/vetdata/docs/FY1948.pdf.

U.S. Veterans Administration (1950). *Annual report: 1949*. Retrieved from: www.va.gov/vetdata/docs/FY1949.pdf.

U.S. Veterans Administration (1951). *Annual report: 1950*. Retrieved from: www.va.gov/vetdata/docs/FY1950.pdf.

U.S. Veterans Administration (1952). *Annual report: 1951*. Retrieved from: www.va.gov/vetdata/docs/FY1951.pdf.

U.S. Veterans Administration (1953). *Annual report: 1952*. Retrieved from: www.va.gov/vetdata/docs/FY1952.pdf.

U.S. Veterans Administration (1954). *Annual report: 1953*. Retrieved from: www.va.gov/vetdata/docs/FY1953.pdf.

U.S. Veterans Administration (1956). *Annual report: 1955*. Retrieved from: www.va.gov/vetdata/docs/FY1955.pdf.

U.S. Veterans Administration (1957a). *Annual report: 1956*. Retrieved from: www.va.gov/vetdata/docs/FY1956.pdf.

U.S. Veterans Administration (1957b). *Annual report: 1957*. Retrieved from: www.va.gov/vetdata/docs/FY1957.pdf.

U.S. Veterans Administration (1964, February–March). Rehabilitative recreation in the Veterans Administration. *Personal Information Bulletin: Special Issue on Recruitment*, 174, 5–7. Retrieved from: https://books.google.com/books?id=1atgCLvDNKoC&printsec=frontcover#v=onepage&q&f=false.

U.S. Veterans Administration (1967). *Annual report: 1967*. Retrieved from: www.va.gov/vetdata/docs/FY1967.pdf.

U.S. Veterans Administration (1969). *Annual report: 1968*. Retrieved from: www.va.gov/vetdata/docs/FY1968.pdf.

U.S. War Department (1945). *Music in Reconditioning in ASF Convalescent and General Hospitals*. (Technical Bulletin MED 187). Retrieved from: https://mountainscholar.org/handle/10217/184765.

van de Wall, W. (1936). *Music in Institutions*. New York, NY: Russell Sage Foundation.

van de Wall, W. (1946). *Music in Hospitals*. New York, NY: Russell Sage Foundation.

van de Wetering, M. (1984). The popular concept of "home" in nineteenth-century America. *Journal of American Studies*, 18(1), 5–28.

Vaudreuil, R. (2020) National Guard and Reserve Questionnaire. [Unpublished raw data].

Vaudreuil, R., Avila, L., Bradt, J., & Pasquina, P. (2019a). Music therapy applied to complex blast injury in interdisciplinary care: a case report. *Disability and Rehabilitation*,19(41), 2333–2342. https://doi.org/10.1080/09638288.2018.1462412.

Vaudreuil, R., Biondo, J., & Bradt, J. (2020a). Music therapy with active-duty service members: Group protocol description and secondary analysis of protocol evaluations. *Music Therapy Perspectives*, 38(2), 167–177. https://doi.org/10.1093/mtp/miaa006.

Vaudreuil, R., Bronson, H., & Bradt, J. (2019b). Bridging the clinic to community: Music performance asocial transformation for military service members. *Frontiers in Psychology*, 10, 119. www.frontiersin.org/articles/10.3389/fpsyg.2019.00119/full.

Vaudreuil, R., Langston, D., Magee, W., Betts, D., Kass, S., & Levy, C. (2020b). Implementing music therapy through telehealth: Considerations for military populations. *Disability & Rehabilitation: Assistive Technology*, 1 (July), 1–10.

Vaudreuil, R. & Reuer, B. (2013). *MusicWorx Toolbox Series: An Introduction to Military Music Therapy Programming: Working with Active Service Members and Veterans* (3rd ed.). San Diego, CA: MusicWorx.

Vaudreuil, R., Walker, M. Freeman, E., Hogue, J., Betts, D. (2020c). *Standardization of Clinical Operations for Creative Arts Therapies Disciplines to Support and Drive Clinical Research across the Creative Forces®: NEA Military Healing Arts Network*. The National Intrepid Center of Excellence Research Fair. Virtual Conference. Poster Presentation.

Vergun, D. (2016). Survival rates improving for Soldiers wounded in combat, says Army surgeon general. Army News Service, Washington DC. Retrieved from: www.army.mil/article-amp/173808/survival_rates_improving_for_soldiers_wounded_in_combat_says_army_surgeon_general.

Vergun, D. (2020). Medical improvements saved many lives during World War I. Feature, Know Your Military. U.S. Department of Defense. Retrieved from: www.defense.gov/Explore/Features/Story/Article/2115192/medical-improvements-saved-many-lives-during-world-war-ii.

Villanueva, J.A. (n.d.). 24 *Notes that Tap Deep Emotions*. Retrieved from www.ausa.org/history-taps.

Waldon, E.G. (2001). The effects of group music therapy on mood states and cohesiveness in adult oncology patients. *Journal of Music Therapy*, 38(3), 212–238. https://doi.org/10.1093/jmt/38.3.212.

Waldon, E.G. (2015). Music therapists' research activity and utilization barriers: A survey of the membership. *Journal of Music Therapy*, 52(1), 168–194. https://doi.org/10.1093/jmt/thv001.

Walker, M., Kaimal, G., Myers-Coffman, K., Gonzaga, A.M.L., & DeGraba, T.J. (2017). Active duty military service members' visual representations of PTSD and TBI in masks.

International Journal of Qualitative Studies on Health and Well-being, 12(1), 1267317. doi: 10.1080/17482631.2016.1267317.

Wellman, R. & Pinkerton, J. (2015). The development of a music therapy protocol: A Music 4 Life® Case Report of a veteran with PTSD. *Music & Medicine*, 7, 34–39.

West, M. (2000). Music Therapy in Antiquity. In P. Horden (ed.). *Music as Medicine*. New York, NY: Ashgate Publishing.

Wheeler, B.L. (2014). Music in Psychosocial Training and Counseling (MPC). In M.H. Thaut & V. Hoemberg (eds). *Handbook of Neurologic Music Therapy* (pp.331–359). Oxford: Oxford University Press.

White, W.C. (1944). *A History of Military Music in America*. New York, NY: The Exposition Press.

Wikipedia contributors (2020, June 15). Call and response (music). In *Wikipedia, The Free Encyclopedia*. Retrieved from: https://en.wikipedia.org/w/index.php?title=Call_and_response_(music)&oldid=962696424.

Wilson, L.G. (1989). Dorothy M. Schullian 1906–1989: A humanist historian of Renaissance medicine. *Journal of the History of Medicine and Allied Sciences*, 44(4), 421–429. https://doi.org/10.1093/jhmas/44.4.421.

Winkelman, M.J. (2017). Shamanism and the Brain. In N.K. Clements and J. Kripal (eds). *Religion: Mental Religion* (pp.355–375). New York, NY: Macmillan Reference USA.

Winters-Fisher, A. (2019). Dance/movement therapy and warrior wellness: A pilot case study. *The Arts in Psychotherapy*, 62, 52–60.

Wolfe, L.R. (2016, January 25). *Korean War Music*. Cold War. Retrieved from: https://coldwarstudies.com/2016/01/25/korean-war-music.

World Health Organization (2010). *Telemedicine: Opportunities and Developments in Member States. Report on the Second Global Survey of Telehealth*. Retrieved from: www.who.int/goe/publications/goe_telemedicine_2010.pdf.

Yellow Ribbon Reintegration Program (n.d.). *About Us: Goals, History and the Team*. Retrieved from: www.yellowribbon.mil/cms/about-us.

Yun-Springer, A.B. & Silverman, M.J. (2014). Levels of evidence in the *Journal of Music Therapy* from 2000–2009: Descriptive analyses by year and clinical population. *Music Therapy Perspectives*, 32 (2), 185–190. https://doi.org/10.1093/mtp/miu020.

About the Editor

Rebecca Vaudreuil, EdM, MT-BC, MSW Candidate, '22 is a board-certified music therapist who earned a bachelor's degree in music therapy at Berklee College of Music and master's degree at Harvard Graduate School of Education with a focus on educational neuroscience. She is currently working on a master's in social work at Fordham University. She has earned certifications in the areas of neurologic music therapy (fellow), neonatal intensive care music therapy, and music therapy assisted childbirth. In 2010, she founded a music therapy model for military populations that she implemented on military installations throughout Southern California. Since 2014, Rebecca has worked for Creative Forces®: NEA Military Healing Arts Network, a national initiative that develops creative arts therapies best practices for military populations. As lead music therapist, Rebecca provides clinical and research mentorship for the music therapy team, supports increased access to creative arts therapies research across military and veteran healthcare systems, and promotes community-based arts partnerships. Her work has been published in scholarly journals and highlighted by CNN, ABC, PBS, and in a White House Blog. Rebecca is a featured lecturer at various national and international symposiums, conferences, and universities, and serves as the special interest group coordinator for the International Association of Music Medicine. She is the resident music therapy supervisor for the Jamaica Field Service Project, where she supervises U.S. music therapy students in Schools of Hope, hospitals, infirmaries, and homeless shelters in rural areas across Jamaica.

About the Contributors

Claudia Avila is a proud Army wife, mother, and advocate for service members, veterans, and their families and caregivers. She believes in the power of interdisciplinary collaboration as the foundation of patient-centered comprehensive treatment and the integration of creative arts therapies into military, veteran, and civilian healthcare systems. She is the caregiver for her husband, Captain Luis Avila, who serves in the United States Army.

Mack Bailey, MM, MT-BC is a board-certified music therapist and award-winning singer-songwriter. After a career in professional music, Mack earned his master's degree in music therapy, specializing in neurologic music therapy. Mack's combined passion for communication, expression, and the intersection of neurology and music drives his work with military veterans with PTSD through his non-profit organization, Music Therapy of the Rockies.

Donna Betts, PhD, ATR-BC is the clinical research advisor for Creative Forces. She served as President of the American Art Therapy Association (2015–2017). Formerly Associate Professor and Research Director in the George Washington University Graduate Art Therapy Program (2009–2018), Dr. Betts is an award-winning scholar.

Hannah Bronson, MT-BC is a doctoral student in clinical psychology at the University of Denver, Graduate School of Professional Psychology. Her areas of clinical interest include trauma, substance use, co-occurring mental health diagnoses, and integrating creative arts therapies into treatment. Hannah has provided music therapy for active-duty military populations, and has authored publications and presented nationally on this topic.

Demi Bullock, BA is a music wellness facilitator and consultant. She graduated from the University of Massachusetts Amherst with a bachelor's degree in interdisciplinary studies with a focus on trauma, music, and mental health. Demi advocates for interdisciplinary treatment modalities and has earned certifications spanning the domains of health and wellness.

SSG Brittany Costa, MMT, MS is a Staff Sergeant in the U.S. Army, Colorado National Guard, where she plays clarinet in the 101st Army Band. She holds degrees in music performance, arts administration, and music therapy. She has professional experience as a musician, mental health coordinator, arts administrator, and music therapist. She aims to provide music therapy with military populations.

Chief Warrant Officer Two Jonathan L. Crane is currently a researcher for the U.S. Army Band's program focused on how music effects people across all domains. He has served in various roles from performer to commander in many locations across the globe, including a one-year deployment to Iraq in 2011.

Jason Danley served six years in the U.S. Navy as a Fleet Marine Force Corpsman. He deployed to Iraq in 2008 and Afghanistan in 2009–2010 with the 3rd Battalion 4th Marines from Twentynine Palms. While in the Navy, Jason met his wife, Christina. Together they have three sons: Caleb, Christopher, and Cameron. They reside in San Diego, California.

Lisa Fagan is the daughter, aunt, and mother of Marines. She understands military life and its challenges. Raised in Pensacola, Florida, she moved to California where she achieved a national gold medal for public speaking. Lisa is the training manager at Steadfast REIT and she lives in Spring Branch, Texas, with her husband Kevin, son Ben, Saint Bernard Frank, and cat Queen Latifah.

Donna Faraone, MPA, MT has served the Department of Veterans Affairs for more than 38 years as a music therapist, performance improvement coordinator, and currently, as a Whole Health implementation lead. Donna is an experienced presenter and a published author and is committed to the transformation of veteran healthcare to a Whole Health approach, aimed at optimizing veteran health and wellbeing.

Justin Francis, DMH, MA, MT-BC is the music therapist and internship supervisor for the New Jersey Veteran Healthcare System. He has presented at national and regional music therapy conferences. In 2020, Justin earned his doctorate in medical humanities from Drew University. He currently serves in the New Jersey National Guard.

Elizabeth K. Freeman, MA, BC-DMT is the lead dance/movement therapist for Creative Forces. She provides dance/movement therapy services in an integrative treatment program for service members with traumatic brain injury and associated psychological health conditions at the National Intrepid Center of Excellence, a directorate of the Walter Reed National Military Medical Center.

Lori F. Gooding, PhD, MT-BC is a music therapy faculty member and researcher at Florida State University. She currently serves on the Creative Forces Technical Working and Technical Review groups and as President Elect of the American Music Therapy Association.

John D. Hogue, MS, MM, MT-BC is a board-certified music therapist and statistician with a decade of experience in program evaluation. He earned two master's degrees from Illinois State University in quantitative psychology and music therapy. He currently serves as the senior informatics specialist for Creative Forces.

Sara Kass, MD is a board-certified family physician. Sara earned her BS at Pacific Lutheran University and her medical degree from George Washington University. Sara served 23 years in the Navy, dedicating much of her career to advancing care for military-connected populations. Sara is the Creative Forces' senior military medical advisor.

Diane G. Langston, MM, MT-BC is a board-certified neurologic music therapist. Diane graduated from Florida State University with bachelor's and master's degrees in music therapy. Her clinical practice, research, and advocacy focuses on music therapy with veterans and their families. Diane has presented on the delivery of music therapy via telehealth at conferences worldwide and is a published author.

CAPT Moira G. McGuire, BSN, RN-BC, CSC is a nurse officer with the U.S. Public Health Service at Walter Reed National Military Medical Center where she serves as chief of their new Arts in Health Program. She has spoken extensively in military and community settings about the importance of creativity and expression in the treatment, healing, and prevention of illness and injury.

Nathaniel McLaughlan, MA, MT-BC is a board-certified music therapist with Creative Forces. He earned his master of arts degree in music therapy and counseling at Drexel University. His work focuses on behavioral health and brain injury rehabilitation for active-duty service members and their families, as well as caregiver and provider resilience.

David Otto, MME, MT-BC is the Executive Director of Recreation Therapy Services for the Department of Veteran Affairs. He has worked in the VA for over 25 years, dedicating his career to serving our nation's veterans and advocating for program development and policies in recreation and creative art therapies. David has co-authored articles in professional journals and presented extensively at national and international conferences.

Natalie Quintana, MM, MT-BC is a neurologic music therapist at James A. Haley Veterans' Hospital in Tampa, Florida. She provides music therapy for brain injury rehabilitation, transitional programming, and geriatrics. She engages in professional advocacy through presentations, curating for the National Veterans' Creative Arts Festival, and building partnerships that support community arts engagement.

Barbara Reuer, PhD, MT-BC internationally known for her expertise in music-centered wellness and music therapy, is Founder/CEO of MusicWorx and Resounding Joy. Dr. Reuer has served as President of National Association of Music Therapy and is a recipient of the American Music Therapy Association Lifetime Achievement Award.

Danielle Vetro-Kalseth, MM, MT-BC is a board-certified music therapist for Creative Forces at Joint Base Elmendorf-Richardson in Anchorage, Alaska. She earned a bachelor's in fine arts at Shenandoah University and her master's in music therapy at Florida State University. She provides music therapy services to active-duty Air Force, Army, Alaska National Guard, and Alaska veterans.

Karen Wacks, MEd, LMHC, MT-BC is a board-certified music therapist and a licensed mental health counselor. She earned her master's in education at Harvard University and is a professor at Berklee College of Music in Boston, MA. The emphasis of her global work is community music therapy, specifically for peace and reconciliation for those experiencing war and conflict.

Melissa Walker, MA, ATR is the lead art therapist for Creative Forces. Melissa joined the DoD in 2008 after earning her master's at NYU and is currently the Healing Arts program coordinator at the National Intrepid Center of Excellence, Walter Reed Bethesda. Melissa's work has been highlighted via outlets such as *National Geographic* and TED talks.

Megan Wong, MA, MT-BC is a board-certified music therapist and Neurologic Music Therapy Fellow. She received her bachelor's degree in music performance from Westmont College and her master's degree in music therapy from Colorado State University. Megan is the music therapist at the Intrepid Spirit Center Camp Pendleton.

Lisbeth Woodward, MT-BC, NMT is a board-certified music therapist who received her bachelor of music in music therapy from the University of Eau Claire, WI in 1991. She is trained in neurologic music therapy and has worked at Salem VA Medical Center for 30+ years, where she has held a national roster internship program since 1996.

Subject Index

Page numbers in *italics* refer to figures and tables.

Author Index